5 Minutes with God

A 365 Daily Devotional

Brett T. Gilford

WESTBOW
PRESS®
A DIVISION OF THOMAS NELSON
& ZONDERVAN

WestBow Press books may be ordered through booksellers or by contacting:

WestBow Press
A Division of Thomas Nelson & Zondervan
1663 Liberty Drive
Bloomington, IN 47403
www.westbowpress.com
844-714-3454

Scripture taken from the King James Version of the Bible.

ISBN: 978-1-9736-7816-8 (sc)
ISBN: 978-1-9736-7817-5 (e)

Library of Congress Control Number: 2019917262

Print information available on the last page.

WestBow Press rev. date: 5/10/2021

Spending time with God is vitally important to the believer. Without it, we would be like a ship without a rudder; aimlessly drifting through life. I am excited about Elder Brett Gilford's devotional, 5 Minutes with God. It is a guide to helping us connect with God in a simple yet transformative way. Elder Gilford is a devoted husband and father and a faithful Elder at The Potter's House of North Dallas. His life is a testimony that spending 5 Minutes with God reaps countless rewards.

Pastor Sheryl Brady, Sr. Pastor of The Potter's House North Dallas

Acknowledgements

Bishop William Murphy III wherever mentioned about the prayer call
Wherever mentioned about Daily Readings; Devotional: Jesus Calling Sarah Young
God's Creative Power For Healing by Charles Capps - Pg. 299
AA Big book - Pg. 331
Steven Covey Seven habits
Bible versions: AMPC, NIV, NASB, KJV, ESB, NLT

January

1

Giving God The First Fruits Of Your Day

When I began my relationship with Christ, I remember my Pastor saying something that I will never forget. He said, "it is better to ask God for direction in the morning than to ask for a whole lot of forgiveness at the end of the day."

David said, "early will I seek thee." Keeping that in mind, I've made it a daily practice after I awake every morning, to spend at least an hour with the Lord in prayer and in His Word. It started with my spending *"5 Minutes with God"* and eventually progressed into an hour. Those first five minutes went by so fast that I didn't even realize I had spent as much time as I did. That prompted me to go to bed early in order to get up earlier, because I enjoyed that time with the Lord and wanted more of it before I started my day.

When I give God the first fruits of my day, the day seem to go much smoother than the days I don't. When life happens, as it most assuredly will, I have a peace about most situations.

Today know that the biggest payoff you'll ever receive from spending time with God and reading His Word comes when you give voice to His Word as it causes your faith to increase. Angels are activated and along with the Holy Spirit, together they bring into manifestation of what you've been speaking.

Psalms 63:1-2   Philippians 4:6-7 AMP   Romans 10:17 AMP   Mark 11:23-24

2

Put Your Plans Into Action

Now that we've entered into a New Year, what are some of the things that you would like to accomplish? What are your goals? The best way to see them come into fruition is to put it in "black and white", write them down. The Prophet Habakkuk tells us to write down our vision because in doing so it makes it clear and gives us a tangible target to "shoot" for.

What do you want to achieve? Think about where do you want to be spiritually, financially or even career wise. If you're serious about it, then begin to put your plans into action. I used to work for someone that once said, "A plan without action is nothing more than a good idea." Write it down and set timelines and benchmarks. Begin with the end in mind and start from there. For example, say you desire is to move into a new home, place on a timeline a date. Then every two or three months have small goals written down and review them periodically to help guide you along the process.

Seek God's guidance by acknowledging your need for Him upfront. He's eager and waiting to help you get what you want because He also wants it for you and the things He wants to give you are good. All you have to do is walk right.

Habakkuk 2:2-3 MSG   Proverbs 3:6   Psalms 84:11 AMP

3

It Was All A Setup

All of last year was nothing more than a setup for what is about to happen in our lives this New Year. Although we might not understand it all right now, every encounter we had with people, no matter how brief or whether it was good or bad, was divinely orchestrated by God. It has been and will be used by God to help fulfill His call on our life, while further propelling us toward our destiny. Understanding our experiences is like putting a puzzle together. Every piece has a purpose; we just need to see where and how it all fits. When I look at everything from this perspective, things that occur take on new meaning. God is using it to help mold me and "perfect that which concerns me" as it works for my overall good.

God has a purpose for your life that has yet to be fulfilled. That's why you woke up this morning and didn't die or get consumed back in your before Christ (BC) days, like some of your "homies" did. It was only God. I know in my life it had to be, because I didn't have to be here today, given the path I could have followed. Why is that some of the guys I grew up and ran the streets with are either in prison or dead, but not me? Why did the big disease with the little name miss my doorstep but took others when I was just as guilty? I look back now and see some defining moments where God intervened in my life and just like the old folks used to say, "He was saving me when I didn't know I needed to be saved."

As I embrace this New Year, I'm full of expectation, because I know the things that God has spoken to me and I'm excited to see how it will all unfold. What about you? What has God spoken to you? Our part is to continue praying and seeking him. After all, He has a plan and this is all a set up.

Psalms 138:8 AMP   Romans 8:28 CJB   Jeremiah 29:11-13 AMP

4

The Battle Within

When it comes to making changes in our life, the greatest battle we'll ever have to face most often comes from within. Breaking free from the way we used to think is a major hurdle that requires a lot of effort on our part. One of the things I had to overcome was fear of the future. The old was so familiar that even if it wasn't always good, it was predictable. Which leads me to ask a legitimate question: What will I be like if I do this?

My wife and I were talking about something we were watching on television about people making changes. I shared with her some sayings I have picked up along the way about change: "When the pain of staying the same becomes greater than the pain to change then we change." Another saying, "it is not until we get sick and tired of being sick and tired do we change."

It takes the act of renewing your mind with the Word of God if you're to break old paradigms. Renewing your mind is not a onetime event but should be an ongoing process done daily. As long as you're alive, change is always going to happen. Change is the only permanent thing in life. What's important to keep in mind is how we embrace those changes. We have to let the Holy Spirit have free reign in our lives if we're truly going to be available for the Masters' use. God has a plan, and when we seek Him about the plan, He unfolds it to us little by little, step by step.

Go ahead, make the changes you know you should make. You've got the greater one living big on the inside of you, that will help you overcome every internal battle you'll encounter.

Ephesians 4:23 AMP   John 16:13 AMP   Jeremiah 29:11-13 AMP   1 John 4:4

5

Getting Back To Basics

When it comes to our relationship with God, how effective we are is contingent upon our spiritual maintenance, and if you've been slacking off, then it's time to get back to the basics.

In football the basics are blocking and tackling. As a born-again Believer in Jesus Christ, the basics for us are spending time daily in His Word, praying, and listening for His voice. There will be distractions that come up. When they do, you have to work at it especially when you don't feel like getting up early or laziness attempts to creep in. It's in these times that you have to push past them, tune out the negative voices and influences that try to speak into your life and go to the Word of God.

We are constantly facing new challenges and we have to follow what the Word of God says. In order to know what it says you have to spend time in the Word seeking it. It's the best way to let the Word of God be the final authority in your life.

As you begin this New Year ask yourself, "Where do I need to get back to the basics in my relationship with Christ?"

Jeremiah 29:11-13 AMP   2 Chronicles 15:3-4   Matthew 6:33 AMP

6

You've Got It All

God has made available everything we'll need. Whenever we need healing or direction, if we go to His Word it can be found. His ultimate design is for us to live our lives through His Divine Providence, in such a way that we lack nothing. The key to enjoying this kind of life can only be found in and through our giving. As we give it comes back to us. I want to be clear that I'm not only talking about money. God has given us plenty of resources-as the Spirit leads-to share with others. What about sharing the Gospel with someone, volunteering your time to help out somewhere or maybe donate the clothes in the back of your closet you haven't worn in years. The list can go on but do you see the point I'm trying to make. If we have it to give, then give and it will come back to you. After all, God has given us all things, so be a distribution center and let it flow through you. When you do this, what you're really doing is making room for more!

2 Peter 1:3 AMP   1Thessalonians 4:12   Luke 6:38 AMP

7

Love Gives

God is love and Love gives. The greatest gift He gave us is His Son. Wrapped up in Him is eternal life, redemption, salvation, and healing. That's what love is and what it does. Love gives. Look at what love has done for you on a personal level. Every now and then it'll do you some good to reflect on the moments you now recognize as love.

God's love can only be expressed to others thru you and that's tied up in how you carry yourself (i.e. talk, respond and react). Love is always gracious and kind no matter what. The Bible is a love story. From Genesis to the Book of Revelation it depicts God's love for His creation, humanity. Regardless of how far to the left man steps, Love is always right there to forgive and pick up the pieces of our lives.

God loves you so much that He protects your right to miss heaven. People don't miss getting into heaven because of a sinful act they committed. If that were the case, none of us will ever have an entirely clean slate. People put measurements on it, whether there are big sin or little sin, but God sees it all the same. From stealing an apple to committing murder, sin is sin. People miss it because they fail to see the need for a Savior, thinking they can do it on their own. That comes from either being improperly introduced to Him [witnessed to, being offered the free gift of salvation] or they flat out rejected Him.

Take the time to meditate on 1John 4:17-21 it'll change your perspective. Challenge; will you share the love of God with an unbeliever this week? Can all those you come into contact with see the love of God thru you?

1 John 4:7-21 AMP

8

Changed By God's Word

I noticed recently that I've changed because familiar situations look entirely different. As I go along my life's journey, the changes are becoming more pronounced.

Periodically, before I open God's Word, I ask Him to give me a Word that'll provoke me to make the necessary adjustments, so that my life mirrors His Word. God's Word is alive. There is life in the Word. Everything that we will ever need God has already provided and can be found in His Word. The key is to actually read the Word, which means spending time in the Word so that you know it. I've found that by spending time daily in God's Word is not a waste of time. Actually, it's the best use of my time every morning. I heard a speaker once say that he read his Bible and the newspaper every morning so that can see what both sides are up to. Reading the Bible daily arms you for the day that lies ahead. God has a plan that is revealed to us in His Word. Another benefit from reading the Word of God daily is that it gives the Holy Spirit something to work with. There are times when a situation will come up and the Holy Spirit will bring back to your remembrance a Word that you read just for that situation.

Searching the Scriptures daily gives the Holy Spirit something to work with and allows you to get the news from God "hot off the press."

Ecclesiastes 12:13 AMP   Hebrews 4:12 AMP   2 Peter 1:3

9

Being Led By The Spirit

If we are truly striving towards getting to know God on a more intimate and personal level, it's going to require that we surrender our wants and desires while simultaneously submitting to His. We've experienced God on one level and now it's time to embrace this new level we're at. We might not have fully arrived and it seems kind of uncertain, that's only because it's new. Being on a new level is like riding on a boat and the first time you get up to walk while it's moving, you have to learn a new sense of balance. That's where you are, unbalanced. We have to continue seeking God. As we trust and follow His gentle leadings, everything is going to be all right. This is not to say we won't face opposition because as sure as the sun rises in the east and sets in the west we will. What we have in our favor is that God has commanded a blessing on our life. As long as we give heed to what and where the Holy Spirit says to do and go, everything will fall into place.

All along this journey are little lessons that we'll have to go through and learn from for the next level. It's not a waste of time because God doesn't waste anything! If you happen to be going through something just know "you have to go through in order to get out" and it won't kill you because it was designed to prepare you for your next level as you propel towards your destiny!

Make a decision today that you will seek and follow after God with all your heart and not get distracted by tricks of the enemy. You have only begun to scratch the surface of what He has prepared for you. This is only the beginning. I'm going to trust God as He guides me, because I know that the best is yet to come. What about you?

Isaiah 43:15-19 NLT   Jeremiah 29:12-14 MSG   Deuteronomy 28:8

Romans 8:28

10

Changes

I learned a long time ago that the only permanent thing in life is change! With that in mind, I usually handle change pretty well. I go through the initial emotional adjustments and usually get to acceptance quickly.

This time around is entirely different......

I was about to turn 55 and eligible for retirement. It's a change I knew eventually I would have to make. What I wasn't prepared for was the emotional upheaval that went with it. I have been with my employer for over 34 years, which amounts to more than half of my life. Feelings of uncertainty tried to overwhelm me, but God.

When you retire other things come into view. One of which is having to prepare for when I die so my family will be taken care of is a doozy. Death is a sobering thought. Learning to accept physical limitations (I really am not 16 anymore) along with day to day life, leaves me feeling like that guy sitting at his desk where they keep stacking work on him and he shouts "If you put one more thing on my desk I will explode!" Couple that with having to deal with the attacks that accompany being called into the ministry, leaves me sometimes thinking I am at Wrestle Mania underneath a pile on! Sometimes I feel like running away, but to where? I could go on, but I don't want anyone asking do you want some cheese to go with that whine? LOL

My reading one particular day talked about walking this path with God and how it is both a privileged and perilous way, and how if I stay close to Him, my work although hidden right now, will blossom and produce abundant fruit. This reminds me of something I heard once, that "Roots grow down before you'll see anything come up." My roots must be deep and grounded in love, in order to bring forth the harvest God promised me!

John 15:4-5 AMP   *Ephesians 3:17-19 NLT*   *Romans 8:28 NLT*

11

Giving God Something To Work With

In order for us to receive anything from God, we first have to bring Him something to work with. If there's a Promise in the Bible and you're believing to see it manifest in your life, have you incorporated it into your daily confessions? Have you sown a seed or given an offering in that direction? You have to give God something to work with. Some of God's Promises come with conditions. If the conditions are met the Promise is fulfilled.

When we look at Luke 6:38, we tend to associate this Scripture with money and rightfully so. Yet, if we back up and look at verse 37, Jesus is talking about the characteristics of love. In this passage He talks about judging, condemning, and forgiving. So, if you were to substitute the thought of money and replace it with forgiveness, it adds a different perspective to forgiving and being forgiven. The condition of this Promise is that which you give, will be given back to you, not necessarily the same way and amount you gave to others. There are other examples throughout Scripture that are conditional.

You have to give God something to work with. It can be as simple as your obedience, money, time, talents, treasures or faith. Give Him something to activate the promise.

What will you give or offer?

Luke 6:37-38 MSG   *Deuteronomy 28:1-14 AMP*   *Malachi 3:10-12 AMP*

Mark 11:23-24

12

Staying The Course

Don't deviate from the course you're on because of what things might look like. The Spirit world isn't based on how you feel but on what God has said in His Word. The Word works, and if your faith is "shaky" then it's time to double up on your Word intake, confessions and prayer time.

Don't allow things in life to overwhelm you. When things start to get crazy just step back and assess the situation. Ask God what needs to be changed and make them. Divide and conquer is a key to winning when things start to pile up on you. Your enemy, the devil, doesn't want you to succeed and will try everything that he can (i.e. symptoms of sickness, conflict with others and money issues) to distract and /or discourage you. They might come one at a time, one right after another or simultaneously. Remember what Christ suffered on the way to and on the Cross. He did it all for you to enjoy the victory that He secured for you. Because Christ went through some stuff and came out with your redemption, whatever you might be facing you've already won.

Emulate Christ and endure. No matter how tough it might get, the Blood of Jesus has secured your victory!

Psalm 34:19   Revelation 12:11 AMP   Isaiah 53:7

13

Keep Moving

When I heard the following statement it really gave me something to meditate on: "When God gives you an opportunity, work that which has been given to you and stop looking for a finished product, because the tree is in the acorn." That got me thinking about trusting God, His process' and how we shouldn't "*despise small beginnings.*" We all have to start somewhere, with a vision of what we want the end to look like. As you meander towards your goal, it takes trusting God's direction when it seemingly doesn't make sense, and letting him work out the details, and remaining steadfast.

God has placed inside all of us certain passions and desires. We are pre-wired to fit into a plan that He has custom designed for us. It's up to us to make the best use of what He has given us. The main stumbling block that we'll face is fear, and we can't allow fear to hold us back nor keep us from maximizing our full potential. Successful people still have fears. The only difference is they push past those fears and they don't allow fear to prevent them from attaining their goal.

You have an ability that is uniquely designed to fulfill Gods plan for your life. All you have to do is keep moving forward!

Psalm 37:23   1 Corinthians 15:58 AMP   Jeremiah 29:11   Philippians 3:14

14

Unforgiveness and Forgiving Ourselves

Have you ever noticed how hard it is sometimes to forgive yourself when you need it? Unforgiveness in any form whether it is for us or someone else, is nothing more than an attack from the enemy. If allowed to fester it can become toxic. Before you know it, another situation comes along that adds to the "pile of emotional turbulence" you might be experiencing. For me, I have to stop beating myself up first and foremost by rehearsing the things that I am grateful for and remembering that God loves me. No matter what might have transpired, it's not fatal, and surely there's a lesson to be learned.

On a recent prayer conference call, the leader talked about unforgiveness. I had to ask myself am I harboring unforgiveness toward anyone in my heart? I have to forgive the people who have hurt me because there definitely are people whom I have hurt and I want to be forgiven. The leader talked about how God has forgiven my debts and if I look back over my life, I'll see that there were things that could've destroyed me, but God forgave my debt.

God deleted those files, so I now have the responsibility of pursuing peace and forgiving my debtors and myself.

Psalms 34:14 AMP   Matthew 6:12 AMP

15

Mid Month Check Up

We are at the midway point in the first month of this year and it's time that we do a mid-month check up on our goals for this year. So, go pull them out for review. We have to keep in mind that we are now at the next level we have been talking about for so long. This is the new level and it brings more change. There is going to be a whole lot of "moving and shaking" taking place in your life. People are going to be coming in and out of your life. New relationships will be forged that are divinely appointed and strictly for helping fulfill your God-given purpose. Family and friends are going to make their transition to be with the Lord and there's nothing we can do about it except celebrate their life and keep moving onward in our journey.

All of this is why we have to keep our goals in the forefront of our mind. We have to change the way used to think and do things. I can tell you for me personally it is not easy. My wife and I are repairing our house and things are not where I was accustomed to them being. I can't get bent out of shape because it's part of the process, which means letting go of the past for the new. Something I heard recently that stuck with me is: "The passivity of your present has its roots in past paradigms." That tells me the biggest obstacle facing me today is yesterday. The Apostle Paul put it more succinctly when he said that he is forgetting those things which are behind, and reaching for what's in front of him, as he presses toward the mark for the prize that's found in Jesus.

God has inspired our goals for this year. He has already given a snapshot (vision) of what it's going to look like. Just watch it unfold as He does a new thing in your life!

Philippians 3:13-14 AMP   Isaiah 43:17-21 NLT

16

Keep It Flowing

The key to blessings flowing is giving. Once the flow of blessings begins, you can dare to believe and ask God for bigger and better. At this level our focus has changed, and our thoughts and desires should be geared more toward others rather than self. We have to keep it flowing, and the best way to do it is to be led by the Spirit, and not guided by our emotions. Emotional giving might cause you some regret down the road, even if your intentions were in the right place. Let me give you an example. There are people who have either heard or seen others get blessed in certain areas because of a seed they have sown. They might have given a car away and got blessed by a new and better car, debt free. Then when some see the fruit of their harvest, they go and give theirs away, looking to get the same harvest, and when it doesn't manifest, they get angry with God and fall away from God. What they failed to realize is God prepared them to be in a position to give on that level, which led to that subsequent level of manifestation. To get there, you have to be led by the Spirit and not the flesh.

The blessing is perpetual, and we have been called to be distribution centers. If God gets it to you, His intent was to get it through you, and when you bless others, keep God in the mix. By that I mean always talk and brag on Him. Squeeze in a partial testimony if you can about something He's done for you.

If your desire is to bless others on the level I described above, then let God prepare you. You can start right where you are. What about the clothes in your closets? As long as they're in good condition, ask the Lord to show you who can you bless. Take them to the cleaners, and then sow them. Remember, your capacity to receive is predicated on your level of giving.

I heard it said once that there is no way water can go through a pipe and the insides not get wet. When you give, God is going to make sure you get a return on your giving; you have His Word on it.

2 Chronicles 1:7-12 NLT   Mark 11:24   Romans 8:1 AMP   Luke 6:38 NLT

16

17

Show Your Appreciation

With the busyness that seems to consume everyone these days, many people don't show, and people aren't shown any appreciation for the things they have been done.

When we show people that we appreciate them and the things they do, we are in essence acknowledging the great things God has done for us through them; so how can we not do more than say "Thank You" to them.

God has given me prime examples on how to conduct myself in this area. When I had job interviews for promotions, my brother encouraged me to send "Thank You" notes. A few years ago, my parents went to China, and the Lord placed a couple on the trip with them. The wife assisted my father with my mother immensely, as my mother was progressing in the early stages of dementia. Upon their return, my dad sent them a gift for their house to express his gratitude.

It's a classy thing to articulate your appreciation in a tangible way. When we give cards, a gift or money, it makes people really feel appreciated and that they have done something good. When we bless others, we make room in our lives to be blessed. Keep in mind that when you activate this level of spiritual growth in your life, it becomes perpetual or rather a constant state of exchanges.

We don't bless others just to get blessed, but by blessing them we in turn get blessed. Your being blessed is directly tied to your giving.

Remember this is the next level so adjust yourselves accordingly!

Psalms 103:1-5 AMP   Galatians 6:7 AMP   Luke 6:38 NLT

18

Praying With and For Our Children

When I was in school, I remember the only drills we used to practice for were in the event if we had a fire or tornado. One day as we all were sitting around the dinner table, my daughter told us they had a drill in case someone came into the school with a weapon and tried to harm them. I told her that's why we pray every day before they leave out of the house, so that nothing or no one will hurt or harm them. I told her she can tell her teacher with boldness that doing a drill is good, but nothing is going to come in and hurt them because we prayed, and my Father said the safest place any of you could be is in here with me because I'm going home after school today.

Every morning before our children leave, we pray together. Sometimes I let them pray or they will step up and ask to pray. At the time both my girls were nine and five years old. It is my assignment as is every born-again parent to teach our children to know God for themselves and how they can access God 24/7. When they fall and hurt themselves, I pray, and lay hands on them according to the Word. Any time when one of them got hurt I'll have the other one go pray for them. The best way I know to teach them is to let them see me walk this thing out day-by-day and not just in case of an emergency because ours is a walk by faith and not by sight. There was a time when my wife wasn't feeling good and my oldest one went and began praying for her on her own. This is a direct result of the seed we've sown into her. Our children won't learn this in the public schools. When my son was in pre-kindergarten, the school called and said he had something in his eye. He wouldn't let anyone look at it and he wouldn't stop crying. By the time I got there he had stopped and was better. I told the nurse that she should have prayed with him and he would've been all right. She said, "pray with him?" and I said yes. The look on her face was priceless. When I got in the car headed home it hit me that I probably should've shown her right then how and probably could have led her to Christ. I won't let another opportunity like that slip by me.

Today, I urge you to begin praying daily with your children or when you get the chance pray with your grandchildren, nieces and nephews. This is a different kind of world we live in today than when we were kids. If you can't pray with them every day you can surely pray for them because the blood is still in effect covering and protecting!

Mark 16:18   2 Corinthians 5:7   Proverbs 22:6 AMP

19

Read The Book!

Good Morning to you! If you're reading this then God still has something for you to do and your work is not done. Everybody you come into contact with today ought to be infected and affected by the love of God flowing from you. All it takes is a warm smile. Say "hello" to someone you don't know or hold the door open for someone who may or may not say "Thank You." Let's make today a day full of "Intentional Random Acts of Kindness."

I remember when Chick-fil-A lines were literally out the door as people of faith gave an overwhelming show of support for the owner's stance on same sex marriages. The next morning, I just happened to check my phone and saw where a friend of mine voiced their opinion on Face Book about the issue, which of course led to several other people chiming in one way or the other. What was interesting is that the dialogue, from what I gathered, was amongst Christians. Without going into detail, suffice it to say, it was interesting; especially to hear Christians supporting same sex marriages or rather not opposing them. Part of me wanted to join in but the bigger part of me said "No." Then I heard that still small voice say, "Read the Book."

No matter where you stand on the issue, whatever God wrote about homosexuality that should be our stance. As children of the Most High, who we are is more than being narrowly defined by who they decided to have sex with. That's not the way God planned it. As always, I have to add the addendum that I am not anti-gay but pro-God and His Word. I have, as I am sure a lot of you have, family members who subscribe to that lifestyle. So far, I've had three family members, my younger brother included, who died directly or indirectly from being gay.

If you have any questions talk to the Author of the Book. I'm pretty sure He's available to take your questions! He enjoys talking with us, He looks forward to it every day.

Just read the Book. It's not open for debate or to legislate. It is what it is.

Hebrews 13:1-2 NLT   2 Timothy 3:16 NLT   Romans 1:22-27 NLT

20

A Safe Place

Being in the will of God is a safe place. Stepping outside of His will is dangerous, and when we do and try to go on our own we always seem to get into trouble. It's in our best interest to live a life according to the Word of God, which is His will for us. Like the title of a television show from back in the day puts it; "Father Knows Best."

I know someone who is trying to find their way in this world. She has decided that she knows better than her mother how she is supposed to live her life. She refuses to conform to mom's rules and has been making unhealthy choices. The most recent one having dire consequences when she left home while her mother was at work and caught the bus with some friends to go across town. While there, she attempted to cross the street and was struck by a vehicle going approximately 30-35 mph. She was knocked unconscious and woke up in the hospital with a fractured hip and other related bruises and injuries. It was the grace of God that kept her from being seriously maimed or killed. I shared with her that there is a price to pay when we do wrong. Although we might not pay immediately and seem to get away with it for a moment, down the road at some point we have to "pay the piper." In some way, shape, form or fashion I said you have to settle up, and you just did.

It's moments like these where we get the opportunity to take inventory of our life. God has designed life in such a way that there are laws in place to govern every area of life. A law is an established principle that will work for everyone who gets involved with it, such as the law of gravity, seedtime and harvest, reciprocity etc. Some laws once enacted there is no way to avoid the inevitable outcome except by another law that will supersede it. The point I want to make is, that you can't escape what you put into motion. Once you realize this is not going the way you wanted and repent, God's grace and mercy can step in and supernaturally smooth things out.

It's never too late to stop the madness and make a course correction. God already put in the budget for your life all the favor, grace and mercy you'll need. Always keep in mind, that the safest place that you can ever be in is the perfect will of God.

Psalms 91AMP   2 Peter 1:3-4 AMP

21

Let The Word Do The Work

Have you ever caught yourself trying to do something to ensure that the Word you're standing on will manifest itself, only to have no results? If so, let me "pull your coat" and tell you to stop right where you are! There is nothing you can do in the natural to cause God's Word to manifest in your life except confess it and believe it.

The Bible talks about entering into the rest of God. At some point we have to cease from our labor, like God did on the 7th day. Take advantage of God's rest and let the Word do the work. The point I want to make is this, God sent His Word and in doing so has given us everything we'll ever need.

There are a couple of things paramount to us effectively entering into God's rest and they are:1) Fine tuning our sensitivity to the Holy Spirit (the voice of God); 2) Spending quality time in the Word; 3) Obeying the gentle leadings of the Holy Spirit can help chart the path for success in every area of your life, along with quickening a Word to you when a Bible isn't handy. This only comes from spending time reading and confessing what God's Word says. Your Bible is a living thing and will speak to you when you take the time to get intimate with it, so get a pen or highlighter out and start marking up your Bible, making little notes in the margins.

Today give yourself a break, and rest. You'll get the manifestation of rest when you let the Word do the work!

Hebrews 4:9-11 AMP   2 Peter 1:3   John 16:13-14 AMP

22

They Are One In The Same

One morning I was meditating on how the Father, Son & Holy Spirit are one and live in me. To the unbeliever they are inexplicably tied together, working in concert with one another, but we who are born again, understand the relationship that exist between them and know they live inside of us.

When we pray, we ask the Father in the name of Jesus for what we want, and the Holy Spirit along with the angels bring it to pass. Look at it this way; the Father thinks it, the Son says it and the Holy Spirit gets it done. The Holy Spirit within you is a guide ordering your steps. God has a plan for your life and it's not by accident that you're reading this right now. What is He speaking to you? What desire or dormant passion in you has been awakened? That's His gentle nudging. You have a destiny to fulfill and an assignment to complete. There has been so much deposited in you and it needs to be released because at the end of the day it's all about other people and how you can be a benefit to them.

When you pray in the morning it should be a trigger that begins a daylong dialogue between you and God. It's not a one-sided monologue but rather a time where you and God can commune together. There is a shift-taking place right now in the spirit realm and time spent communing with God will enhance your sensitivity to His leadings, as He impresses into your spirit specific things that are unique to you and the calling on your life.

The first thing every morning start the spiritual ball rolling by spending time with God in His Word and in prayer. As I heard someone once say, always make sure you have a notepad and pen with you to take notes about the things the two of you will be talking about throughout the day.

John 14:10-20 AMP   Psalms 37:23

23

Sabotaging Success

This current phase of transition is full of events. Little life lessons have been learned and sometimes I feel like I am on one of those big exercise balls, about to fall off. I roll to the other side only to have the same experience from a different perspective. The emotional "kitchen sink" was even thrown and almost hit me in the head (if it had not been….). As I travel along this journey (and that's just what this is a journey) I can see how God has me in a state of perpetual preparedness. Every step taken has a purpose even though I might not readily see it.

I trust God, and from where I sit it's the best choice. My track record before I answered His call leaves no room for doubt that this is the correct way. If I remain diligent in doing the basics: reading my Bible daily and praying, it seems like God is leading me with nuggets from His Word. I'm following, like the kids had *ET* in the movie doing with candy. Every time I get one a nugget it's revelatory. Messages from the pulpit bring me comfort and confirmation that this journey is in direct alignment with His Word.

One of the most recent nuggets I received said God will only show me step-by-step, one at a time. If He were to show me the end right now, I couldn't handle it without experiencing my current phase of preparation, then the next and the next one. I'm doing the best I can, and God knows it. There is a part of the old me that I am learning can't go with me any further. It makes me sad. The old me is kicking and screaming, "No! I want to go!" You ought to see him throwing temper tantrums, wanting to really act out and sabotage my success. The only thing is, I've been there, done that and all I got was a t-shirt? No thank you, I have enough of those t-shirts already!

I continue on this journey, I am learning how to stop, smell the roses along the way and enjoy the trip without sabotaging my success!

Romans 8:28   Jeremiah 29:11 AMP

24

The God Kind Of Faith

Jesus tells us to have the faith of God or rather the God kind of faith. It's the kind of faith that exercises its authority by speaking, and whatever is spoken to or about comes to pass. We know that the world was framed by the Words God spoke, and we, being created in the image of God (another speaking spirit), have the same faith power available to us. Jesus tells us that if we speak to things and believed what we say, then those things will obey us. He even challenges His disciples after they awoke Him thinking they were going to die while in the middle of a hurricane. Jesus calmly rose, rebuked the wind and told the sea "Peace, be still." The wind ceased and there was calm. They knew He could do something about it, which is why they awoke Him from His sleep in the first place. He was telling them they could've done the very same thing. If you listen to the words that others around you speak, you can tell where they are in the faith process, especially if they are facing some type of challenge.

My question to you is, what does your faith say? Faith speaks to the end of a matter and not the beginning or middle. No matter where you are or whatever it is you might be facing, what do you want the end to look like? Are your words or faith lining up with it? We create the things we're believing to see manifest by speaking it. Today, let your faith speak to it and not your emotions!

Hebrews 11:3 AMP   Mark 4:37-40 AMP   Luke 17:6 AMP

25

Being Restored

You're valuable to God and He wants to restore you. In the natural, people don't restore things if they have no value. You are important and valuable to God. He loves you, and that's why He wants to restore you back to the place where you were and recover what you lost.

Could it be you've made some bad decisions in the past? Maybe you took a wrong turn that has taken years from your life and you still haven't fully recovered from it. If so, I want you to rest assured that God is a restorer and He will allow you to recover all that you've lost.

Being restored is a process. You have to trust God in and through the process. Sometimes it might not feel like or look like things are going your way, but they are. We don't base the things of God on how we feel, because our feelings can change just like the weather here in Texas. God's Word is our final authority. When challenges come, the first words that come from our heart and out of our mouth should be "What does the Word say?" You can only get like that when you make an investment of your time in the Word. That old saying of "no deposit, no return" is true. If you don't put it in, you can't get it out. The only thing that will come out is what you've been spending time with. The question is, what have you been spending time with?

We have to be Kingdom-minded and that takes a constant renewing of the mind if we're to get to the point where we think of others more than ourselves. When God restores you, keep in mind that it's not all about you, but for the Kingdom. On the prayer call one morning, the Elder talked about how God is restoring us for the real harvest that is out there-the souls of the lost.

God is not against us having nice things, but there is something out there more precious to Him than us having a new house or car. He wants us to go out, claim the lost and lead others to Jesus. Pastor Sheryl Brady put it best when she said, we should clear the path and point them to Jesus.

So I ask, are you clearing and pointing?

Joel 2:25 AMP   1 Samuel 30:8   Ephesians 4:23 AMP   Luke 10:2

26

My Smart Phone

One day my smart phone started acting up. Some of my calls were going straight to voice mail and when I called someone using speed dial their number wasn't there. That's when I noticed some of my contacts were missing. All of the people that I text daily were reduced to a lists of telephone numbers. The following day, I went to the store to see if they could help. The technician told me the only way to correct the problem was to do a factory reset because my internal memory was low. So when I got home, I waited until I got ready to send the text message for the day, and I sent an additional text for people to respond back with their name; that way I could recover & rebuild my most important contacts. After I sent everything out, I deleted some apps I wasn't using, cleaned out my emails and text messages. Guess what? My contact list was divinely restored! The next morning, I began thinking about it and how grateful I was because I didn't know whose number I thought I had lost forever, and how the problem was simply rectified by throwing some stuff away. Around the same time, someone I follow on Twitter said, "that it's time to un-clutter your life. Too much clutter and your mind can't think straight!"

My smart phone experience reminded me of something that I desperately needed to deal with, which brought me to this thought: What do I need to throw away in the natural, character-wise, that could be clogging up the flow of the Spirit, causing me to be distracted in a real subtle fashion?

Ask the Holy Spirit to show you what is cluttering up your own life. When you do, just know that it will produce some sobering results, so be prepared!

Philippians 3:13   Matthew 7:7-8   John 14:26 AMP

27

Assigning Your Angels

Over the years I've come to learn more about and appreciate the ministry of angels. There are two angels that God uses regularly. God uses Gabriel when He wants a Word sent to someone and Michael when there is warfare.

We have angels assigned to us, that are waiting to hear the Word of God spoken out of our mouths in faith. They are on point and ready to go to work to bring the Word of God to pass. Angels exist in heaven and are innumerable. They are ministering spirits sent to minister to us, the heirs of salvation. We have a covenant with God and it's our responsibility to know what's in it. God cannot get involved if we don't know what we've got coming. Once we know, angels are God's covenant enforcers and it's their responsibility to establish God's Word in the earth. They are waiting on the Word of God to be spoken so they can go to work.

Angels are not some sort of genie ready to come out of a lamp when you rub it, but rather they are always on their job 24/7 - 365 days of the year, waiting to be activated by the Word of God. Just like God did for Daniel, He will send angels to those who trust Him, and they will defend us in the time of trouble.

Today, give your angels their assignment. Get into your Bible and read up on your covenant to see what you've got coming, then speak the Word of God over your situations. Angels are waiting on the sidelines with their Nike's laced up, ready to go!

Psalm 103:20   Hebrews 12:22 AMP   Daniel 3:13-28 AMP

28

Engrafting The Word Into Your Heart

When we take God's Word and put it into our mouth, it then goes into our heart. If we are diligent about doing this daily, the Word becomes engrafted into our hearts, which is our spirit.

Just like when a doctor performs a skin graft. He takes a piece of skin from one part of your body and surgically places it over another part that is damaged. After a certain amount of time, that new skin becomes a part of your body where it was attached. The same thing happens when we consistently put the Word of God in our mouth, it becomes engrafted, planted and rooted into our hearts and becomes a viable part of our being.

If we need healing, we confess "by His stripes we are healed." Every time you get a bad thought, pain or take your medicine, that Scripture should be the only thing coming out of your mouth. We are exercising our faith just like God did Abram when He changed his name to Abraham: "The Father of a multitude." God was calling things that weren't as though they were already in existence. When we confess God's Word, we're doing the same thing until we get the total manifestation of the things we desire.

Today, I want you to remember that it's in our best interest to search the Scriptures daily and discover what God has to say about whatever might be concerning us. Take that Word and deposit it into our heart/spirit man by confessing it. When we do, it will cause our faith to grow as that Word eventually becomes an engrafted part of us.

James 1:21   1 Peter 2: 24 NLT   Romans 4:17 AMP   Romans 10:17 AMP

29

Does God Have Your Attention Now?

When we follow the Holy Spirit, we basically give God permission to interrupt "our life" with what He wants to do. Learning His voice takes practice. You may want to go one way, and something says "No." You do it any way only to realize you shouldn't have, then wind up saying "I should've listened to my first mind." That's God in the person of the Holy Spirit, fulfilling the prophecy Jesus gave when He told us that He will be your guide. As our guide, God knows how to get our attention.

If you look around at what's going on in the world today. There are subtle urgings being sent as reminders that you need to get it together, because God's way is the ONLY way to maneuver through this maze called life and have real fulfillment. Everything on television is sex-related in some form or fashion, straight or gay, it's illegal and out there. It won't be long before the shows our children watch has regular gay characters. They're starting out now by hinting that they might be gay, but just wait. Once the LGBTQ folks start pressuring them it will be "two snaps and a twirl" (remember the gay characters from "In Living Color") in our kids' faces on a regular basis. Our elected officials, no matter what side of the aisle, seem to have lost their purpose and just don't care. Natural disasters are on the rise worldwide and weather patterns are doing the Macarena across the country as temperatures plunge to record lows everywhere including down south. People in the church are falling by the wayside and church leaders are committing suicide. Jesus said that we would go through some things, but to be of good cheer because He overcame them. Once again, this is all prophecy coming to pass.

So, I ask again. Does God have your attention now? You either get serious or get sifted. The choice is yours: but as for me and my house, we will serve the Lord! What about you and yours?

John 16:13 AMP   John 16:31-33 MSG   Luke 22:31 AMP

30

Don't Let Your Emotions Rule You

Now-more than ever-we have to watch our feelings. The way things are moving can be overwhelming as we're being faced with positive opportunities juxtaposed with negative challenges. If we're not careful, fear and resentment will begin to creep in if we don't "nip it the bud" immediately.

We can't allow distractions to throw us off our game. Don't be surprised when serious conflict has an opportunity to arise with people, especially family members. Expect it, keep your mouth shut and take it all in stride. You have an assignment to complete and your enemy doesn't want you to succeed. He is going to hit you where he thinks you're the most vulnerable-in your emotions. You can count on it. This is the new level and we will not let fear dominate us. Successful people have fears. What separates them from the rest is they push past those feelings for what lies ahead because reaching their goal is more important than being stuck back in "I wonder what would've happened if I had just kept going" land. You can do it too, just get focused on the Word and keep moving. My Grandfather used to say "a rolling stone gathers no moss", so keep the momentum. You've come too far and been through so much and survived it, so why stop now? One of my Pastors used to say, "the devil is a lie" and that is so true. Fear and all of its cousins (anger, resentments, procrastination etc.) come straight from the enemy.

Avoid petty distractions and arguments. Speak to that mountain of fear and tell it where to go in Jesus name. Don't let the enemy talk you out of what God has in store for you. You're in the will of God. Exercise your blood-bought authority and walk this thing out.

Mark 11:23   John 16:23-24 AMP

31

The Report Of The Lord

I started meditating on this early one morning. At the time, there were a couple of things going on that I had no immediate control over. I had to really trust God for the outcome and not the "what ifs" the enemy was attempting to disturb my peace with.

I've been walking with God just a little bit too long not to exercise complete faith in His Word. When things start to "concern" me as this was doing, I go to the Word, read aloud what it says and then begin praying in my heavenly language, tongues. When I pray in tongues, I pray the perfect prayer. The Spirit-to-spirit connection is established between His Spirit and mine when I pray in the spirit. It's the only thing I know to do. Praying in English allows me to only pray what I know mentally but the Spirit of God knows everything and is always ready and able to make intercession for me. Couple this along with the fact that I refuse to open my mouth and say anything that I don't want to happen. Like my brother always says, "If God didn't write it, I'm not going to say it." There is no way I am going to start verbalizing the "what ifs" when I have the same opportunity to speak Gods Word over it. That just doesn't make sense to me. I have to let my spirit man hear me speaking God's Word in order for my faith to increase. Which also means that I can't let my demeanor change, because surely as the sun rises in the east and sets in the west, challenges will come today that require me to really walk in love towards all that come across my path. I already know the test is coming and guess what? I aim to pass it. Faith works by love and that means no matter what the situation is, when I look at how Love acted all the way to and up on the cross, I know I can win just like Jesus did.

As you go through your day today, walk in love. Remember, we only believe the report of the Lord!

Philippians 4:8-9 AMP   Romans 8:26-27 AMP   Romans 10:17 AMP

Galatians 5:6 AMP

February

1

This Is A Faith Fight

Paul told Timothy to "fight the good fight of faith." There is only one thing the enemy wants from you in this fight, and it's your faith.

This is a faith fight or rather a fight for your faith, and your mind is the battlefield. If the enemy can get your faith, then he's got you. He will use everything in his arsenal to attack you. His attack is going to come in the realm where he operates best, through your senses. If he can get you to feel or see, then the potential is there for you to begin thinking contrary thoughts, which if not captured immediately, will progress into negative speech. James tells us to "resist the devil", not fight him and "he will flee." I haven't found it in the Bible yet where it tells us to fight the enemy. We have to acknowledge that our weapons are mighty through God and use them. Since we are made in God's image (another speaking spirit) and we're told to resist the enemy, then we have to open our mouth and begin speaking God's Word in faith, not fear. The Word of God will assign angels to go to work on our behalf.

This battle is a spiritual one and it's the Lord's, so why not let Him use what He's got to fight it. All we have to do is speak what we want into existence and it's already done.

1 Timothy 6:12 AMP   2 Corinthians 10:4-5 AMP   James 4:7-8

Psalms 103:20

2

What Are You Thinking?

The book of Proverbs says we are what we think in our hearts. So, the question is, what are you putting into your heart or what are you feeding your spirit man? Do your thoughts line up with the Word and the will of God or are they all over the place like a ship in the middle of a storm being tossed to and fro? The best way to get and keep your thoughts in alignment with the Word of God is to constantly renew your mind in God's Word.

The only power Satan has is the power of suggestion. I want you to meditate on that and let it sink in. The only power your adversary has over you is the power of suggestion. Little-by-little, he will introduce subtle thoughts of doubt and fear into your life to torment you, to point you in a direction that is based on fear. A prime example is extended warranties and the protection plans they offer when we make a purchase. Some of them are good. If you bought a computer and they offer an extended warranty for $35 that might not be a bad idea. On the other hand, if you purchase a microwave for $65 and they offer you a plan for $15 that's not a wise investment. If something goes wrong, you might have to pay for a service call, that in the long run, would be cheaper if you purchased another one. The point is, society has increasingly become fearful, and organizations are feeding off of those fears by making people pay for something they don't really need. We have to be on guard and vigilant over our thought life.

Consistently taking in the Word of God will thwart the enemy's designs and allow the Greater One, who lives big on the inside of you to take His rightful place. Watch as His thoughts and ways eventually become yours.

Proverbs 23:7   Ephesians 4:22-24 AMP   1 John 4:4 NLT   Psalms 119:59-60

3

Spiritual Laws

Recently we talked about laws and how they are established principles that will work for anyone who gets involved with them. They can't be stopped once put into motion except by another law that supersedes it. All laws have to be obeyed. In the natural, we have the law of gravity and once put into motion only the law of lift can supersede it. The laws of nature have to be obeyed (i.e. when it is cold outside, the law of nature dictates you have to dress for it or else you'll get sick). Then we have spiritual laws, which work in the natural, such as sowing and reaping, and confessions. Without fail, Spiritual laws will work when you put them to use coupled with your faith.

Doing things God's way ensures success every time. This means you do everything above board, no shortcuts. You have integrity, but most importantly you have your faith, so exercise it. When things don't seem to be going as planned stick with God's Word. You're the Kings kid and live on the winning side, it's time to lose that defeated-life mentality and rise above it. Do you believe God and His Word? If so, then walk in the blessing that accompanies it.

God has promised you the good life, a life filled with abundance. It's been set up for you. All you have to do is activate spiritual laws. Take the Word of God that fits your situation, speak that Word, mix it with faith and watch it work for you every time.

Joshua 1:8   Mark 9:23   Ephesians 2:10 AMP   1 John 5:14-15 AMP

4

Forgiveness and Avoiding Strife

There was a time when someone I knew, established a business venture that was in direct opposition to an organization they belonged to. They were subsequently relieved of their duties and they were unjustly upset about it. Some other "events" transpired, and I had a front row seat unbeknownst to them. As I watched it unfold, I couldn't believe this person was acting in such a manner. I contacted them about the situation. Their response was evident that they were in the throes of a stronghold, of which is difficult to escape without renewing your mind.

As time passed, they resorted to various social media outlets to garner support and promote their venture, while making misstatements, inaccurate, and one-sided portrayals about the organizational leadership they were formerly a member of. I sat down to write them another email about it-against the advice of my inner circle-but I didn't send it. That day the Lord led me to the topic of forgiveness and showed me how if I had sent that email, I would be in strife, no matter how "justified" I felt. The only thing that will "heal my wounds" is the Word of God and time.

You might find yourself in a similar situation one day and I want you to know that God will give you the grace to work through whatever issues life brings. None of our actions has taken God by surprise, and I've learned that everybody is doing the best they can even if I don't necessarily agree with them. Sometimes the best way for me to handle a situation is to keep my mouth shut, along with the restraint of tongue, pen and keyboard, and just keep moving, because God has bigger fish for me to fry!

Ephesians 4:23 AMP   Galatians 5:19-21 AMP   Ephesians 4:32 AMP

5

Christian Under Construction

As I was reading the Book of Romans one day, something came to me where Paul tells us that it's the goodness of God that makes us want to change. A relationship with Christ is not a bunch of "do's and don'ts" but rather a change of heart, where certain activities we used to enjoy doing we don't do any more. It's not because we can't, we just don't want to. These types of changes are subtle and don't require a lot of effort on our part to initiate but we still have to work to maintain. This is where renewing our mind comes into play. We are constantly being shaped and molded by God. From the inside out we are becoming more Christ like. Subtle changes like our reactions have now turned into responses. We don't get as angry-if at all-like we used to. Anger is fear based and perfect love cast out fear. Those little things that used to be irritants don't even faze us anymore!

Keep reading your Bible and praying because you're a Christian under construction and God isn't finished with you yet!

Romans 2:1-4 AMP   1 John 4:18 AMP   Romans 12:2 AMP

6

Walking This Thing Out

The past few mornings, I've been reading and meditating on the blessing and how God will bless all the work of my hands. No matter what comes your way or how it may look, you have to walk this thing out. This course you're on has been pre-arranged, custom designed for you and is the will of God for your life.

The greater the battle the bigger the blessing. That's why you're going through all of this. God allows these things to occur for reasons that are obscure right now, but if you stay the course, in time, it will all come to together like a jigsaw puzzle. There will be challenges and all types of distractions that you'll face and overcome. Just keep putting one foot in front of the other. The distractions might be your children acting crazy, issues at work, insane thoughts or maybe even symptoms in your body. Don't fall for it. Stay prayed up and in the Word. There will be times when the road might not look like you anticipated. That's when you have to exhibit pit bull tenacity and hold on to the promise God-made specifically to you. Look it up and put Him in remembrance. He hasn't forgotten and really wants to see if you know what He said. Rehearse past victories by testifying to yourself. Tell people how great a day today is and that God has been good to you.

If you do these simple things, your demeanor and perception will change. Hope will begin to invade you as your spirit man rises up big on the inside of you and overtakes your fleshly thoughts. God has commanded the blessing on your life and it's on the other side of this. Just keep walking.

Deuteronomy 28:8-12   Isaiah 43:26 AMP   Ephesians 2:10 AMP

7

The Pity Pot

There are times when I have to become transparent and this is one of those times. I'm somewhat embarrassed to share what follows. One day while getting an oil change, I was sitting there with headphones on and playing on my tablet. All of a sudden, because I allowed one bad thought about some old stuff I had dealt with come in, the flood gates literally opened. The "negative committee" showed up. You know how it goes, one little thing after another. Then that one thought, "This is going on and how are you going to do that, what about this and I don't really feel good & blah, blah, blah." I'm telling you in the course of two minutes I was sitting on a "pity pot" the size of The Cowboy's Stadium. Feeling sorry for myself, I was nursing a mild case, on the way to becoming a severe case of the "Oh woe is me." Here I am, a man of God, full of faith and power, thinking and feeling like this. Then the Holy Spirit shows up and says, "Whoa wait a minute, what's going on here? You know better and you know what to do, so turn the game off." What's embarrassing is, at the time, I was listening to a sermon about the Blood of Jesus.

I turned the game off and began to make my confessions about the Blood as it relates to my finances, health and family. Once I got started it was on. I put God's Word in my mouth. Whatever His Word said about what I was facing, I spoke. That's why the Apostle Paul tells us we should be "Casting down imaginations, and every high thing that exalteth itself against the knowledge of God and bringing into captivity every thought to the obedience of Christ." That Scripture is one that is in my arsenal to be used, and not just sit there and gather dust, while I am out here beating myself up. **His Word is my final authority**. Which got me to thinking, nowadays everybody is going through something and I want you to know that you're not alone. The day of judgment for the enemy is getting closer and he is attempting to turn up the heat and make us think that somehow God has forgotten us. Of course it's a lie, because my Bible tells me that I'm on God's mind, so how can God or any of us forget someone that is on our mind? It's impossible, so don't go for it.

If you find yourself in a similar situation open up your mouth and immediately speak the Word of God and kick those negative thoughts out. Should you need some reinforcements, shoot me an e-mail, Tweet or Facebook message; I will get into agreement with you. Together we will give the devil some much-needed resistance and laugh while we watch him flee.

Oh yeah, by the way, I got off the pity pot and back in the fight.

2 Corinthians 10:5 AMP   Psalms 115:12   Matthew 18:19   James 4:7

8

Trusting God

One morning in my "Daddy time" with the Lord, we talked about trust. There comes a time in our walk with the Lord where we have learned to trust Him. David and Solomon encourage us throughout the Psalms and Proverbs to trust God. They tell us that increase of direction, protection, wisdom and blessings are available to those who trust in the Lord. These are some tough times that a lot of folks are going through. I'm talking about times when tough decisions have to be made. This is why we are told to trust God and lean not to our own understanding.

Development is a process. We are put in "situations" that are uncomfortable, but as we continue to develop our trust in God, we eventually get to the point that when things come up, you immediately know God has already got it covered. No fretting and no worrying. That's the place Paul tells us about; the peace that passes all understanding. People around you can't understand why you're not tripping out over a situation, but you know in advance, that God has a plan and it's going to work out for your good. Before you knew you had a problem God already had the solution. We just need to ask Him "What do you want me to do?" and then do it. Trusting in the knowledge that God loves you. Just like a Father loves his children and He is not out to get you. God loves you. He really does. Our Senior Pastor said this one-day and I never forgot it, "God loves everybody in the movie, both the good guy and the bad guy."

Have a great day today basking, enjoying a pleasant situation, in the love of God!!

Proverbs 3:5-6   Philippians 4:6-7 AMP   Romans 8:28

9

God Is Getting You Ready

I'm going to share an experience I had with today's message. Back in the mid 90's was when I learned about prayer, and a book by Germaine Copeland titled *"Prayers that Avail Much"* was instrumental to my foundation. At the time I was married to my ex-wife and there was a prayer that I found concerning your wife, so I began praying it over her. When the marriage subsequently fell apart, I couldn't understand what was going on. I had some questions, like why weren't my prayers answered and what did I do wrong? I still held on with hope that one day I would find the kind of love that makes the artist Babyface write love songs.

I can look back now and see God was at work behind the scenes bringing it to pass. God allowed circumstances to improve my character and integrity because I wasn't ready for the answer. There were some things that had to be worked out of me in order for me to be in position to receive the kind of woman I was praying for. I am a living witness that He does answer our prayers through the ministry of angels. When God answered my prayer with my current wife, He went way past what I thought it would look like. I tell people it's almost like I asked for a Cadillac and He gave me a fully loaded Rolls Royce.

You might be standing on a promise you found in His Word and things don't seem to be lining up like you think they should. Your prayer has been heard and the answer is on its way. If I had gotten mine before I was ready, I would've messed it up, so hang in there. God is using all of this activity that doesn't make sense, so at the right time, you'll be in the proper position to receive it. Always keep this in mind, the answer to your prayer doesn't always look like you think it will.

Psalms 103:20   Ephesians 3:20 AMP   1 John 5:14-15 AMP

10

God Will Judge It Fairly

Have you ever been done wrong and you know you didn't deserve it? If so, you've been upgraded, and I want to welcome you to Christianity 2.0.

Being mistreated will happen more frequently as you go further and higher in the things of God. You'll face attacks from people you never thought they would come from. All of this is confirmation that you passed another phase of the Holy Ghost's vetting process. You have to stay focused, keep moving, don't react and definitely, don't respond.

At this stage we trust God to judge every misunderstanding, false accusation, and unjustly suffered wrong fairly. Listening and following the instructions of the Holy Spirit is extremely important, especially when the overall situation might seem insignificant. You're anointed for this time because you have been called and chosen. Yes, there is a call on your life that is accompanied by the commanded blessing of God. He will and is blessing the work of your hands. You might not see it readily. In my experiences, He sends little nuggets of encouragement right when I needed them.

When attacks, injustices, or accusations present themselves, give it to God in prayer because at the end of the day we know that He will judge it all fairly.

1 Peter 2:18-23 MSG   Deuteronomy 28:8   Colossians 3:12-15 AMP

11

Interceding For Others

One of the responsibilities we have as Christians is to pray for others. There are times when we'll be asked to pray for someone who has a specific need and then there'll be times when someone you know will suddenly come to mind. Friend or foe, the Holy Spirit is prompting you to pray for them.

When the Holy Spirit impresses upon you to pray for someone, you don't stop until you get a release from the Holy Spirit to do so. You can either pray the perfect prayer by praying in the Spirit or you can pray by asking God to do in their life, specific things you want Him to perform in yours. The latter is the best way to come to grips with someone whom you might be at odds with, and asking God to bless them, even when you don't feel like it is the best way to release the hurt and obtain peace.

There is a spirit of deception that has come upon the earth and people are being duped all around us. As the Word of God increases so will lawlessness. Our nation is at a spiritual crossroad with more and more states legalizing same-sex marriages. Things you used to hear about happening every now and then are commonly being reported on the news. For a while, just about every morning, it was reported someone got it in their heads the night before that they can steal a truck and ram it through the front door of a business that has an ATM machine. Thinking they can steal it and not get caught, but they wind up getting caught anyway.

We have a front row seat as we witness prophecy being fulfilled in our life. Jesus said all of the things taking place would come to pass (i.e. wars, commotions, famines, earthquakes in divers places, out breaks of pestilences' etc.) He tells us don't be terrified by them because the end is not yet. With all of the events taking place globally, our prayers need to be focused on what's transpiring with a special emphasis on praying for our leaders, especially the President of the United States. We need to pray for their safety and that of their family. The enemy is stepping up his game by attacking where they live, but we can thwart his attempts with our prayers.

This is nothing but spiritual warfare. We need to suit up, get armed with the Word of God in our mouth and in prayer, use the Name and the Blood of Jesus. Let's go into battle. We've already won. It says so in the back of the book!

James 5:16 AMP   *Luke 21:9-11 AMP*   *1 Timothy 2:1-2 AMP*

Revelation 12:10-11 AMP

12

Moving Targets

I remember when I had a brief moment of naiveté, where I thought the attacks from the enemy would maybe not dissipate entirely after I get ordained, at least subside. No sooner than the words came out of my mouth the Holy Spirit reminded me of something Bishop Jakes talks about all the time: new levels bring new devils!

As I was fellowshipping with the Lord that morning, we talked about how the Apostle Paul had a messenger from Satan harassing him so much that he became like a thorn in the flesh. The thing I was shown is how throughout all of his epistles, Paul only mentioned it once. He was so focused on his mission of spreading the gospel, that nothing else really mattered.

We have a job to do, and the Bible tells to stay the course and in doing so, our work is not done in vain. You might not always get to see the fruit of your labor, but every now and then God will give you a nugget from someone you have touched to remind you that you're on the right path.

Today, I want to encourage you to *"Keep moving because moving targets are much harder to hit than those standing still doing nothing!"*

2 Corinthians 12:7-9 AMP   1 Corinthians 15:58 AMP

13

Watch Out For Petty Irritants

Have you noticed how lately it's not the major, earth shaking things of life trying to invade your space, but rather the little things that pop up seemingly at the most inopportune time? It could be something that you've overlooked in the past and now today it "takes you there." I'm here to tell you, Don't Go for It!

It's nothing more than a sign and confirmation. The Bible clearly tells us "no weapon formed against us will prosper" so don't start tripping. We are not ignorant of Satan's devices nor are we low hanging fruit just waiting to be picked by him. Large or small, we know and understand that it's an attack. The attitude I try to maintain is; whatever goes on or goes wrong, none of this stuff is fatal. When at work, I would always tell my employees that if something happened, don't lie to me about it. If you did it, you did it. We'll fix what we can and if we can't, we'll move on because it is not the end of the world. Do you remember you remember hearing: "Don't sweat the small stuff because it's all small stuff?" If you can develop and maintain this type of attitude, no matter what the enemy throws your way, this is one sure fired way you can keep him on his heels and frustrated.

On this level we have to be free from strife. There's too much at stake. We haven't even begun to scratch the surface of what God has in store for us. The promise you found in God's Word is your prize. Stay focused. Ministry sometimes is like serving a good meal to people; they eat and get up from the table without leaving a tip. God sees your work and He will reward your faithfulness. He knows that you're making an impact in the lives of people while simultaneously destroying Satan's kingdom.

Song of Solomon 2:15 AMP   1 Corinthians 2:9 AMP   James 3:16

14

God's At Work In You

God deals with us internally where both He and the real you co-exist. God is a Spirit and we were made in His image, which by default, makes us spirit-beings also. We are a spirit, who possess' a soul, and we live in a body. We're spirits having a human experience, and when it comes to us, God works from the inside out.

What He has deposited in us has to come out in order for us to do the work He has planned for us. When we spend time daily reading and meditating on His Word, God downloads updated information into our spirit man. The Holy Spirit has been sent to guide us to that place God has prepared for us right here on earth. That place is the good life. It's a life filled with promise, hope, and full of joy. That's not to say there won't be difficulties because there will, but whatever God allows to cross your path, know He has already prearranged enough grace for you to get through it. Notice I said "get" and not "go" through. I want you to start thinking past tense. "Get" means you have made it through. We can only get like that when we take the Word and deposit it on a daily basis into our spirit man. We have to put the Word in, in order to get Word results out. Becoming God inside minded allows His love to be expressed in everything we do, no matter where we go or who we encounter.

The greater one lives big on the inside of each and every one of us waiting to be expressed to the world. Today let the love of God be expressed to others in all that you do. Remember it's an inside job!

John 4:24   John 16:13   Ephesians 2:10 AMP   1 John 4:4

15

Have You Prayed About It?

This following may seem like a generic question, but it's a valid one: "Have you prayed about it?" There are times when we can have our faith out there, believing God for something, but haven't sought Him in regards to us getting or having whatever it might be. We've taken for granted that it was all right to be desired. We've began making plans and moves in order to get it. Then we experience a few minor hiccups. We started to feel a "tad bit" disappointed and realized we haven't prayed about it.

Thinking we're so in tuned to God that we can ignore basic fundamentals will cause major problems and heartache somewhere down the road. It's called being out of the will of God. This trap can easily be avoided by simply seeking the Father in prayer about everything that concerns you. We all should have an effective prayer life just like Elias. He prayed that it wouldn't rain and for 3 ½ years and it didn't. Then he prayed for rain and it rained.

God wants us to have and enjoy the good life, heaven right here on earth, as long as our request is in alignment with His will to further advance The Kingdom. Be confident that He hears your prayers and they'll get answered. We've got His Word on it!

Proverbs 3:5-6 AMP   James 5:16-18 NLT   Ephesians 2:10 AMP   1 John 5:14-15

16

When God Says All

As you read your Bible and come across the word "all", do you get the full impact of what it really means? This is how *Webster's 1828* define it: The whole quantity, completely, wholly, the whole entire thing. Basically, it means everything, nothing left. "All" means all. When you ask someone have they eaten all of their food and they say yes, they can show you an empty plate.

When God says that He will bless "all" the work of your hands that means you've met certain conditions and what you're working on is in alignment with Kingdom principles, making it an overall benefit to the Kingdom. I've learned that God doesn't bless mess. There is a plan and purpose for your life. When you're fulfilling it, God blesses and causes to prosper the work you're doing. You can't do just anything, pray, expect God to bless it, and voila it's blessed. Why do you want whatever it is and if you get it, what will you do with it? Going back to talking about the Kingdom again, how will it affect people for Kingdom purposes?

If you keep running into roadblocks, it could be this isn't what you're supposed to be doing or the way you're going about it is incorrect. There's a difference between the challenges you face in and out of the will of God. It has to be spiritually discerned. You can do something with good intentions, and if it's not approved by God, no matter how hard you try, it goes nowhere real fast. There are times when you're in His will and you will face hazards and traps on the road. That's when the Holy Spirit will speak to you, more than likely give you advance warning, and give you what steps to take. If you pay attention, all will be well. If not, then you'll have to make a course correction and get back on track.

When you read your Bible and see the word "all", underline, highlight or circle it. Whatever your norm is when you mark up your Bible, do it. Take a moment to meditate and ask God how it applies to your life.

Deuteronomy 28:12   James 4:2-3 AMP   John 16:13 AMP

17

Being Steadfast

No matter what comes your way know that you're not alone. Everybody goes through challenges at some point in life, but you have to remain steadfast in your faith. Those around you might not be up to the same speed as you but they're on board, so don't get discouraged.

What God has spoken and shown you in His Word to do-do it. The fruit of your labor will come to pass. You are so close to the manifestation, any and everything that your enemy can throw at you he will. His strategies haven't changed, only the vehicle he uses has changed. It's still the same old lust, not necessarily sexual, greed and envy, to name a few. If you drill down, you will find some sort of fear at the root of it.

When your faith is out there, you don't have to fear losing or missing out on anything or anyone. God is still in control and hasn't forgotten you. He definitely won't let you go without, regardless of what thoughts might run through your mind. Every now and then it'll do you good to look back and see how far He has brought you. Think of the times when you didn't see a way, yet there was one. Look at you now. The only reason we ever look back is to reflect, because we no longer live in or for the past. Neither do we repeat the same mistakes while expecting different results. The enemy will attempt to deceive you into thinking otherwise, by dressing it up real nice and pretty. We know that if it was good and worked so well back there, why did we ever leave it?

Faith in God's Word, trusting what He said will surely come to pass is all we need to remain steadfast and move forward in doing the things He's assigned us.

1 Peter 5:6-9 AM   Mark 4:19 AMP   1 Corinthians 15:58 AMP

18

Making Plans

Recently, I began thinking about some things I wanted to do. Making plans and trying to figure out how to bring them to fruition. Wondering how this will work, does it fit, what about this…and then that still small voice reminded me of something I'd read earlier about how control can be turned into an idol if I fail to incorporate God into the mix.

We can make all the plans we want, but we have to remember that He inspires most of our plans. God already has in place how they are to be carried out. The key to plans being successful is found in this one little thing: We have to let God work out the details. You might have to take unplanned twists and turns or perhaps have to do something that doesn't make sense to you right then, but it will in the end. God wants our will to be submitted to Him. When we can do this, things flow much easier. That's not to say you won't meet certain challenges, because you will. Anything that God's elect does for His Kingdom will encounter resistance from the other kingdom, but you cannot be moved. Distractions will come from some of the most unlikely places. Sometimes people you never imagined will come right out of left field over something that is so mundane, it's almost comical.

God has had a plan and purpose for His man since the foundation of the world. We have to discover our part, be submissive to the Master's designed plan for us, and simply stick to the plan.

Jeremiah 29:11   2 Timothy 1:9 AMP

19

Words Frame Your World

A while ago, a friend of ours had an issue with her computer and we went over to their house to help them out. While there, she repeated a few times how she didn't know anything about computers. She called my wife the other day and asked if she could come over and have me copy a CD for her because she couldn't get her computer to work correctly. Mind you, this is after she has made several trips to the store where she purchased it and invested in a protection plan from a well-known mobile computer repair company. When that didn't work, she bought a brand new one and was fixated on the idea that with the prior one, she was sold a lemon; yet she still had the same issues with her new one.

I copied the disc for her and while she watched, explained how easy it is and that she could do it. She started talking about what she didn't know and couldn't do. After a couple of times of her saying what she said I told her, "Stop saying that." The next time she said it I elevated the tone of my voice and told her of course she couldn't because that's all she says, and you know the Bible says; you can have what you say, and you've got it. Then she said, "but I'm telling the truth." I told her so what, ask the Holy Spirit to give you the wisdom to do what you don't know what to do. She said "ok" and left to go home and try what she saw me do. The next day she called my wife and left a voice mail all excited because she was finally able to copy a CD and didn't know how she did it, but God gave her wisdom to do it.

The lesson here is that we frame our world with the words we speak. Our conversation might be so innocent that we overlook the impact our words have on us. For example, you might be facing sickness in your body. Stop saying what the diagnosis from the doctor is and start saying what the Word says about you. Speak to the end of the thing and call what you want into existence. You're not denying that you have whatever it is, you are denying its right to live in your body. Start calling it symptoms and in the same breath speak healing. If you have been prescribed medication say, "I'm healed" every time you take it.

You were created in the image of God, with the same creative power to speak whatever you say into existence. You believe what you speak, and what you say-either positive or negative-will eventually come to pass. If you don't want it, don't say it!

Mark 11:22-24   Romans 4:17 AMP   Genesis 1:26-27

20

The Report Of The Lord

Whose Side Are You On? / Whose Report Will You Believe? The reason I pose these two questions is because the world we live in is getting really crazy. When I read the news one day about potential meteors falling from the sky and how one about 62 feet in diameter burst over the skies in Russia with the same type of impact that 40 Hiroshima type atom bombs has, it made me go hmmm, I am so glad I'm on Gods side! Even going to the movies or the mall isn't as safe as it used to be. This is just the tip of the iceberg. I could go on and on, but that would only fuel the fire I want to extinguish. If we don't take a stand and get on God's side, which means believing His report, the enemy's terroristic threats will overwhelm you.

I know a guy who is a professed atheist, and it amazes me the level of deception the enemy has on people. As an atheist he flat out says there is no logical proof that God exist and there is nothing you can say to dissuade him. Satan has this guy so caught up he doesn't even believe the devil exists, which doesn't surprise me. All while I talked with him about God, I could hear the Holy Spirit telling me not to cast my pearls before swine. My stance is this - at the end of this road when I die, find out that I was wrong and there was no God, then I will have lived an amazingly good life. But if I'm right, woe unto you because life isn't a game of golf where you can get a mulligan. With life there are no extra innings or overtime periods. You're one and done. As a buddy of mine used to say, "you only go around once in life and this is not a trial run."

When I go to the Word of God and read what the psalmist wrote, I am more than confident that no matter what, God has my back! We know upfront certain things are going to happen all around us, but we won't be afraid and none of it is going to come near us, because we trust in God.

Today, open up your Bible and read what God said, because it's better than what this world is saying.

Romans 10:13-17 AMP   Matthew 7:6 AMP   Psalms 91:5-9

Jeremiah 17:7-8 AMP

21

Be A Blessing

I remember a message preached that provoked me so much I sent them a Tweet saying the message set off an explosion on the inside of me. The message was titled "It's a Family Blessing." It was about the eight promises God gave to Abram.

For me there was one point that really stood out and that was when God told Abram that He would make him a blessing. What I related to is that I will be a blessing or a benefit to others. Basically, I'm supposed to help others be blessed. The pastor went on to say that we should have a "make me attitude and have already lost the spiritual welfare mentality. I am different and not a zero, and if we're not doing that already, then start now in small ways. Start small-little by little-you will be making a difference." That just sent me over the edge. It put me on a search for how I can be a blessing to others.

There is a myriad of ways to accomplish this. One way is by intentionally performing random acts of kindness. As an example, when you're eating out, leave a much bigger than normal tip for the wait-staff or buy the people at the next table's meal and they not know it was you. Another way is to buy groceries for the person in front of you at the supermarket (not in the 20 items or less line) and when the cashier gives them the total, you immediately swipe your card or pay with cash. Have you ever given someone a "holy handshake" with a couple of fifty- or hundred-dollar bills? The feeling you get from blessing people cannot be explained in words. I know that just by reading this some may get the "I can't do that" thoughts, but remember to start where you are. Don't despise small beginnings. Blessings are perpetual and they're cyclical. It's a spiritual law. Once you get started blessing others, blessings come back to you in ways that exceed what you gave. I was talking to a friend one day about this and how you can't beat God giving. When we give, it provokes God to give back to us even more because He can now trust us to be what He designed us to be, a distribution center. Ready to give at a moment's notice, to distribute when and where He prompts us to.

I'm a living witness that in doing so, it's not a loss, and God will restore back to you more than you could've ever imagined, as long as your heart and motives are correct.

Genesis 12:1-3 AMP   Psalms 112:9 AMP   2 Corinthians 9:6-8 AMP

22

All Eyes Are On You

You're being watched. The moment you were born again, your life went on public display for the whole world to see. People everywhere are watching to see just how you live, and you never know who's watching. I remember once I was at the grocery store and I had an opportunity to step out of character, but I didn't. Don't you know that as soon as I turned around, I ran into one of the elders from church. You never know. People where you work or play, who know you're a Christian are watching. They might be on the same side of the fence as you or not. They might be quietly sitting on the fence, just watching to see if you act like they think most Christians act or are you different and reflect the type of life that is drawing them to Jesus.

For Christians, love for one another is our main focus as we walk this thing out. That's why we have to renew our mind every day in the Word of God, so that we keep our inner man built up. What you take in is what comes out, especially when things aren't going right, and the pressure is on. Will the Word rise up on the inside of you and be larger than your circumstances or will you "drop the ball" and have to regain your footing? It's happened to all of us, so don't beat yourself up. I didn't get to where I am overnight and given the right set of circumstances, I'm subject to respond in a non-loving way just like the next person. Most of the time I don't, because I keep my mind renewed daily in the Word of God. I know firsthand that if you put the Word in, when the heat is on, the Word is going to come out.

As you go through your day today, let the Word of Christ dwell richly in you as you walk in love toward everyone you encounter. You don't have to be "preachy" all it takes is a smile and a Hello.

Colossians 3:16-17 AMP   Ephesians 4:23 AMP   Matthew 22:37-39

23

Keeping Your Mind Renewed

Keeping your mind renewed is a maintenance step. Life and your enemy will constantly throw things your way and if you're going to be all that God has designed you to be, then you have to stay in close contact with the Source through His Word.

Back in the day, if you were traveling somewhere and didn't know how to get there, you used a map to plan your course and you constantly referred to it so as not to lose your way. Today, we have Global Positioning Satellites (GPS), and when in use, it gives you timely and accurate updates. When you get off course in life, just like a GPS, the Word of God instructs you on how to get back on track. What do you do when you need a Word and don't have a Bible handy? The Holy Spirit will quicken a Word, that you spent time reading out loud, and bring it back to your spirit man. I've had times when I gained a new revelation from a particular verse of the Bible that I was familiar with, due to the events transpiring in my life at the time. This is why it's important we renew our minds, so we stay current and up to date with the what, the where and the how of God's plan for our lives. He knows the correct paths to take.

Another benefit of a renewed mind is God's Word will increase your faith when you speak the Word as you read it. Taking God's Word in visually is good, but when your spirit man hears you speak the Word, the dynamics change and puts the enemy on notice because speaking the Word has creative power that he doesn't want to see manifest. Myron Butler has a song titled "Speak into the atmosphere" and there's a line in the song that says, "I shall have what I decree." Being able to decree or speak a thing is only accomplished in someone whose mind is renewed with the Word of God.

Don't look at renewing your mind daily as a sacrifice, but rather time spent communing with the Father. It pays enormous dividends. It'll heighten your spiritual awareness, allowing you to fine tune the voice of God when He speaks.

Ephesians 4:22-24 AMP   Romans 10:17 AMP   Job 22:27-28

24

Trust God and Be Flexible

I remember back in the late 70's, when I was working as a temp for the United States Postal Service, there was an older gentleman named Ralph whom I worked with. He used to tell me all the time, "Gilford, you've got to be flexible working for the Post Office." I never forgot those words and it's a principle that governs my life today.

God has placed inside of us desires and passions that are to be used to fulfill His plan for our lives. When we act on them, and come up with plans and strategies to bring them to fruition, we have to trust God as He works out the details. This can and most likely will involve a drastic "looking" setback as you lay aside your way of doing for His. I put an emphasis on looking, because it will appear that way, but remember we are walking by faith and not by sight. Yes, you may experience some disappointments, but you have to keep in mind that your steps are being ordered. If you keep at it, over the course of time, the sting of a disappointment lessens because you see the bigger picture as the Word of God is in your heart. One thing I've learned is that there is a thin line between due diligence and my will. Due diligence is doing all that I'm supposed to do. My will kicks in when things start to change, and I want to do something that will force it back into what I believe to be alignment. When things get like this, I have godly counsel that I go to and they help me navigate through it, keeping me on track.

As you walk this thing out, remain flexible and disregard the petty distractions life will throw your way. Walk in love and keep God's Word in your mouth.

Proverbs 3:5 AMP   Psalms 37:23 AMP   Mark 11:22-24 AMP

25

Staying Inside Of Today

Have you ever found yourself mentally all into the future? Every now and then it happens to me. I'm trying to figure how things are going to work out, what about this and before I know it, I'm about to be overcome with worry. That's when I have to put the brakes on and start speaking the Word, telling God that "I trust you and according to your Word, when I do, you'll direct my path. I thank you for direction. I thank you that I have all I need on the inside of me. The answer to every situation is in me. I got it." I then start reading and meditating on Scriptures which relate to seeking God and staying inside of today. As long as I stay inside of today and deal with today, everything is okay. Tomorrow's problems will take care of itself when tomorrow gets here, just like yesterdays did on yesterday. There's no need to take today's "what ifs" into the future.

If you ever find yourself doing the same, just remember to stay inside of today, that's where everything is okay. All of that other stuff will work itself out, as long as we put our trust in God, follow the gentle leadings and direction of the Holy Spirit, He won't lead you wrong!

Proverbs 3:5-6   Matthew 6:34 AMP   John 16:13

26

He's The Same God Every Day

I remember once when my day started out differently. There is the normal day-to-day stuff that has to be accomplished, plus any "honey do's" my wife has assigned me to. Coupled with some of the things I'm believing God to manifest in my life with their fast-approaching due dates on the horizon, all of this had me feeling a little discombobulated.

The closer I get, the more I have to guard my mouth and my love walk, because I don't want to have come this far and miss it. It's the little things that the enemy will send your way to throw you off your game, yet I have come this far by faith. I know what God has done in the past and that fuels my faith for the future. He's the same every day and won't change.

It all boils down to this, after I have done all that I can do in the natural, I commit it to God and trust Him for the results. He will bring it to pass.

Song of Solomon 2:15   Hebrews 13:8   Psalm 37:5

27

God Knows Where He's Taking You

God has a plan for all of our lives. Every detail is worked out. All He needs from us is our obedience. Every step we take has a purpose which take us closer to fulfilling our destiny. Remember, our lives have been pre-destined by God, which means the good life has been pre-arranged for us. God knows the way. The question is are we entirely ready mentally and spiritually, when it comes to letting our steps be ordered? Adverse things will happen; it's called life. We have to get to the point in our walk with God, that we learn how to accept what He allows. God doesn't use the works of Satan to teach us. When He allows certain circumstances to manifest in our lives, they transform us. We can learn from it and watch God turn those situations around to work for our good.

Are you in transition? Do events seem to be going in the wrong direction? Relax. This setback is only a course correction and that's not a bad thing. Sometimes there are things that have to be worked out of us if we're going to be truly effective in our walk of winning others to Christ. At this new level in God, the way we used to think and respond has to change. Some of the things we got away with back there won't fly now.

Renewing our minds is not a onetime event, but rather an ongoing process in the life of every believer who continually makes the necessary adjustments God requires. God has an expected end, so enjoy the journey and stay focused on His Word, you'll get there.

Jeremiah 29:11   Ephesians 2:10 AMP   Psalms 37:23   Ephesians 4:23 AMP

28

Now It's His Turn (The Holy Spirit)

Lately I've noticed that I have a heightened awareness of the Holy Spirit operating in my life and have come to rely on Him more each day. When we look back at the progression of the Trinity's work, we see the Father and His different character names at work, from creation until the time Jesus came into His ministry. For three years we see firsthand through Jesus, what is expected of man and the things we can do here on the earth. Fifty days after His work on earth was completed the Holy Spirit descended. He is in full operation in the earth today. He is our guide sent to help us on this last leg of life's journey. He is talking to each and every one of us more and more. He's that still small voice talking to you while you're driving telling you which way to go. He's behind those inspiring thoughts you have, the ones where you say, "I don't know where that came from." That's Him fulfilling the prophecy of the Christ.

One sure-fire way to watch Him work is when you have misplaced something and can't find it. One day my wife was looking around the house for something and couldn't find it. I watched her go over the same locations in the house a couple of times before I asked, had she asked the Holy Spirit where it was. She said "no." I told her to ask Him, pray the answer in tongues and then say I believe I receive. She did it and not even five minutes later she found what she was looking for. She was amazed at the results. You can have the same results in your life, not only when you've misplaced something but when you have a situation or circumstances come up and you don't know what to do. Just ask. Pray the answer in tongues and then say, "I believe that I receive my answer." If you don't pray in tongues, just ask. Thank Him for the answer. Say "I believe that I receive" and you will!

God in the person of the Holy Spirit is no respecter of persons. If He did it for me, He will surely do it for you. All you have to do is ask.

Acts 1:8   Acts 2:1-4 AMP   1 Kings 19:12   John 16:13-14

29

Interceding For Our President

One morning on the prayer call the leader touched on something that had been rolling around in my spirit for a couple of days. There is a lot going on in the world today and now more than ever The President needs our prayers. You don't have to agree with some of the stances that he's taken because I sure don't, but he is still the person who was elected to lead our country. I've yet to see one person who has held that office be perfect, and we have to always keep in mind that it is the office and not the person that is divinely appointed.

God tells us to pray for our kings and all those in authority over us. He didn't say whether or not we voted for them or agree with their every decision to do it, He said to pray for them. When we follow God's command and pray for them, not only is this pleasing and acceptable in His sight, it also puts us in direct alignment to live an inwardly quiet and peaceable life. This tells me no matter what goes on, as long as I pray, I can be at peace. We should also take it a step further and be interceding for leaders on a global level. With all the unrest over in Russia, Ukraine, North Korea and elsewhere, we can intercede for the leaders of those countries. The events occurring in the world today are simply fulfilling a prophecy. The stage is being set. Remember the sign that we are looking for Jesus' return is the spreading of the Gospel throughout the world, not all of the chaos going on in the world. The wheat and tares will grow up together. The better it gets on one hand, the worse it will be on the other. That's why we must pray, so we can be at peace.

If you're reading this, I want you to think long and hard about all of the liberties you have that you take for granted; some of which you don't even give a second thought. I'm talking about your basic freedoms like speech and the ability to move freely throughout this country. When it is all said and done, this is our country. It's our responsibility to pray for our leaders. Not only the President, but our local, city, state and national leaders. They help shape the policies and laws that govern our land. They all need our prayers!

1 Timothy 2:1-4 AMP   Matthew 24:4-14 AMP   Matthew 13:24-30

March

1

Activate The Blessing

God has commanded the blessing on your life and it's your responsibility to appropriate it. We have defined "blessing" as an empowerment to prosper or succeed. Once you acknowledge that the blessing is on your life, your whole demeanor should change. The way you speak, think and act should reflect that the blessing is on your life. Your attitude should not be one of arrogance, but of confidence and full assurance that the blessing is activated and in full effect in your life. Thoughts of failure and defeat will no longer plague you because you know in your "knower", that you are able to overcome whatever obstacles come your way. You should be just like the guy in the auto insurance commercial who wants the guy juggling chainsaws that are running, to throw them and let him juggle them because he can handle it, with seemingly no experience. Our confidence in the blessing should be as great or more than the guy in the commercial displayed because we keep renewing our mind in the Word.

With the blessing comes a certain condition that must be met. You have to obey God's instructions, even if they don't immediately make sense and you don't understand the how and why of it. That's where trust comes in. You have to trust God that it will all work out in the end. My grandfather used to tell me "hindsight is always 20/20 vision" and that is true. When you look back at certain events in your life, you can now see what part they played in the overall, grand scheme of things to get you where you are today.

When the blessing is on your life, your main function is to be a blessing to others. You have to pass it on and let it flow, like water running through a pipe, into the lives of others. Don't entertain thoughts that you're losing something by passing it on. Just like water flowing through the pipe, even the inside of the pipe gets wet. God will make sure you have more to store.

"The blessing of the Lord, it maketh rich and adds no sorrow with it." You don't have to work to get the blessing; God has commanded it on your life. Accept, acknowledge and activate it. There's work to be done and lives to be touched, so pass it on.

Deuteronomy 28:8   Ephesians 4:23 AMP   Romans 8:28   Proverbs 10:22

2

Seek God

Have you sought God about it? It's a perfectly legitimate question. There are times when we do things or plan to do something; especially if it's legal and moral, but have failed to seek God about it.

Having come this far in our walk with God, we should have a twofold purpose for the things that we do. Our first purpose should be to please God. Secondly, we should purpose to be successful so that the Kingdom of God receives a benefit. If we're to do that, then we have to stop moving without considering or consulting God, unless you enjoy running into brick walls. Moving too fast or in fear ultimately leads to failure. God has a plan that won't fail. If we do things His way, which goes against the grain of the world, it is so much easier, less stressful and enjoyable. I heard one day how God has a perfect plan for the earth and in order for us to get the revelation of His plan, we have to spend time in prayer and in His Word.

To get clear instructions and be successful, we have to commit all we do to Him. This will establish our thoughts. Keep in mind that God has a perfect plan in place for your life. Every step and misstep have been accounted for. His plan includes a good life. Not a trouble free one but a worry, stress-free life if you seek Him first, and follow the plan He lays out for you. When things aren't going the way you think they should, don't jump out in front of God and try to fix it. Be patient and keep trusting. This is not the time to act or start speaking contrary but rather hold on to your faith because God is faithful.

Manifestation may not come immediately, which is okay, because it gives God time to get everything in alignment. When the manifestation comes, it definitely will be better than you thought or asked for.

Jeremiah 29:11-13 AMP   Proverbs 16:3 AMP   Ephesians 2:10 AMP

Hebrews 10:23 AMP

3

God Is The Knot At The End Of Your Rope

After we have exhausted all of our resources and done everything that we know to do in trying to fix our situations, when we're at the end of our rope, God is telling us to tie a knot and hold on because He is that knot. We have to hold on and rest in this moment because He's got us. He sees and knows everything that is going on with us and understands exactly how we feel. His Word comforts us as it reveals what our Great High Priest Jesus experienced here on earth. He was tempted but did not sin.

At times we might be faced with an opportunity to assuage our situations by taking some unethical shortcuts, but if we just hold on, we get to see God work it out better than we ever could. Hart Ramsey's "Uplift" message one day hit the nail on the head with this: "It's going to be ok. God has plans that you are not even aware of yet. Trust this: He always has a Ram in the bush. You'll see!"

Christ voluntarily restricted His use of certain attributes so that He could be the perfect example of how we are to conduct ourselves while here on earth. By remaining in constant communion with the Father through prayer, Christ only did things He saw the Father do. As for us, we should only do and say what God directs us.

Today, keep your focus on God who is the hope, the knot at the end of the rope you're holding onto. He's got your back. Rehearse some of your prior victories. If He did it once, He'll surely do it again.

Hebrews 4:15   Philippians 2:5-8 AMP   John 5:19

4

The Promises Of God

Is there a promise you found in His Word that you're standing on? If so, you can rest, for it'll surely come to pass. Some people like to say, mistakenly, that when it comes to getting prayers answered, God will either say "Yes", "No" or Maybe, and that is far from the truth that we find in His Word. God always says yes to His promises. ALWAYS! You can be confident on this truth; that if you found it in His Word, the answer is "Yes", and the moment you prayed in faith, your prayer was answered.

Most people lose it in-between believing and receiving. Your prayer is answered in the spirit realm the moment you pray. Until it manifests here in the natural, we give God thanks as if we already have it. We don't keep asking God for the same thing over and over. That says you don't believe you already have it. As a parent, if your child asks you for something and you tell them yes, if they keep coming to you asking for it, that immediately tells you they didn't believe or have faith in you. If they asked once and come to you saying "Thank you" for it before they actually receive it, then you'd be inclined to think that they believed they are going to receive it and they believe you'll do what you said.

Whenever you're standing in faith on the promises of God, don't lose faith in-between the believing and receiving phase. Just like Daniel's prayer took some time before the Angels showed up with his answer, Angels are at work on your request. There is a battle going on, just hold on, the answer is on the way.

2 Corinthians 1:20 AMP   1 John 5:14-15 AMP   Mark 11:22-24

Daniel 10:12-13 AMP

5

Doing God's Word

When you hear the Word of God, you receive instructions and information that you can act on. Then you have to do it. It's on you to do what you hear and if you don't, you'll wind up forfeiting the blessing attached to it, which would be a terrible mistake.

We've heard the saying that our "steps are ordered." They are not ordered "of" but ordered "by" the Lord. This tells me that there is a certain level of specificity involved. God strategically guides our steps, placing us where He needs us to be. This is the reason why God speaks specific instructions to us. People are still in need of healing, salvation and deliverance. The only way God can get it done is through us. At different times, we are His eyes, ears, hands and His mouth in the earth. If the work has to be done, then we have to do it as He leads. We have to be like Jesus, only doing what we hear the Father wants done and when He wants it done. There's a rhythm to God. We have to "fall in line" with God, so that we can meet the needs of the people in a timely fashion.

One of the blessings of God is prosperity. God delights in your prosperity, so go for it. When I mention prosperity I'm not talking about money, but rather your success. There are promised blessings for being obedient. Take the Word you receive and run with it. God has nothing but the best for you and everything has been laid out, so go for it!

Psalms 37:23 AMP   Deuteronomy 28:1-14 AMP

6

The Expiration Date

One of the first things we do when grocery shopping for a loaf of bread or milk, is to check the expiration date. It's a common practice when dealing with perishable items because we want to know how long it'll last. In life, your problems have an expiration date. They're perishable, just like a gallon of milk and when they come your way-check the date.

The Psalmist wrote that many are the afflictions of the righteous, but the LORD delivereth him out of them all. The Lord delivering you is the expiration date. This tells me there are going to be some challenges along the way, but they won't last forever. They'll come and go, so please don't get caught up in the "hype." I have a little exercise I want you to try. Can you remember what was a "problem" you had six months ago? Three months? What about two weeks ago? Can't even remember, can you? They came and then they expired.

As long as we're living, challenges will come our way. What we're required to do is maintain the proper attitude. The Apostle Paul encourages us when it comes to tribulations, we should glory or be full of joy in them not because of them. This is the attitude and mindset of a victor. Knowing that we have an assured victory should ignite a certain amount of boldness and confidence on the inside of you. That's why we have to remain diligent when it comes to our spiritual maintenance. Praying, Bible reading and studying is critical. We don't want to get caught slipping and forget, that whatever situation comes up, it's going to pass. If you can't find an expiration date, then you need to give it one. Exercise your Blood-bought authority by speaking to that mountain and casting it into the sea. As long as there's no doubt in your heart and you believe what you say, you'll receive. It's going to come to pass.

Don't start "tripping" when life happens. Just kick back, watch the Word of God work and relax, because there is an expiration date to your problems. We win in the end.

Psalms 34:19   Romans 5:3-5 AMP   Mark 11:23-24

7

Where Are The Cracks?

One night we had a ministry meeting with the leadership of our church that included all of the elders and ministers. To say that they poured into our lives is not giving it justice. Our Bishop gave us such an impartation as it relates to church authority, the anointing, our assignments and the responsibility that comes with it. It was a while before I went to sleep that night because I was so full.

As I was driving home from the meeting, the Holy Spirit began ministering to me certain points that Bishop spoke on. This brought three questions immediately to mind: 1) who am I. 2) what do I believe? I had no problem with those two it was the third one that made me pause: 3) does my life line up with what I believe? I'm not just talking about the part of me everyone sees, what about the cracks, the invisible me that no one can see, like in my thought life and love walk. Do I gossip? Could my cracks be hindering my anointing and periodically render me ineffective? Am I so indifferent when it comes to my cracks that they have become a tolerable part of the inner-me that needs to be examined?

The Holy Spirit prompts us to examine ourselves and the Apostle Paul gives an excellent illustration. In his letter to the church at Corinth, he's talking about partaking in the Lord's Supper. He says *"But let a man examine himself..."* When you make the decision to seriously examine yourself, you might need some tissue and time as it could be rather intense. It is nothing to be afraid of. This process is similar to step four of the twelve steps in a recovery program. In taking an inventory of their lives, participants do it morally, fearlessly and searching, trusting that God will help them clean house. Out of His love for us God will reveal the cracks and help us seal them. It's not like we don't know what they are. I challenge you to write them down. There is no denying what's in black and white. As they are revealed to you, let the Holy Spirit show you how they can be sealed and stay that way.

Question: If you were to do this, what's the worst thing that could happen to you? Answer: You would become a better person and more effective in the Kingdom! Go ahead, take inventory, it won't kill you; it'll just make you better!

1 Corinthians 11:28 AMP   2 Corinthians 3:5 AMP

8

Relationships Are Divine Connections

God created the earth and man. He gave dominion of the earth over to man. In order for God to accomplish anything in the earth, He needs people and permission. If He violated any one of these, He would be a liar and we know that He isn't. This is why we need each other. I need you and you need me. Each one of our relationships has been strategically prearranged for a specific time and purpose. We may not understand the "why" at first but through the course of time, God will make it perfectly clear. I'm a firm believer that we are blessed to be a blessing to others, and God is always trying to get something to you, so He can get it through you, so others can be blessed. For example, you might know me personally and there are some whom I've never met, but this message or these daily messages have found you. As God speaks to and through me, I share it with you. It's all a setup. There are people in your life whom God has sent to encourage or help you navigate through the obstacles of life. If you have been blessed to have someone, then by all means pick up the phone and call them if you need to. Don't feel like you're a burden to them and by the same token if you're called on to help, do it eagerly as unto the Lord. If you don't have someone, ask God to show you who that person is. He's got somebody specifically for you.

You are God's greatest asset in the earth. God said that He would bless you, the righteous, and His favor will surround you like a shield. When you get blessed it's always for you to bless someone else and be God's distribution center right here on earth.

Numbers 23:19 AMP   Colossians 3:23   Psalms 5:12 AMP

9

Being Grateful

Many of you don't know my story, but I have a lot to be grateful for. Right now, I should either be dead, buried, in my grave or in prison. I should be anywhere, doing anything, other than sitting here talking with you about God. I am so grateful to God. My soul says thank you.

One morning as I was walking my dog, I began thinking about being thankful, and how when we approach God in prayer, one of the first things we say before anything is, Thank You. Being thankful is an attitudinal characteristic we develop and fine tune along this journey. Sometimes just a quick glance back at how things used to be is sufficient to make you grateful for the things you have or don't have today. If you dare look back a little longer, you'll see God at work, keeping you when you didn't know you needed to be kept. Before I answered God's call on my life, there were instances that if it had not been for His hand on my life, I wouldn't be here today telling you that I am grateful for everything that I went through back then. Unbeknownst to me at the time, He had a plan, which includes my sharing this with you today.

In the Old Testament days when the priest went before God, they had to bring an offering of an animal sacrifice. The Psalmist talks about coming into the presence of the Lord with thanksgiving. The work Jesus did on the cross means we no longer have to make animal sacrifices because we now have God's Grace. When we approach God, we simply say "Thank You." Before we ask Him for anything in prayer, we say thank you.

Whenever you're feeling down and whiny, write a gratitude list. Think of ten things you're grateful for and watch your feelings transform into thankfulness. Go through the day telling God "Thank You" every chance you get. Over and over just do it. God says you're welcome in awesome ways!!

Psalms 100:4 AMP   Psalms 95:2   Ephesians 5:20 AMP

10

Don't Shortcut Your Time With God

Ever had one of those days when it seems just a little harder to get out of the bed, and when you finally do, your whole routine is thrown off. I've had days like that. As I started moving, I realized that I had an extremely busy day ahead. When I started my time of fellowship with God, thoughts of today began to flood my mind and then the spirit of compromise showed up, because I have my normal flow. Thoughts of cutting out this time now and catch it later in the day wouldn't leave me alone. I know if I do, later will never come, and the next time it will be easier to cut. Therefore, I took a deep breath, prayed, pushed past those thoughts, and decided something elsewhere would have to be adjusted, but not my time with God.

I refuse to be deceived into thinking that it's all right to put God on the back burner every now and then because "God knows your heart." When I hear people say things like that, I know they have cut God short somewhere and are trying to justify what they did. I immediately tell them "Yea He knows your heart, but He knows His Word."

We have to take the Word of God and hide it in our hearts. That takes consistently spending time in His Word to accomplish. One of the lesson I learned the hard way, a long time ago is, I have to do it early or my day is all "jacked up." I can prevent it by simply doing what I know to do, when I'm supposed to do it, and that is giving Him the first fruits of my day.

Don't shortcut God, because when you do, you're really shortcutting yourself. Set aside some time, preferably in the morning to fellowship with Him. Get your news early and hot off the press. God has a plan for your life and He's waiting to tell you how to go about it!

Psalms 119:11   Psalms 63:1   Jeremiah 29:13 AMP

11

Psalm 56:4

One morning in my prayer time, I was lead to *Psalm 56:4. In this passage the psalmist writes: *"In God I will praise his word, in God I have put my trust; I will not fear what flesh can do unto me."*

Meditate on this passage. Roll it over and over in your mind about how trusting God, no matter what you might be going through, is the smartest thing you could possibly do.

Nothing you'll ever experience will catch God by surprise. He knows and Jesus has felt the pain you're feeling right now. The Bible tells us that Jesus was touched with the feelings of our infirmities and temptations, so know that you're not alone. This thing won't last long because it has an expiration date. It will expire the moment you esteem God and His Word over your circumstances, no matter what it might be or look like.

Remember, we don't walk by what we see or our senses, but by what the Word has to say about it, because, for all practical purposes, Gods Word is etched in stone!

Hebrews 4:15   2 Corinthians 5:7 AMP

* KJV

12

Off Balance

Have you been a little off balance lately? I remember once, of having to let go of some old things while at the same time learning new things to replace them. For instance, my old trustworthy Dell laptop had reached what the techs call, after five years, "end of life." I finally became a Mac guy and purchased a Mac notebook. To say it was challenging is an understatement. It took me twice as long to do simple things. While I "enjoy" the learning process of navigating through different keystrokes, the changes made it hard for me to get into my familiar flow of things. I learned a "new normal." This all being juxtaposed with constantly getting new information that's good, enlightening and fits with the other areas of my life God was working on. I was developing new spending and eating habits which was causing me to look at making changes elsewhere.

I keep getting those little promptings to do more, so that I can get into alignment with where I believe God is taking me. The one thing that keeps me centered is, I'm still making my confessions because I have no doubt that the Word works regardless of how I might feel. I am not in fear and have a sound mind or rather clear thinking.

Renewing the mind and speaking the Word of God holds off the enemy while he tries to play mind games of intimidation. Something I learned a long time ago is that the only permanent thing in life is change. No matter what adjustments you find yourself making at this stage of life, God has provided enough grace for you to be successful.

Hebrews 10:23 AMP   2 Timothy 1:7 AMP   Romans 12:2 AMP

13

What Do You Desire?

Have you ever read a Scripture so many times that you know it by heart and then one day get the revelation of one particular word found in it? It happened to me as I was reading "what things you desire when you pray believe..." that's when the word "desire" jumped off the page, and it helped me "connect a dot" to another verse I happened to be meditating on.

This is how "desire" is defined in Webster's dictionary: to express a wish to obtain; to ask; to request; to wish for the pleasure or enjoyment of, with a greater or less degree of earnestness. As born-again believers we have to keep it in proper perspective. By that I mean, we don't desire anything that doesn't further advance the Kingdom of God. You can desire things personally, like healing in your body or that a specific financial need be met, because the Kingdom receives a benefit from your testimony.

The Psalmist wrote the best way to receive our desires is to delight or take great pleasure in the Lord. We delight or express pleasure in the Lord when we fellowship or commune with Him in prayer and His Word. You have to take the Word, keep it in the midst of your heart by meditating on it throughout the day, and let it get into your heart or spirit man. Faith grows exponentially when your spirit man hears you speak the Word. Your heart is the soil; His Word is the seed you plant and water by speaking it.

What do you desire? God wants to fulfill all of the desires He's placed in you. When we give Him credit, the Kingdom is advanced, and people are drawn to Him. This gives them some much needed hope.

Mark 11:23-24   Psalms 37:4 AMP   Proverbs 4:20-21 AMP

14

Don't Sign For The Package

With the way things seem to be going on in our lives today, there are times when it can be a little overwhelming. When it gets like this, we have to be vigilant about the things we say, and if we're not careful, the words coming out of our mouth will be more about the situations than the Word of God. Therefore, if you don't want something, then don't say it i.e. "Don't sign for the package!"

If the mailman brings you some mail that requires a signature and you don't want it, you don't accept it. Without signing for it, you send it back to the sender and you don't give it a second thought. We need to take the same stance when the enemy tries to deliver something to us with a negative thought. It could be when you start to get symptoms of sickness in your body or a bad report from the doctor. Maybe your money is "getting funny" and the thought comes, "I don't have enough to do this or how am I going to do that." Don't agree with the thought but speak what you want it to be by faith. It's at this point where you can either sign for it or refuse it. What are you going to do; or better yet, what are you going to say? Will you speak a promise or the problem? Are you going to speak faith or fear? We already know the negative, but can we see by faith the promise?

I have a covenant with God that's intact, and as long as I do my part, God has to do His. I believe it by faith, and I can't see anything other than all of my needs being met. There is no way that money, health, relationships or any other situation will not be handled according to God's Word, as long as I keep His Word in my heart and it comes out of my mouth first. I believe this with every fiber of my being. Remember, you were created in the image of God. You are another speaking spirit, with the same creative power He has when he spoke the world into existence. Make sure your words are in alignment with God's Word and what you want to see manifest in your life because when we speak, we create our world and you'll get it.

The next time the doorbell rings and it's the messenger from Satan with a delivery that needs your signature in order for you to have it, simply tell him to send it back "refused" or better yet send it back "unknown" because that person doesn't live here anymore.

Malachi 3:10-12 NLT   Philippians 4:19   Job 22:28 AMP

Mark 11:23-24 AMP

15

Life

Are you really living and enjoying the life you want or is your life like "Texas hold em" where you're making the best out of the card's life dealt you? If the latter is where you find yourself, it is never too late to right the ship of your life. You can turn it around today.

How are you walking and is your life pleasing to God? This is a question that only you can answer and requires some soul searching. When I ask about your walk is it in the spirit or the flesh? Is it according to God's Word or the world? Starting right where you are, you can begin to live the kind of life that pleases God. As you prepare to read your Bible, ask God to "Give me a Word that will help me make the necessary adjustments so that my life will mirror your Word." The Holy Spirit will illuminate a passage of Scripture for you and it will address a particular area of your life.

Something that I've had to do is quit living in the past and stop digging up dead situations. Past things are nothing but distractions. What's important is staying in the "here and now" by focusing on life today. Doing the best I can means making mistakes and when I do, fix what I can and if I can't move on. There is a battle that takes place in our mind and emotions. When we slip up, the sooner we can forgive ourselves the quicker we are to getting on the road to recovery. My grandfather would say, "you can't put spilled milk back in the bottle." That is true. God is sovereign, and even He can't undo the past because it would make him a liar. He gave us dominion over the earth and when we mess up, we seek Him out to help clean up the mess we made. He will have people give us favor and extend grace. This gives us an opportunity to learn from our mess ups, but He won't undo it.

Today, make the most of your life by walking in the spirit and not in the flesh. Jesus came to give us the abundant life, that's an overflowing with good kind of life. Receive it.

Ecclesiastes 12:13   Romans 8:1-2 AMP   John 10:10 AMP

16

You've Already Got It / Go Get It

The moment you were born again, everything you will ever need for life on earth was provided. God has made available to you all things that pertain to life and godliness. We used to sing a song that said, "Everything you'll need, He's already provided." Makes no difference whether it's healing or some other type of need; it's already been made available. We have to bring it into this world or make the transfer by speaking the Word of God in faith about it, and when we do, manifestation is sure to come.

Lately, the Lord has been dealing with me to become more aggressive with my faith. If I pay close attention to those around me, I can see that there are opportunities to share my faith in one form or the other (i.e. praying with or for people.) Maybe speaking a kind word or just saying "hello" and "have a good day" to the stranger pumping gas at the pump next to me. I have to get the word about the love of God out of me and into those around me because it feels like a fire shut up in my bones.

Our whole Christian walk is geared toward helping others. For three years, Jesus was our example as He walked the earth. He went about doing good and only saying what the Father told Him. The same power Jesus operated in has been bestowed to those of us who believe on His name.

You've already got it. Pass it on!

2 Peter 1:3 AMP   Acts 10:38   Jeremiah 20:9   John 14:10

17

You Are Not Defeated

People who always talk about how hard of a time they're having, or negative things going on in their life, are folks who have a defeated mentality in that area of their life. Yes, you will go through some things, but you don't have to put it on blast (incessantly talk about it).

The Bible says you have what you say, and with speech like this all you're doing is adding fuel to the fire of what you really don't want. It never produces victorious results. If you've been consistently going to the doctor year after year for the same illness, and it never gets better, something's wrong. If you are born again, defeat is not of God. What do you confess or take ownership of with the words of your mouth? Are you signing for packages that you don't want? When we talk like that, in essence we're sub-consciously saying God is a failure. In our mind, we know He isn't but in our heart the connection hasn't been made. Sometimes the few inches from our mind to our heart (spirit man) can become an endless highway if we don't change our speech. What does God's Word have to say about who you are and what you can have if you meet certain conditions? You have to know these. Look up the Scriptures for healing and prosperity. Confess them and then go to the Scripture that says you can have what you say. Claim healing and prosperity in your body according to the Word you just confessed.

If you don't get anything else, look at yourself, determine if some adjustments need to be made, and by all means make them. If you do, the worst thing that can happen to you is you'll be healed and enjoying all the benefits of Kingdom living.

Mark 11:23-24   1 Peter 2:24 AMP   3 John 2 AMP

18

It All Begins With A Seed

Everything you are is a by-product of the seeds sown in your life. I'm not just talking about things you've said or done, but about the way you were raised or things you encountered along the way. One way or another, whether you did it or it was done to you, all of your experiences have been deposited into your life and now you have the manifestation of those seeds sown.

God has designed life in such a way that certain agricultural principles and metaphors when put into motion govern our life. One really old saying, "you reap what you sow" immediately comes to mind. Every day is seedtime for us. This is when we should endeavor to sow seeds of kindness, peace, money and love. I'm a living witness that if you put it out there it'll definitely come back to you. When you look back, you will see how God strategically set the whole thing up. It came back to you right when you needed it. I want to caution you about sowing money. The number one rule is to be led by God, not your emotions in your giving. Sometimes we can get caught up thinking that we will receive the same type of harvest someone else did so we give for no other reason than to just get it. On the other hand, whenever you have a financial need the best way to get that need met is to sow a seed as the Holy Spirit directs.

Maybe you've sown seeds yet no manifestation. Just be patient it takes time. The deeper the roots the bigger the harvest, and when harvest comes it will be your "now" moment.

Genesis 8:22   Galatians 6:7-10   Mark 4:26-29

19

It Wasn't A Waste Of Time

One day in my quiet time with the Lord this came up: From time to time I mention how everything that we experience at some point in our journey is for the road up ahead. The relationships you have with different people who cross your path aren't by accident but rather by divine appointment. It's all a set up for bigger and better things. I'm talking about destiny being fulfilled. Your calling was established while you were still in your mother's womb. Everything has led up to this point. All you have to do is look back and see how every step has prepared you for the next phase of your life. In this season things are going to turn around in your favor because God can now trust you.

Whatever God has spoken to you in your spirit, will now come to fruition. Every step has led to this point in your life, and you are now ready to step over into your new season and claim the biggest part of your inheritance. It's not coming, it's here. You've been praying and sowing in tears. God heard you. He will reward your labor of love, which you have shown towards His name. Stay sensitive to the Holy Spirit. Your mind is filled with so much these days that when He speaks strategies and concepts to your spirit you might not remember. Get in the habit of writing down what He speaks to you.

Where you're at right now is another step. It's not a resting place!

Jeremiah 29:11-13   Hebrews 6:10 AMP   John 16:13 AMP

20

Is God's Word Your Final Authority?

Here is a thought provoking yet very serious question; is God's Word the final authority in your life. One afternoon, I had my children in the car. My son who is the youngest was three years old at the time, said "its morning outside." His older sister told him it wasn't and that it was afternoon. They debated for a minute and then he asked me was it morning or not. I told him "no it's the afternoon" and He said, "Oh ok." My word settled the issue for him. He trusted that I would tell him the truth and that I knew more than she did. Even though she might be right, he had to confirm it with me. This started me to thinking about the Father and how we should be the same way. His Word should be the final authority in our life.

The way things are going in the world today, God's Word has to be our final authority. The ever-shifting moral compass, the legislating of immorality (i.e. same sex marriages) or the instability of our economy. Additionally, taking little "shortcuts" that would immediately enhance your finances, while you tell yourself "everybody is doing it, who's it going to hurt or nobody is going to know." All are causing people to make decisions and take stances they normally wouldn't. God has written a book with very clear, detailed instructions and directions about His stance on everything from how we relate to Him, to our relationships with parents, spouses and children, how to handle our finances, and His position on sex. Since the book has already been written, He won't go back and change it or give us a revised version. All of those issues have been settled. The Holy Spirit is gently nudging us to get it together and read the book. Spending time in His Word leads to a renewed mind, where you will be equipped and able to resist the enemy when he brings thoughts that don't line up with the Word.

Something I learned a long time ago is that I can't change the Word to fit my life, but I can change my life to fit the Word. God is "the same yesterday, today and forever." He won't change and neither will His Word. You've got His Word on it!

Psalms 119:89   Ephesians 5:13-17   Hebrews 13:8

21

Look Out For The Kitchen Sink

"New levels bring new devils" is a saying I've often heard and it's so true. Along with the new devils, one thing I've come to notice is the enemy will also bring up some old stuff too. He will throw any and everything he can at you. It's all an attempt to distract and discourage. Hence "Look out for the Kitchen Sink."

The day you got born again a target was placed on your life. The best thing about it is it's hard to hit a moving target! If you're busy doing what God called you to do you'll be okay. The safest place to be is in the perfect will of God. That's not to say challenges won't come because they will. Your relationship with the Holy Spirit will help you navigate through the minefield of the enemy as you sidestep his traps. He will literally throw the kitchen sink at you through your thoughts. It could be an old boyfriend or girlfriend whom you haven't seen in years and you see someone or something that reminds you of them. It could be an opportunity to steal something, maybe a spam email of the x rated nature or an old habit God delivered you from like alcohol or drugs. The enemy is aware of your triggers and he definitely knows what has worked in the past. Anything that he can use to distract you, he will. Remember the greater the attack the closer you are to your breakthrough. That's when you kick back, laugh at the devil and tell him, "Thank you for the confirmation, because obviously you can see in the sprit realm that I must be closer than I know."

There's only one way to deal with him and it's not fighting, but rather doing what the Bible tells us to do, *"submit to God, resist the devil and when we do he will flee."* A good definition for resist is to stand firm against, refuse to give in. My favorite is say "no." Being submitted to God, doing the things He called us to and doing it His way, when the devil comes along and make no mistake about it he's coming, we won't have the time to entertain him because we're too busy doing Kingdom work to give him a second thought. When he launches his attacks against you in your thought life remember: the only power he has is suggestive thoughts. The mind is the battlefield.

Your enemy will throw everything he can at you and when he gets to the kitchen sink and tosses it your way, remain steadfast and unmovable and tell him "thank you" for delivering my breakthrough confirmation.

2 Timothy 3:12 AMP   Psalms 91:1 AMP   Psalms 34:19   James 4:7

22

Studying The Word

You don't have to be a minister or preacher to study the Word of God. "Study" is defined in Webster's 1828 as setting the mind or thoughts upon a subject for the purpose of learning what is not known before.

When you study God's Word, it doesn't matter how many times you have read something, what's transpiring in your life at that time determines the revelation and understanding you gain. God's Word is so pregnant with revelation that sometimes you have to approach it like a thirsty man needing a cold glass of water on a hot Texas day.

Studying God's Word will help you make sound decisions, control your thoughts, and determine your actions. They'll be based on the Word. There are benefits to taking time to study the Word of God. You'll be rewarded with not only wisdom and a deeper understanding, but you'll get to see different facets of God. Like I mentioned earlier, a lot of what you gain will be predicated on the stage of life you currently enjoy. You have to want God's Word to speak to you, especially when things are a little tough. On many occasions I've had the Word come down my street and park right in my driveway. It was just what I needed at the appropriate time.

When you study the Word & apply it to your life, it'll help you stay focused. You want the Word to take root and bear fruit in your life-the kind of fruit that remains.

2 Timothy 2:15 AMP   Proverbs 4:5-7 AMP   John 15:16 AMP

23

Dealing With Change

Scripture tells us that God never changes. He is "the same yesterday today and forever." That's reassuring to know when you're in the midst of change which seems to be happening more frequently these days. Sometimes I feel like a shapeable piece to a puzzle that I have no idea what the final picture looks like. I know I have a destiny to fulfill and God is behind the scenes working out the details.

My pastor once said something that was so profound. She said, "God doesn't have to explain anything to us. Our responsibility is to simply obey. The more we obey, the more He will give us vision." Obeying when things are changing, and you are trying your best to maintain is not easy. You might get those nasty little distractions that want to garner your attention and if that doesn't work, doubt tries to nudge its way past security and come in uninvited. That's when our faith kicks in. Spending time daily in the Word of God reading, confessing, and praying in the Spirit are the best tools I know of to help you stay anchored. This is what I have to do in order to stay built-up or else I become short- tempered, easily irritated, wanting to express myself verbally and I then wind up having to apologize later. I personally don't get a thrill out of apologizing for something I shouldn't have done or said but I do apologize. There's an old saying "crow goes down better when it's warm" so I apologize quickly!

As you go through the changes and challenges of life there's nothing to be afraid of. God will hold your hand. Just remember there are only two permanent things in life: Change and our unchanging God!

Hebrews 13:8 AMP   Jeremiah 7:23   Isaiah 41:10

24

God and Our Children

One morning I let my oldest daughter lead our prayer before they went off to school. I usually do it but felt led to let her. I was thinking about a message I did awhile back on praying for our children's safety while they're at school and how we need to keep it up daily. We can't afford to get caught slipping when it comes to covering all of the children in our immediate and extended families. Our covering and stance is one of protection by faith and not out of fear. We know things are different today than it was when we grew up because it was unheard of for anyone to come into a school and shoot up the place. God and prayer have been replaced with armed guards, metal detectors and pistol packing teachers. Since we can't immediately put God and prayer back into the public school system, the next best thing is to put the Word of God in our children. We have to teach it to them and that goes much further than just lip service. They have to see us not just talking the talk but also walking the talk.

Today's children are inundated with images from a variety of sources; some of which we have no immediate control over. For example, during one season of *American Idol* my youngest daughter asked whether or not the girl performing was a boy or girl. We told her. This is not the first time she's asked this question. I told my wife it looks like we might have to give "that talk" to her sooner than expected, especially if she ever asks why they dress and look like that. My wife asked what was I going to say. She immediately chuckled and said, "Good luck." At the time she was only six years old. When the time comes the only thing I know to do is ask the Holy Spirit to give me wisdom and the words to speak.

We need to put more effort into exposing our children to the Word of God in action. Children need to see how we handle good times and bad. How do you handle and resolve conflict when your children are around? Do you explain to them all of the various options available and if you could've handled it better, are you willing to "eat some crow" and be transparent? They need to see God in the flesh through us and how we deal with life on life's own terms. These are the things we have to do if we're to properly equip our children to go out in this world.

Today you can be the example that not only your children need to see but the world also. There are souls out there to be saved and not a lot of time left to do it.

Deuteronomy 11:18-21 AMP   Ephesians 6:4 AMP   Proverbs 22:6 AMP

25

The Word Will Find You

God's Word will find you right where you are. Whether you're in need of encouragement or guidance, it can be found in the Word of God. The Bible tells us God's Word is *"alive, powerful and sharper than any two edged sword. The Word pierces and divides the spirit from the soul and discerns the intents of our thoughts and heart."*

God knows where you are and more importantly, He knows where you're going and how you're going to get there. When we read the Word, it will do one of three things: It will expose to our spirit man things that need to be worked on in our character, provide guidance and comfort during challenging times or it will be the confirmation needed for a specific situation. When the Word finds you, apply it to your life. There's a reason why God gives us a Word in the particular season we might be in and it is to fulfill the plan He has for our life. Reading your Bible daily is critical because it will keep the spirit of your mind renewed and provide fresh revelation.

Today when you spend your five minutes with God, meditate on the Word and let it marinate into your spirit man. Rest assured, His Word will find you and park right on your doorstep.

Hebrews 4:12 AMP   Ephesians 4:22-24 AMP

26

In Between Believing and Receiving

You've prayed and believe that the Word of God is true yet no manifestation. This is where most people tend to lose it. Some people repeat the same prayer request over and over thinking it will provoke God to finally hear them and give an answer. As we mature in our walk with God, we pray and ask Him according to His word ONCE, and then thank Him as if we already have it in full manifestation until we do; that my friend is faith.

The moment we ask in prayer by faith our prayer is answered. Just like it took the angel Gabriel three weeks to bring Daniel an answer to his prayer due to warfare, don't think your enemy is going to just let you "have it all" without resistance. The tools he likes to use the most are doubt and discouragement. In an attempt to get you to "feel something," things will go awry in totally different areas of your life, which add to whatever else you might be going through. It's nothing but a trick where he can whisper lies in your ear about faith not working. Don't go for it. We can't get emotional and get over into fear. God has given us a sound mind, where we can think clearly, take it all in stride and throw it back on him. Thank him for the confirmation because you are closer than you know to your manifestation.

There's an old saying, "delayed doesn't mean denied." Take this and apply it to your life as you allow God the opportunity to work out the details, get everything and everyone in the proper order for the manifestation.

Mark 11:24   2 Timothy 1:7 AMP   Galatians 6:9 AMP

27

Back To Love Again

Back in the 70's there was an R&B group named LTD. One of their hits was a song titled "Back in Love Again." I was reminded of this as I was studying one day. To partially quote one of the lyrics "Every time I turn around, I'm back to love again." I'm convinced there's no way around it. When you break it down, love is at the core of everything God stands for because God is love.

Initially in the Old Testament we were given Ten Commandments by which to govern our lives. Jesus simplified it by showing us two commandments that we have to live by and they are; "Love God with all your heart, soul and mind, and love your neighbor as yourself." All of the law hangs on these two and when you do them you have done the other eight by default. Picture love acting like a curtain rod and your faith the hooks, because faith works by love. Attached to the hooks are your anointing, healing, peace, prosperity, protection and money. In order for them to stay attached and not fall off we must develop our love walk.

Developing in love is a process and the best place to begin is at home. The Bible is full of instructions on how to love your spouse, children and then move outside of the house to friends, and a host of others including your enemies. We're told why we do it and when to do it. As we move through the process and we need to make course corrections to stay on track, God has included a provision called grace. As you progress, you'll begin to notice subtle changes in your demeanor. You've become easy going and are suddenly more tolerant of others and forgiving when their mistakes affect you. It takes time and practice, but I can tell you from my own experiences this is the place to be. You become more God conscious and less self, thinking of others before you.

The payoff is great when you show God's love to others through daily practice. This is a lifestyle not an event.

1 John 4:16-21 AMP   Matthew 22:36-40

28

Overcoming The Obstacles Of Life

Over the years, I've been privileged to enjoy the counsel of some elderly men at key points in my life. When I was child it was my grandfather. He spoke volumes into my life that I still recall to this day. When I began the transition that brought me to this point in my life, there was a guy named Ron. He once told me that success isn't measured by what you achieve but by what you overcome. That's something I never forgot. When I look back over my life, along with recalling the testimonies of others, we all at some point have had childhood issues that helped mold certain parts of our character that quite possibly still haunt us. Today I want to let you know that no matter what your "it" is, "it" can be overcome, and you can go on, be successful, live a productive and meaningful life.

Our parents did the best they could with the information they had available to them. I'm not condoning any type of abuse, but at some point we have to move on and not let the past continue to hold us hostage. We all, parents included, are a sum total of our past experiences in life. We acknowledge mistakes were made and begin the process of healing by forgiving them. This includes whoever did, not just parents, what they did to you. How long are you going to replay what they did? I used to work for a guy who was a terror on two feet. Everywhere he went his reputation preceded him. He was abusive and real tough over the phone and in emails but never face-to-face. One day the Lord spoke to me about it and told me that somewhere down the line this is what he witnessed and was subjected to as a child. Couple that with fear and 50 years later, if it's not addressed this is the finished product. Once I understood that, I became more tolerant of his shortcomings. Every now and then, I catch myself dwelling on some part of that experience. I say a prayer for him and move on.

Know that God has placed tools in your life so that you can do better. You have the Word of God and the Holy Spirit as your guide. Remember love is key to everything we do and is tied directly to our faith working for us.

Philippians 3:13   Matthew 6:12   Galatians 5:6 NLT

29

This Is Warfare

There is a war being waged against us right now. It take place right between our ears. I've heard it said before and it's so true "the battle-field is our mind" and our soul is the spoil. If you take an honest look at what's going on in the world, the enemy is steadily trying to gain control over us through our thoughts. My brother and I were talking the other day about how in another 50 or 60 years they probably will have legislated that heterosexual sex is outlawed. They are calling right wrong and wrong right. People are so lawless that when you turn on the news you hear of someone else opening fire and killing multiple people randomly with no rhyme or reason. Now is not the time for us to get into fear but rather to draw closer to God.

If you really want to stay encouraged during these times, become intimate with Psalm 91. Get to know this passage like you know your name and watch your faith rise during these seemingly tough times.

2 Timothy 1:7   James 4:8

30

Grace

We have always defined grace as God's unmerited favor. That definition is one of about twenty that *Webster's 1828 Dictionary* gives, but I want you to think of it like this: grace is the ability or capacity to endure.

All through this journey called life, we are going to go through some things. Whether you know it or not God has given us the grace, the ability to endure, and to go through it. My challenge to you is to put a demand on grace. Since it has already been provided for us free of charge, let's increase our knowledge of Him by spending more time in the Word and then bringing it to the forefront of our consciousness as we give voice to His Word. If you do this you'll be adding another layer of confidence while you walk this grace life out. The Apostle Paul sought the Lord three times about his "thorn in the flesh" and was told *"My grace is sufficient for thee: for my strength is made perfect in weakness."*

If Paul had challenges in his walk, then you know we're not exempt from them either. The same grace given to him has been extended to us. All we have to do is walk in it.

2 Peter 1:2-4 AMP   *Acts 14:3 AMP*   *2 Corinthians 12:7-9 AMP*

31

The Seasons Are Changing

There is a saying I picked up a few years ago that I'm sure you're familiar with. It refers to the people who come into our lives. It goes like this, "Some people come for reasons, some for seasons and others for a lifetime." The reason I say seasons are changing is because several of the people I minister with at church, God has shifted them to different locations. When they first started moving I thought it was due to this or that and it kind of bothered me. Then one of my former classmates whom I have been real close to for the past several years moved to another location. That's when I realized it's all a pre- arranged, divine shift.

Sometimes I feel like we're pieces to a moving jigsaw puzzle, not realizing once again, that we all have been called to an assignment. God has pre-arranged our purpose and destiny while our responsibility is to let Him work out the details. Like the cabinet members for The President of our country serve at his pleasure, we too also serve at the pleasure of our God. Ours is on a much grander scale. The work we have been called to do is extremely sensitive and life changing. Only those whom God has thoroughly vetted and properly prepared are given the clearance that allows them to perform in this arena.

God has a plan and purpose for all of our lives. We all might not be seen or heard by millions, but the work we have been called to do is no less important. If you reach one person today and share the love of Christ with them, then you've done a great job in this season of your development and your reward waits.

Proverbs 16:3 AMP   Romans 8:30 AMP   Ecclesiastes 3:1-9 AMP

April

1

Acknowledging Will Make It Happen

In defining the word "acknowledge", it means to admit the existence, reality and the truth of a thing. Webster's 1828 records: "to own, avow or admit to be true."

In the natural we admit that we own something after we take possession of it. For example, when you buy a new car and tell people what you've got after you take delivery. As believers, we take possession of the things we want by confessing them before they manifest. We see it as ours before we actually have it. It could be you are believing for healing in your body or a marriage relationship restored. Whatever it is, you have to see it by faith with your mind's eye, in order to receive it. Do you see yourself healed and doing things you couldn't previously do? Can you see you and your spouse back together again enjoying each other's company? Don't be limited by the examples I gave. You can use it in any area of your life. If you want to lose weight, purchase a new car or new home, etc. You have to see it and acknowledge that it's yours.

The best way I know to acknowledge something is to speak it. You can't speak it if you haven't spent time daily in the Word of God to know that it's yours. Get your mind on the Word and your thoughts will be in alignment with it. This is not positive thinking; this is Scripture thinking and you need to confess it. Say to yourself right now, "I'm a Scripture thinker." Whenever you speak words like this to yourself, it's building up your faith.

Today, acknowledge and take ownership of that thing you believe is yours. God made it available to you through the shed blood of Christ, so go get it!

Romans 4:17   Philemon 6   Romans 10:17 AMP

2

Regroup Not Retreat

Webster's defines "retreat" as: "to retire (withdraw) from any position or place." Regroup is defined as "to reorganize (one's forces), as after a battle."

While in the heat of the battle one of the first thoughts that comes to our mind is to retreat and rethink our position. We ask ourselves, "Have I really heard from God?" Don't go for it. It's nothing more than a trick of the enemy. He's trying to get us engaged in doubt and unbelief, which is fear based. When the battle gets like this you have to fall back and regroup, by going into your Prayer closet.

By now you have come to know the voice of God in the person of the Holy Spirit who is sent to be our Guide and Helper. When you're in your Prayer closet the Holy Spirit will provide instructions for any course adjustments and give you an encouraging word as you reorganize and get back in the fight. One of the members of our praise team said something that I've never forgot, "This fight we're in is fixed. We won, so why are you tripping."

I went to the back of the book and it says we won. Hang in there because if you know you're going to win why do you quit?

John 16:13 AMP   Matthew 6:6 AMP   Revelation 12:11 AMP

3

Are You In A Relationship With God Or Having An Affair?

Are you in a relationship with God or are you having an affair? In your relationship with God do you just drop by and check in to see what the temperature is or are you committed?

Any relationship we have, whether it is with God, at home with our loved ones, those we work with or play with - relationships take work! The reason why affairs are so exciting is because they don't require any work and there's no commitment. Those who put more effort and time in their relationship with God get more out or as the Bible tells us "we reap what we sow!" No matter where we are there is always room for improvement. Personally, there are some days when "I just don't feel it" but thank God I've learned that my relationship with Him, just like being married is not based on how I feel but rather on the covenant He made with Abraham.

Feelings can change as quickly as the weather in Texas, but God always remain the same. He holds up His end of the deal even when we don't!

Galatians 6:7-8 AMP   Genesis 12:3 AMP   Hebrews 13:8

4

Being Specific In Prayer

Have you ever had someone ask you to pray for them without giving you any specifics? I have and what I started doing is ask them what exactly do you want me to pray about? You'd be surprised at how some people don't have a specific request. They just know I have a relationship with God and maybe I can "get a prayer through" on their behalf. I politely let them know that if you want me to pray for you then I need to know what you desire or else I'd be asking for nothing and that's just what you're going to get. It's not my intent to come off harsh or cruel. When we pray, if we're to get them answered then our prayers should be based on the Word of God or have Kingdom purpose.

Praying according to the Word of God will have laser intensity and will zero in on whatever problem or need we have. Take for instance you need healing in your body. Asking God to heal you should be: I need healing in this area for... When it comes to praying about finances, don't just ask an overall "fix it" type of prayer. Instead be detailed about what it is you desire. If you need a specific financial situation rectified in your life then ask for it.

Keep this in mind, when we pray the Word of God angels are listening and when they hear the Word come out of our mouth, spoken in faith, they immediately go to work, causing the corresponding manifestation to occur.

Philippians 4:6 AMP   1 John 5:14-15 AMP   Psalms 103:20 AMP

5

Let It Flow

Have you ever done something for someone, they offered you some money and you tell them "you don't have to" and you refused to accept it? If so, what you quite possibly could have done is stopped the flow of blessing into their life. God is not going to rain money down from heaven and drop it in our hands. It's going to take a person operating in the earth to do God's will and carry out His purposes. When you bless someone financially why is it wrong for you to receive the same? If God impresses upon you to sow money into someone's life could He not be doing the same for you? I know some people feel bad about taking money from people when it's offered. Don't feel bad about somebody being used by God to bless your life. They are blessed in return. You don't know what God is up to when He allows things like this to happen. Keep in mind it's a flow. You have to keep the flow going and not create a dam. Our mindset should be one of "I am a distribution center." When money comes, we tithe, save and pass some on. We are here on the earth to help one another not only by giving but also by receiving. When the Spirit of God moves, we have to be in the right position i.e. on the giving or receiving end of things for it all to work. Don't get me wrong there might be times when God will impress upon you not to receive something and to be a blessing to them in that way. That's where your relationship with the Holy Spirit comes into play. Be sensitive at all times to His gentle leadings and let Him guide.

Today continue to let the blessing flow in and through you into the lives of others. Follow the Holy Spirit because He won't lead you wrong. Let it flow!

Luke 6:38 NLT   John 16:13 AMP   Psalms 32:8 NLT

6

What Are You Doing With Your Time?

Think about how you spend your day. It seems like people everywhere are asking, "where has the time gone"? There are still twenty-four hours in a day and sixty minutes in an hour so why does it seem like it was just Christmas? Yet the month of May will be here in a couple of weeks. The reason is largely because of the amount of time we spend using our electronic devices as we Google something, cruise Facebook, and send out Tweets or text messages. Have you ever logged onto Facebook "just for a minute" to look up and an hour has gone by? It's happened to all of us. The next time you go someplace look around and count the number of people on their smart phones and you'll see what I'm talking about.

The question is this: How much time do you spend in the Word of God and in prayer? You say "I don't have time." You know what, you'll never have time until you make it. I heard Christian teacher and author Gloria Copeland say "You can either spend time with your Bible or spend your time and money in the doctor or lawyer's office. The choice is yours." The Word tells us to *"pray without ceasing."* That doesn't mean we do nothing except pray all day every day, but rather as we go through our day in constant communication with our Heavenly Father. Remember prayer is a dialogue and not a monologue. Prayer is a two-way street. There is a transmitter and a receiver. At some point we are one or the other. It's on us to keep the lines open because the Holy Spirit is always trying to guide us. We have to recognize His voice and respond immediately when He speaks.

Today, start looking at prayer as an ongoing conversation with God in the person of the Holy Spirit. He was sent to do a job and the two of you have to be on the same page if you're to enjoy the good life God pre-arranged just for you. It's not too late you still have time.

1 Thessalonians 5:17   John 16:13-14 AMP   Ephesians 2:10 AMP

7

Pray and Keep Moving

After a series of events I have come to the realization that transition is an ongoing process of life. Somehow in my mind I thought that things would settle down for a minute and I would get a break so I could catch my breath-not! Remember I shared with you on February seventh about the "pity pot." That was just a precursor of things to come. I am convinced that God has a sense of humor. He let me go through a phase of feeling sorry for myself along with a mild case of "woe is me." Once I got that out of the way, the real work began.

As revelation knowledge increases so does the challenge of that revelation. If you're standing on God's Word about healing in a specific area of your body and then you get a flat tire on your car, thank God the money was there but now a different part of your body starts to ache. The devil is playing mental gymnastics with you. One of your children decides today is going to be the day they choose to engage in boundary-testing behavior; like you really need that to happen right now! On your way to deal with that you pull up to the gas station and gas seems to have jumped another twenty cents per gallon overnight. Here comes more mental gymnastics. Mind you it is only ten in the morning. I am not even going to bring up the affairs of this world that will make you at this point reach for either your Bible or some Xanax.

Now more than ever we need a Word from God to help us turn down the noise volume of life. I can't stress it enough "You have to spend time daily with God in His Word!" People say, "I just don't have the time." You can either spend the time with God or you will spend time in a doctor or lawyer's office. You choose.

Don't let all of this noise distract you from your God-given purpose.

Life is going to happen like it or not. Pray and keep on moving!

Psalms 63:1   Psalms 34:19   Romans 8:28 AMP

8

Being A Christian Is More Than Lip Service

I was standing next to a guy one time at an event and the person waiting on us mentioned they were selling t-shirts to help some efforts in Africa. The guy mentioned ISIS. I told him they are not the ones, its Boko Haram you need to be concerned with. That's when the guy next to me said "they were the ones killing people in malls and that if they asked were he Muslim or Christian he would say Muslim." I immediately told him "I'm not. I'm a Christian and will stand for mine." I had no idea he claimed to be a Christian but he backpedaled so quick it would make you dizzy. He immediately jumped on my bandwagon and agreed with me. That's when I told him exactly where I stood and that you can't scare me with death. How can you scare a Christian with the very thing that is going to usher you into the presence of the Lord? I made it clear that I'm not trying to get out of here too quickly, but I'm not afraid to die. I've settled it in my heart. The next morning in my prayer time I thought about the incident and the Holy Spirit began telling me how Jesus said, *"If you deny me before men, I will deny you before the Father"* and how the sting and victory of death and the grave have been overcome.

We have to give more than lip service and stand for Christ. The world we live in has gotten so twisted and they are so far off God's beaten path, that there is seemingly no way back for some. Stand for your Christian values and refuse to acknowledge or participate in something that goes against your values. You can be sued for discrimination and possibly lose in "a court of law." This is why we can't let fear into our lives. The magnitude of these issues is overwhelming, and they are gaining more ground every day. As I read my Bible and understand where fear doesn't come from, and how in the back of the book it says we win!!

I stand for what I believe in and I've made the decision that to the best of my ability, I will live my life according to God's Word because when it's all over, I want to hear well done my *"good and faithful servant ... enter into the joy of the Lord."*

Matthew 10:32-33 AMP   1 Corinthians 15:55   Philippians 1:27-28 AMP

Matthew 25:21

9

Becoming Salty Again

I was on a prayer call one morning and the leader was talking about all of the recent events and how God was using our voice as intercessors today to bring about change. Because we are the salt of the earth, God has allowed all of these events to get the Church and intercessors inspired to get back in position. God is making me salt again. I am the man in the gap and *"the effectual fervent prayer of the righteous avails much."* If we pray it has to happen. When we declare and decree a thing by faith it has to come to pass. Don't let the enemy trick you into thinking that the wrongs you've done in the past disqualify you from praying and having your prayers answered. What you pray and declare, it shall be.

All of the recent events will cause a revival in the church where we all come together and break the spirit of racism in the church. He mentioned a few well-known televangelists who are actively engaged in this with their multi-cultural congregations. The enemy is trying to keep us divided but what this is really doing is causing a spiritual awakening in the body of Christ. We all have to do it together.

God is making us salty again. If our salt has lost it strength, then we need to get it back. This can only be accomplished when we stand in the gap, pray in the Spirit, and do our part as the Spirit directs.

Matthew 5:13-16 NASB   James 5:16-18 NASB

10

Being A Team Member Is An Inside Job

A few years ago, as I was going through the airport and I received a compliment on the hat I was wearing. The wording was, "Jesus One Way" with a one-way sign. The gentleman and I started talking about the goodness of God. I started thinking how wearing a uniform in this case a Jesus hat and T-shirt doesn't necessarily make you a member of the team because it's all an inside job.

Today's uniforms are great witnessing tools. They're compromised of diverse clothing apparel like a hat or a t-shirt. It might be a Jesus bumper sticker, the fish or a cross emblem on your car. Whatever it is that outwardly tells the world you believe God and His son Jesus, advances that individual further into the battle. Now you're on "Front Street." You can talk the talk but how good are you at walking the talk? Rest assured life will throw situations at you and with the right set of circumstances, just like when pressure is applied to olives it produces oil, what's inside of you will come out. What we take in through our eyes and ear-gate, good or bad, goes into our hearts and minds. It will eventually come out either in the way we act or talk. When it comes out of our mouth it goes right back into our ears, reinforcing our belief system.

If you're spending more time watching television or listening to secular music than you do in God's Word, when you get assaults from the enemy, for instance a bad report from the doctor, what will be the first thing to come out of your mouth? Will it be the Word of faith or words of fear? There are way too many distractions that can affect your focus. God's Word is the best foundation one can have. It's hard to build a house in the middle of a storm. When the winds begin to howl and hit the frame of the house, you become worried about losing something. Water from the rain comes in causing damage. Frustration mounts and you say, "If it ain't one thing it's another."

Don't let things like this happen to you. Fill up on the Word of God. Read your Bible, pray and listen to the still small voice of the Holy Spirit. The next time you put on your uniform, proudly displaying that you're a member of the team as someone who is walking the talk then you'll be a living epistle for the entire world to see. No matter what a storm might bring, you'll be standing in faith on the promises of God.

Romans 13:13-14 AMP   Matthew 7:24-27 MSG   2 Corinthians 3:1-3 MSG

11

You're Not The Same

The moment you were born again, you became a new person on the inside. The things that you used to like doing you don't want to do anymore. It's not that you can't do them because you still can, but the desire to do it is gone. You don't want to. You have a new nature and that old sin nature has been transformed into a righteousness one.

The Apostle Paul tells us to put on the new man that was created in righteousness and then he proceeds to tell us things we have to stop doing; lying, stealing and then watch what we're saying around others. None of this is possible without first renewing our mind with the Word of God. If we're serious about keeping our old desires in check then our minds have to be washed with the water of God's Word daily. It doesn't take much to slip back into the old familiar ways we used to be. With a steady diet of God's Word, when situations present themselves the Word will kick in and override those desires. Your enemy knows what used to work in the past, so don't think for a moment he won't throw everything he can at you-including the kitchen sink. We have an enemy and a fair fight is not in his vocabulary. His task is to wreck our testimony and fill us with a bunch of guilt and condemnation. If he can trick us into sinning, then he thinks he's won. *The only power he has is the power of suggestion.* Who we have is the Greater One living big on the inside of us. As long as we continue to feed our spirit man the Word of God, we can handle the attacks of the enemy.

As you go through your day today remember, you've put off the old man and put on the new man, which is created after the image of God. You have a new nature and you're not the old person you used to be. You've been changed!

Romans 12:2 NLT   Ephesians 4:23-29 NLT   1 John 4:4

12

Paid In Full

I was talking with a friend of mine one day about the goodness of God and how we've changed. He talked about the trappings of life he used to have (i.e. money, new cars every year) and all of the things that go with living fast and being in the game. He said all of it doesn't even matter now because he has given them up and now has Christ in his life. We talked about how Paul said whatever he had before Christ he counted it as garbage. I said, "You gave up some things, but a man laid down His life so that you could give them up for a better life in Him."

Christ paid it all for us on the Cross. Our entire sin debt was paid in full and everything that we will ever need in this Christian life has been made available to us because of His blood. One of my teachers in the school of ministry used to say that God put it all in the budget for your life. What I find so amazing is that I have been forgiven up front, before I sin or make a mistake. God knew in advance and made arrangements just for me. He made available everything I would need to help keep the pathway to Him free and clear. All I have to do is accept it and walk in it.

Salvation, grace, and righteousness are free gifts from God. All we have to do is believe it to receive it. Remember, your debt has been paid in full!

Philippians 3:13 AMP   2 Peter 1:3   Romans 5:15-21 AMP

13

It's Not Always About You

Our whole Christian walk is geared toward being more Christ like. When we look at His life through the four gospels, and look at how Paul walked, they were always caught showing love toward others, especially in the face of death.

We are commanded to love. Loving others means we have to exercise an extensive amount of forgiveness toward others. There are times; however, when I don't feel like forgiving someone. Then the Holy Spirit quickly reminds me that forgiveness is a decision not a feeling, and that I was forgiven not only for the wrongs I have already done but those I've yet to do. How can I not forgive someone who has wronged me?

There are times when we are the only evidence people will have that God loves them. We have to let God love others through us. We must be the example that draws them to Christ. You might have to go that extra mile, listen to someone who's having a rough time, which could be all they need. You don't have to get all-spiritual and try to help them figure out their life. A listening ear that lets them know someone cares can make all the difference in the world. On the other hand, you're going to have challenges along the way and you have to remember that as you go through. It's not about you. You'll get a chance to share it somewhere down the road with someone whom God will strategically place in your path.

Paul describes love throughout the entire 13th Chapter of 1 Corinthians and at the end he sums it up by saying; faith, hope and love abide but love is the greatest of the three. Today, let love be expressed to others in all that you do.

Matthew 22:36-40   1 Thessalonians 1:4-7 AMP   1 Corinthians 13:13

14

The Rules Are Still The Same

God has not changed His position when it comes to how He feels about man's sexual immorality. To be clear, sex outside of the institution of marriage is wrong. It is designed for a husband (man) and his wife (woman) to come together to procreate and comfort one another. Anything other than that is fornication.

In two instances God expresses Himself on the subject. In Genesis before the law and I place great emphasis on that because before the law there was no sin, God poured out his wrath on Sodom and Gomorrah. Fast-forward to the time of the Apostle Paul in the Book of Romans where the law came, and grace replaced it. God was so fed up with this issue when it came to His man that He washed His hands of it and gave man over to sin and saying, "have at it."

Man can change and legislate whatsoever he desires *but it will not change the Word of God*. The Word is the only thing we have that's stood the test of time and hasn't changed. The problem we face today has to do with our mind-set. We have a democratic and not a kingdom way of thinking that needs to be reversed. In a kingdom you don't get to vote on what the king says to do, you do it or else. If you really think about it, all of the recent events with Defense Of Marriage Act and everything related to it, under kingdom authority could be classified as a treasonous offense which is punishable by death.

The King has sent out a decree that is found in the Bible. Read it, He's very specific.

Genesis 19:1-17,24-28   Romans 1:26-28 AMP

15

This Is My Season

One morning I awoke with the chorus of "It's Working" by William Murphy rolling around in my spirit. It goes like this: "This is my season for grace, for favor; this is my season to reap what I have sown. Everything is working together for my good."

This was something I needed to hear at that particular time to help keep my mind on the promises God has made concerning me. God is working it out. With all of the little "events" that seemingly arise out of nowhere and have no purpose other than to distract, this was the encouragement I needed to give me a boost. The old saying "the closer you get to your breakthrough the greater the attack" was in full effect in my life. I refuse to be moved by my circumstances. My foundation is built on the Word of God and my faith is in the finished work of Jesus. He settled it all on the Cross; all I need to do is receive it.

I want to encourage you today and let you know you're not in this by yourself. We all are going through something but the one thing we have in our favor is the knowledge that God is with and for us. When we look at the back of the book it says WE WIN!

Psalms 5:12 AMP   Psalms 34:19   John 19:26-30

16

Spiritual Warfare Is A Reality

All of the confusion and discord taking place not only in the world today but in our own personal lives is nothing but flat out spiritual warfare and must be treated as such. The Bible tells us that people are not our problem; it's the spirit influencing them that is at work.

God has been allowing me to see things from an entirely different perspective lately. What I used to immediately attribute to people I now recognize as spiritual attacks. The body of Christ is under attack. We are being assaulted on all fronts. The enemy has crossed over into our territory and has captured some of our soldiers. Tongue-talking saints of God are now prisoners of war. Jesus warns Simon that Satan wanted to sift him as wheat. There is always talk about taking back what the enemy has stolen; nevertheless, look around, our team members are being snatched right from under our noses! The enemy is separating our brethren like a cutting horse does cows. The time for us to "man up" and get angry enough to fight back is long overdue!

I challenge you today to go into your prayer closet, begin interceding daily not only for the lost but also for our fellow team members. Using your heavenly language will assure that the perfect prayer has been prayed.

Ephesians 6:12   Luke 22:31-34   Colossians 1:9-14   Romans 8:26-27

17

It Can Happen Immediately (All At Once)

The story of the fig tree that Jesus cursed is an excellent example of how quickly thngs can change. Mark's Gospel records how Jesus cursed the tree. The next day when they came by, the disciples saw that it was dried up from the roots. However, Matthew tells the same story with a slightly different timeframe. He tells us that when Jesus spoke to the tree, "presently (at once) it withered away." The point I want to make is this: you don't have to always wait in order to receive manifested results when you pray. Past paradigms could be preventing us from getting the same results Jesus did. We have to change our expectations and bring them into alignment with what Jesus did. That's going to require a renewed mind.

Renewing the mind is a lifelong process, not a onetime event. We have to constantly renew our mind with the Word of God if we're to be of maximum use for the Kingdom of God. That's why I say rather frequently: spend time in the Word of God daily, preferably in the morning. It's a practice that I've come to enjoy over the years. I look forward to hearing what the Holy Spirit has to say every morning before I let the rest of the world into my space.

Take the time to look up and meditate on the "immediately" Scriptures which references the results Jesus got. Meditating on them will surely change your perspective and when put to use, will inevitably affect your outcome!

Mark 11:13-14, 20-21 AMP   Matthew 21:18-21 AMP   Ephesians 4:23 AMP

18

The Last Will and Testament

Have you ever been left an inheritance? If you didn't already know it, allow me the privilege to let you in on a little secret. When Christ died He left you an inheritance. The moment you became born again you officially became a child of God, which made you one of His heirs and a joint heir with Christ. The details of your inheritance can be found in what is affectionately referred to as the "New Testament" portion of the Bible.

Your total well-being was carefully thought out in advance and covered in the inheritance. Everything that you will ever need has been pre-arranged and made ready just for you. All you have to do is receive it. Here are a few details of your inheritance: should you ever come down with symptoms of sickness there's healing; for financial instability there's provision, and for security He has provided angelic protection. Guidance in and for all human affairs ranging from family members, employers, to government officials and next-door neighbors have been provided. If you can't find a specific Word on a subject, according to what is written in His will you have the Holy Spirit to lead and guide you into all truth.

His will is His Word and His Word is His will. That's your inheritance. I said it once and it bears repeating, every aspect of this Christian life has been provided for, through the shed blood of Jesus. Today, take time to read the will and see for yourself what's been left for you and how to go about claiming your inheritance. It's waiting on you to receive it!

Hebrews 9:15-17 AMP   Romans 8:16-17 AMP   Ephesians 2:10 AMP

2 Peter 1:3

19

Are You Thankful?

The majority of the time the inspiration for my writing comes from what's happening in my life at the moment and today is no different. I'm like everybody else who has a lot going on in their life and sometimes you don't know where to start. A buddy of mine used to say "I have more than I can say grace over" when he was faced with a lot of challenges that seem to happen all at once. That's how I was starting to feel, but the Holy Spirit stopped me before I got too invested into that mind-set and simply said "Gratitude."

No matter what's going on we have a lot to be thankful for. We have to find some way to rid ourselves of the tormenting negative thoughts that come with being ungrateful. Take a look at the little things you have. All of the things that we take for granted and don't give it a second thought. Start with telling God you're thankful to breathe, because if He didn't ordain it you couldn't "catch your next breath." Did you get out of bed, go to the bathroom, get dressed and feed yourself unassisted this morning? That's a good place to stop and praise God because there are people everywhere (you might know of someone personally) who couldn't.

We can turn a negative into a positive by simply praising God right where we're are. Praise confuses the enemy and changes your countenance. The enemy's desire is to keep us feeling overwhelmed, less than, and living a defeated life. The Bible tells us to glory (be full of joy) in tribulations not for them, which means that joy is our attitude while going through. If you know in your "knower" that God loves you, then no matter what comes your way, He's got you covered. You can find joy in knowing that He has your best interest at heart.

Today keep speaking God's Word into your life. It will cause your heart to be thankful and your mouth to be full of praise!

1 Thessalonians 5:18 AMP   Romans 5:3-5 AMP   Psalms 63:3-5

20

You Have To Hang In There

A couple of years ago a friend of mine from work called asking me to give another person a call. It seems a mutual friend was facing some challenges and life was coming at him hard and fast. I gave him a call. He answered and asked me to call back later. We hung up. Since I couldn't immediately talk with him, I began to pray in the spirit for him and his situation. When I called him back there was no answer. I left a message. I received a text a couple of days later saying he attempted suicide. His son called me and brought me up to speed on his condition. I told him I would keep the family in my prayers. We never know how people will handle things. On the surface when faced with challenges most of us will say that we can get through it. That's true but you have to go through to get through and depending on where you are in the process you can't always see your way through just yet. My friend was no novice to the things of God. He was saved and has been receiving my daily emails for years. Prior to our retiring he would tell me how much they were blessing him.

At some point in life our problems, whether self-induced or not, will get the best of us if we fail to keep our minds renewed daily in the Word of God. When the enemy launches an attack, he will hit you with everything he can until he finds an opening. If he gets in, he will wreak havoc in your life. He can only get in by what we say. When we speak words of doubt and unbelief, he will hit us the more. This is nothing but an attempt to get us talking about the situation and how hopeless it seems. What we have to do is tell the devil just like Jesus did when He was being tempted "It is written…" The greatest weapon we have in our arsenal is God's Word coming out of our mouth, spoken in faith.

Search the Scriptures or ask the Holy Spirit to show you where you can find a Word specific to your circumstance. The enemy has nothing to combat it and when you speak the Word against him he'll leave you and angels will come and minister to you. Remember, we're fighting the good fight of faith, and a good fight is one where you win!

Ephesians 4:23 AMP   Matthew 4:1-11   1 Timothy 6:12 AMP

21

This Is Your Testimony

The things you're going through right now are nothing but fodder for your testimony. I have heard it said before and it bears repeating, "New levels bring new devils." That's how you can tell you've hit or are about to hit a new level in God, just look at the attacks.

Throughout the Bible we're told it's going to happen. The Apostle Paul told Timothy those who live godly will experience some type of persecution. The key word here is "will." We can't be naive to think the devil is just going to sit idly by and watch us enjoy the manifested promises of God and not experience some opposition from the enemy. A friend of mine once told me something I have never forgotten, "bad things happen to good people." It's inevitable if you're living right. The old folks used to say if you're not going through some type of attack you might need to check your salvation. I know for me, sometimes I feel like the football player that has recovered a fumble and everybody in close proximity is going for the ball. I am on the bottom of the pile, but I have the ball and that's my joy. The "pile" can be symptoms of sickness, money issues and for good measure throw in some challenges with family members. When you couple all of that with the regular da- to-day stuff, this can cause our emotions to take us on a rollercoaster ride that might be thrilling but not enjoyable. What keeps me grounded is my relationship with God through His Word. There is a payoff to spending time daily in the Word.

There are times when faced with something that a Scripture will come back to me and I don't have my Bible handy. I might not immediately know exactly where it's located but it was a Word I read to come back exactly when I needed it. The way of escape for us is always found in God's Word.

Today I want to encourage you that when you get through with this test and get to the other side, you'll have a testimony that'll encourage others because it's not always about you but rather someone else!

Psalms 34:19   2 Timothy 3:12 AMP   1 Corinthians 10:13 AMP

22

Praying One For Another

I had the opportunity one day to get into a conversation with someone about a certain pastor. To make a long story short he was telling me why he didn't like this pastor and what he'd heard this pastor say as it relates to denying the deity of Christ. This definitely piqued my interest because I have been a partner of that ministry for over twenty five years. He proceeded to pull up a "You Tube" video clip on his phone. I listened to it four or five times and didn't hear what he heard which kind of upset him. I explained to him that you can't fully understand what the pastor is talking about if you take a 1:19 min excerpt from an entire sermon. You have to put it into its proper context by listening to what he said prior, after, and what point he was trying to make.

The guy purports to be a Christian and attends church, because I had my uniform on; my Jesus t-shirt/hat, this initiated our conversation. I could tell by the tone of our conversation and the answers he didn't give to the questions I asked that we were on entirely two different levels. We went into our meeting and we ended it in love by agreeing to disagree. There are people, fellow brothers and sisters in Christ, who need our prayers.

Spiritually they don't see what we see or maybe they are not getting fed what we are. I'm grateful for the teachers I've had in the past, for the foundation they gave me, and how they taught me the Word of God and how to know God for myself. The leaders I now have reinforce what I learned as a babe in Christ. I can now enjoy strong meat. Paul's prayer found in the Book of Ephesians is a perfect tool we can use to pray for people. We can ask God to open the eyes of their understanding and grant them the spirit of wisdom and revelation in the knowledge of Him. What I like about this particular prayer is where you see the words you and yours, you can insert a person's name making it a specific laser-like request.

The angels are waiting to hear God's Word spoken in faith so they and the Holy Spirit can go to work behind the scenes, orchestrating the order of events necessary to bring it to pass!

Hebrews 5:13-14 AMP   Ephesians 1:15-23   Psalms 103:20

23

Exposing Our Children To God

When you make the investment of exposing your children to God, no matter how young they are it will produce results. For example, we became foster parents and eventually adopted our children. They have been exposed to the Word of God. We pray, worship, and discuss God together as a family. I read recently about some children being told they couldn't pray before they ate lunch at school. We pray over all of our meals and we take turns, so they are familiar with the practice. I asked the oldest two if they pray over their lunch and they said "yes", I thought to myself good, now I don't have to go down there and make a case. At the time they were six and nine years old and my six-yr. old even said one of her friends is a Christian and she says her prayers also when they eat lunch. Our oldest daughter asked us the other day about speaking in tongues. It seems they are being taught about the Holy Spirit in children's church. That's a good thing because it allows us to share with her our relationship with Him. My son who was four, is my ride or die buddy. When we get in the car, I have been playing Shekinah Glory's Jesus cd#2 for a couple of weeks and when the song "Jesus" comes on, when I hear him in the back seat singing the chorus "Jesus" it is a real joy. I remember eating dinner one Sunday after church he told us as only a four-year-old could, about Jesus walking on the water.

When we expose our children to the Word of God and walk it out before them, some of it will stick. We can't watch over every step they'll make when they're grown and out of the house. We do the best we can while we've got them and trust God that what we've deposited in them will surely bring Him a return.

Deuteronomy 6:4-9; 11:18-19 AMP

24

Getting A Goodnights Sleep

I was talking to some friends of mine and one of them mentioned how this joint venture we were involved with at the time was keeping them up at night. I said it wasn't doing me like that because I've decided to trust God about it. I then shared with them a Scripture that talks about having sweet sleep.

When I look at that verse it talks about not being afraid when you lie down. The enemy uses the only power he has, the power of suggestion. He will attempt to fill your head with so much doubt that you'll go to bed with worry. Worry is nothing but the fear of not being able to control the outcome of a situation to your liking and not trusting it to God. Trusting it to God means we've given up control and fully understand that we can't twist God's arm to make any situation turn out the way we want it to, and no matter how it turns out, it will be for our good.

I'm here to tell you worry and fear are not in God's plan and you need to doubt your doubts. When you get those negative "what if" thoughts, counter them with positive "what if" words coming out of your mouth. Faith comes not by having heard but by hearing and hearing the Word of God. When YOU speak the Word of God, and make positive confessions, your faith is increased. When you lie down at night your sleep will be sweet and worry free because you know that it will all work out for your good!

Proverbs 3:21-24 AMP   Romans 10:17 AMP   Romans 8:26-28 AMP

25

Who Do You Need God To Be?

Consider the different character names of God. At various junctures we all need God to be something different. Who do you need God to be? Some might need Him to be a healer while others might need Him to be their provider. When you get into those tight places of life it's comforting to know that God loves you and He is always there. There are more names than I have the time to share with you right now, however I use as a reference a book titled "The Names of God" by Marilyn Hickey. She offers an extremely insightful teaching on this subject.

God is the *same yesterday, today and forever.* He will never change. You can always count on God and His love for you. As you go through your day ask God to give you a fresh revelation of who He is. Keep in mind that no matter what obstacles life throws your way, God is right there in the midst of it all. He's got it all worked out. That's who He is and He's just that kind of God!

Jehovah Rophe - Exodus 15:26   Jehovah Jireh - Genesis 22:14

Jehovah Shammah - Ezekiel 48:35 AMP   Hebrews 13:8 AMP

26

Making Choices

When it comes to making choices, it's something we do all day every day and some without giving it a second thought. But what about the ones that require us to decide if we're going to obey the Word of God in a specific area or choose to go our own way. Those are the choices I want to talk about today. Scripture tells us to choose life. Choose the voice/Word of God. When we do there are benefits attached to it. God has deposited in all of us His moral compass to go by and when we follow it our choices are more God centered than self-centered. One of the greatest choices we could've ever made was making Jesus the Lord of our life. As you go through your day today let your choices come from the inner witness of the Holy Spirit. He won't lead you wrong nor let you down. It's a choice.

Deuteronomy 30:19 AMP   Jeremiah 31:33 AMP   Acts 4:12   John 16:13

27

Using Your Faith On The Front End

I once heard it said and it is still true today how it's better to build a house before a storm than to start in the middle of one.

Confessing God's Word over your body before you get sick is better than beginning to do it after you get a bad report from the doctor. When you confess God's Word up front, you are refusing to allow sickness or disease the right to invade your body. A couple of years ago I was introduced to a book, "*God's Creative Power for Healing*" by Charles Capps, which I use to confess God's Word over my body every day. I get into agreement with God over my immune system, blood pressure, cholesterol level, arteries, no tumors or growths, etc. All of the things that I don't want to occur in my body, I speak against so that it won't come knocking at my door. I plan to live a long, prosperous life according to the Word of God. One facet of true prosperity is being in good health, and if you get into agreement with the Word over your health and eat right, you can experience it. God wants us to live the good life that He's pre-arranged for us to live. All we have to do is believe to receive it. We have been bombarded with so much of the world's way of doing things that it seems kind of foreign to operate on a level like this. God chose the foolish things of the world to confound the wise.

If you want to build your faith to be used up front, then it's going to take renewing your mind in the Word of God to achieve it. My grandfather used to say "an ounce of prevention is worth more than a pound of cure." Start confessing the Word of God over your body today. There's no time like the present.

Mark 11:23-24   Ephesians 2:10 AMP   1 Corinthians 1:27 AMP

Ephesians 4:23 AMP

28

Being Made Whole

Receiving your healing is one thing, while being made whole is another. Jesus told both the woman with the issue of blood and blind Bartimaeus that their faith made them whole. Webster's 1828 defines "whole" as "sound, not hurt or sick; restored to health or soundness." Their faith completed the healing process and restored them back to their original state of being. Initially faith requires no physical effort on our part except to speak what we believe. When we read their accounts, they were specific in their requests. The woman kept saying to herself that if she could just touch the hem of His garment, she would be made whole. While on the other hand, Jesus asked Bartimaeus what he wanted and he said, "That I might receive my sight." The thing they desired from Jesus, they received.

Could it be God has healed you from cancer, multiple sclerosis or some other type of debilitating disease and you don't feel like it? You might be dealing with lingering symptoms that only need your constant confession of faith that you're healed to keep in check, until your wholeness is manifested. Don't lose heart, you've already been healed and are now in the process of being made whole. Some receive their total wholeness or restoration at once, while others go through a process. Part of your process might require physical therapy or going to the gym to rehabilitate certain parts of your body.

Whatever it takes in order to complete the process, do it. God has a plan and needs us to have a fit body and be in good physical shape to fulfill the work He has predestined for us to do.

Isaiah 53:4-5 AMP   Matthew 9:21-22 AMP   Mark 10:51-52

Mark 11:23 AMP

29

Renew Your Mind

In the Book of Ephesians, the Apostle Paul tells us to be renewed in the spirit of our minds and to put on the new man who is created in righteousness and true holiness or the holiness of truth.

Renewing the mind is not a one-time event. It is a daily process that aids in giving you current data from the Holy Spirit. Familiar Scriptures take on a new revelation, while praying in the spirit allows us to pray perfectly because our spirit knows the perfect will of God making intercession for us.

The entire process results in an increased sensitivity to the gentle leadings of the Holy Spirit. When we obey Him, our journey will be marked with prosperity. I'm not talking money but peace, safety, and good health, which is God's idea of being prosperous!

Today, spend time renewing your mind with the Word of God and in prayer. Get your news hot off the press!

Ephesians 4:23-24 AMP   Romans 8:26-27 AMP   Psalms 139:1-4 AMP

30

Responding Is Better Than Reacting

One of the things I have really come to appreciate about spending time with God in His Word early in the morning is it really helps me stay more God centered and not self- centered. When things come up, as they most certainly do, I've learned the difference between being reactive and responsive.

When I get in reaction mode, my emotions and flesh are in full force. This is where I begin to feel the tug-of-war taking place betwixt the old and the new me. It seems like the floodgates of negative emotions open and more often than not, I wind up apologizing to someone. On the other hand, when I take the time to step back, wait, then respond to a situation, my spirit man is in control. The results tend to be more favorable. I've learned the best way to avoid reacting and to be more responsive is stick to the routine of consistently digging into the Word of God early before I let the rest of the world in.

No matter what comes along your way today, see things from God's perspective and not your own. When you do, there is a peace that comes. People won't understand how you can be like that with everything that's happening, but you know. God gives a peace that comes with keeping your mind on Him and His Word.

Psalms 63:1   Proverbs 14:29 AMP   Philippians 4:4-9 AMP

May

1

How Are You Walking?

If the path you're walking is ordained of God, then you don't have to worry about your steps slipping. Walking according to God's Word will produce results. You might not understand every little twist and turn or why some things happen along the way. If you will trust Him and stay in His Word, watch and see how things will always work to your advantage.

God has a plan for all of us and certain details about the plan can be found in His Word. The safest place you can ever be is in the perfect will of God. He knows the "where" and "how" of your entire journey. We can have our plans but at this level of development we have given God permission to interrupt those plans for something better.

Today allow God to order your steps in His Word. When life throws you a challenge, go to the Word, that's where you can see just how to handle it.

Psalms 17:5 AMP   Proverbs 16:9 AMP   Psalms 119:133 AMP

2

Let It Go

Someone has hurt all of us and no matter what they did, we have to forgive them and let go of the hurt. This is something that requires constant work in my life. There might be others having to deal with this also.

Love demands that we forgive others. Jesus told Peter to forgive his brother seventy times seven. Now when I think about it that way, it means I have to automatically, with no hesitation forgive people. Can you imagine going around with a notebook and every time you get hurt or offended you write their name down along with the time, day and what they did to you? Just the mere thought of it means you have to work hard to keep track of every injustice you suffered. I learned a long time ago and I share this with every newlywed I can that is: "You can't keep score in love because there's no room for it."

Love is the curtain rod that hangs all of the law and the prophets. If we are to keep our faith working then it takes love. If we hold onto unforgiveness, it won't be long before a root of bitterness is developed and we're walking around angry at the world.

As you continue along on this journey of faith, make a decision that you'll walk in a constant state of forgiveness. After all, the blood of Jesus has forgiven you for the things you have yet to do. Surely, you can forgive others for their past transgressions against you. It doesn't matter whether they are alive or dead, let go of what they did to you. You can only do that through forgiveness.

Remember love doesn't keep score.

Matthew 18:21-22 AMP   Matthew 22:37-40 AMP   Galatians 5:6

3

Let Your Angels Do The Fighting

Contrary to popular beliefs, you're <u>not</u> supposed to fight the devil. According to the Word of God we should submit to God, resist the devil and he will flee from you. When he brings suggestive thoughts of sin your way, the best thing I can tell you to do is simply speak the Word against him. The only power he has is the power of suggestion. He knows what you like and will dress it up nice and neat for you. Before you know it, you're all caught up. I heard it said once and it bears repeating, "Sin will take you farther than you planned on going, keep you longer than you planned on staying and cost you more than you planned on paying." This is why we have to resist his attempts to throw us off of our game because it's just not worth it.

When you resist him and pray according to the Word of God, Angels are standing by ready to go to work on your behalf because it's their job. They are servants sent to assist us in the service of God. If there is any demonic interference to your request, know that Angels are fighting for you just like they did for Daniel.

Every morning when you rise, your angels are waiting on the sidelines for you to give them their assignment. As soon as you speak God's Word, they lace up their Nike's and go to work.

The question is do your angels have to dust theirs off because they haven't had anything to do lately?

James 4:7 AMP   Psalms 103:20 AMP   Daniel 10:12-13 AMP

Hebrews 1:14 AMP

4

You Better Tell Somebody

You know how when something good happens in your life and you can't wait to tell it. Do you share that same "tell it" intensity when God manifest something good for you? Do you keep it to yourself because some people might not understand? In the times we're living, if you're the latter, then it's time you get busy and start talking God up. You don't have to get "preachy" because there are ways you can share the goodness of God with those in your circle.

When you talk about God on a regular basis it makes Him bigger than all of your circumstances and situations. In making Him bigger, your faith grows. Your spirit man is best fed when he hears the Word of God or something about God coming out of your mouth. I tell myself every time my thoughts tend to get "squirrelly", that God's commanded blessing is on my life. When I do, it seems like I activate the blessing, then manifestation is usually right around the corner.

Start talking about the little things God has done for you and who He is to you today. We have to proclaim His goodness and tell others all about Him.

Psalms 119:46   Romans 10:17 AMP   Deuteronomy 28:8

5

Making Changes

When it comes to making certain changes in our lives like losing weight, stop smoking etc., we can desire to change all we want, but until the decision to change is made all we're doing is playing mental gymnastics.

Nine out of ten times the only motivating factor in our decision making process seems to be pain. I know for me when it came to stop smoking, I had the desire to stop and since I had already successfully made other lifestyle changes, I thought the process would be the same. It wasn't. I couldn't understand why it wouldn't work until Dec 4, 1995. While still living and working in Detroit, I went out on the dock to smoke. Not wearing a coat I caught a bad cold. That's when the dots got connected and I realized I hadn't made the decision to stop. Once I did, I haven't looked back. That's not to say the urge hasn't come because every now and then it does, but I made a decision and I have decided to stick with it.

You might be in a similar position like I was, in 1995. Whatever it is you need or want to change; you can make the change. It's just as simple as making a decision. I didn't say it would be easy, because you'll be met with resistance. Your mind and body are going to fight against you, but you must stand your ground. Once you make the decision it's important to put parameters around it. Avoid the people, places, or situations that are associated with it. Maybe you'll have to change your routine like I did. I used to have my coffee and smoke cigarettes while spending time with the Lord first thing every morning. When I made my decision, I stopped making coffee at home and spent the time reading my Bible and praying without smoking and drinking coffee. Then on my way to work I bought my coffee and a doughnut from the donut shop. I can say through the grace of God I haven't smoked since then.

I'm sharing this because I want everyone to know bad habits can be broken and you can successfully make changes in your life. Make a decision and get God involved. You can do it. I'm praying and cheering for you!!

Romans 12:1-2 AMP   *Philippians 4:13 AMP*   *Proverbs 3:6*

6

He's Always There

Jehovah Shammah, The Lord is there is my personal favorite when it comes to the names of God. He is always there and as long as you're living and breathing, He'll be there. When He said that He would be with us unto the end of the world, it's so true because the day were born again, God in the person of the Holy Spirit took up residence and moved in on the inside of us. Because He's living big on the inside of us, there's no way He'll leave. This is why we quote Scriptures like *"God has not given us a spirit of fear."* Since His Spirit is living in us we shouldn't be fearful and if it does happen, immediately start speaking against it so that it won't get a foothold in your life. If you're not careful, fear can have you running around scared, making irrational, and emotional decisions that you might regret down the road.

I remember when I began to feel a little overwhelmed and powerless due to all of the things happening in, and around me as my faith was being stretched. Believing God for the manifestation of things sometimes has me feeling like this. When I do, the Holy Spirit reminds me that God is right here with me. No matter what I'm facing, when I start speaking His Word and get into agreement with God's Word, it's not long before I start to feel better, and my perspective changes.

As you go through your day today, know that God is with you no matter what. He's right there on the inside of you, living big!

Ezekial 48:35   1 John 4:4   2 Timothy 1:7 AMP   John 14:15-17 AMP

7

This Fight Is Fixed

Recently I had something I'd been facing off and on resurface. I was becoming slightly disturbed. When I got home it was just in time to hear our radio show "Resting In His Word" with Cheryl Boggs. As I listened to the first segment, I was speaking on "Putting Your Faith to Work" from the book of Mark. Cheryl sang and talked about faith. On Dan Haynes' segment "Kingdom Keys" he referenced the same Scriptures I did. Right in the middle of our segments Cheryl played a couple of songs and one really caught my attention by Janice Peterson "The Fight Is Fixed." The song ignited something inside of me when she sang about "waiting on the Lord and be of good courage. Don't quit just wait on Him; He will come through because the fight is fixed. Just speak the Word, the fight is fixed."

This fight we're in is fixed because our victory has already been won. When we look back to the Cross remember it's not only a place of victory but it also represents defeat, they go hand in hand. Whenever you have a victor you also have a defeated foe. Jesus overcame our enemy and we also have overcome him by the same Blood, and the word of our testimony. We testify or according to Webster's 1828 "we give witness" to what the blood has done for us!

As you go through your "go through" remember what a friend of mine told me once "It's a fixed fight so why are you tripping!"

Mark 11:23-24   Revelation 12:10-11 AMP   Revelation 21:6-7 AMP

8

The Love Test

Warning

If you make the decision to read this, you are subject to experience an opportunity to walk in love.

Proceed at your own risk.

Any time the subject of love is brought up you get the opportunity to exercise it. I had to caution you because it is so true especially when your faith is out there where you believe God for manifestations like never before. Trust me. You'll have a chance to demonstrate it before the day is through and guess what, you'll pass the test. I speak that by faith over your life right now in the name of Jesus. Maybe you're like I was; you're experiencing a major shift that's propelling you towards fulfilling your destiny. Either way challenges will come, providing an opportunity to advance or abort, and that rest in how we respond. The Bible tells us faith works by love. You can't expect to receive from God and you're not walking in love. We no longer operate in reactionary mode when things crop up but rather in a responsive, love-type manner *"always abounding in the work of the Lord."*

One of the beautiful things about God in the person of the Holy Spirit is how He fulfills what Jesus said about showing us things to come. What I have given you is the answers to the test before the test so that you won't be caught off guard.

You will pass the test and give the devil a black eye in the process!

Galatians 5:6 AMP   1 Corinthians 15:58 AMP   John 16:13 AMP

9

Don't Stop Now, You Can Make It

One morning as the Holy Spirit began ministering to me I kept hearing the song "It Ain't Over" by Maurette Brown Clark playing in my head. The next day it was Timothy Wright's "We're Gonna Make It" Pt. 1& 2, both of those songs encouraged me and I wanted to share them with you today.

I know and fully understand how challenging it is today. I also know more than anything else that God has a plan and He will see it through to the end as long as we hold up our end of the deal. I recently talked about how we have to meet the conditions that God has set forth in his Word if we're to receive from him. It takes faith in God's Word, doing what He said, when He said to do it and walking in love. Regardless of how things might look now, you're going to make it. You've come this far by faith and not by sight, that's how we walk. If we're not careful, distractions will quietly slip in and change our focus. Distractions are those petty annoyances that seem to arise at the wrong time. Recognize them for what they are. The key is to respond and not react. Develop a mental checklist and immediately evaluate it based on your destiny and whether or not it fits. The Holy Spirit will reveal it to you if you ask Him.

Don't let go of the promises that God has made. You're going to make it. Look to the Word when circumstances say otherwise. You're the closest when it doesn't look like it. You've got His Word and the blood of the lamb both screaming, "We've already won!" So I ask, "If you know you're going to win, when do you quit"?

Jeremiah 29:11 AMP   2 Corinthians 5:7   Revelation 12:11 AMP

10

The Great Exchange

When you accepted Christ as Savior, your spirit man was born again and saved from paying the penalty of your sin. Jesus paid the cost so that we don't have to. In the final moments of His life, as He hung on the Cross and said "It is finished", His work on the earth was done. The great exchange had begun to take place. Every stripe He received, crown of thorns on His head, nails in His hands and feet, along with being pierced in His side not only paid for your redemption, but also was a symbol of exchange.

He became all that we were so that we could become all that He was. He did it out of love without opening his mouth. He could've stopped it at any time but love wouldn't let Him. As a matter of fact, He counted it as joy because He knew on the other side of all He was going through mankind was going to be reconciled back to the Father. That's what love is and has done for you! He traded all He was for all we were.

My challenge to you today is to share the great exchange with someone who might need to know that it's available. Let the Holy Spirit guide you and use you to offer the free gift of salvation to someone.

Isaiah 53:4-7   Hebrews 12:2 AMP   Romans 10:8-10 AMP

11

No Deposit, No Return

One morning I woke up thinking about God's Word and how to get more from it. The Holy Spirit began a conversation about those who get more out have put more in.

The Kingdom of God is based on the agricultural system of sowing and reaping, seedtime and harvest. That theme runs throughout both the Old and New Testament. The Apostle Paul tells us whether we sow to the flesh or the spirit that's where we will reap or receive our harvest. To get more Word-based returns in my life means more of the Word has to be deposited. Can I spend more time in the Word and less in front of the television or surfing the net? Of course I can. I am not limited to just making it the first thing I do in the morning or listening to the Word in my car. I can spend more time throughout the day seeking Him in prayer about everything that concerns my life along with opening up my Bible and reading it aloud.

God has given us a warehouse full of examples to follow. Look at the fruit in the lives of all the "great" men and women of God today. They only got there by spending time cultivating a deeper, more intimate relationship with the Father. If He did it for them, then He will surely do it for you and me.

Galatians 6:7-8 AMP   Romans 2:11 AMP

12

What Are Your Mountains?

I can't begin to tell you the number of times I have read and quoted about the mountains referred to in the Book of Mark. One particular morning it seems like for the first time, I actually understood and got the revelation about speaking to the mountains!

Jesus tells us to speak to the mountain and command it to be removed and cast into the sea. What are your mountains? Could it be financial, where you get hit with an unexpected expense right before you go on vacation? Maybe you're being hit with symptoms of illness in your body. Those are just a couple of examples of potential mountains. There are more but the point is that we have to speak to them just like Jesus spoke to the fig tree and told it what He wanted to happen, and the next day His disciples saw what He said. The tree was dead.

When we meet the conditions of not doubting in our heart (spirit man) and believe what we say will come to pass, we can have the same twenty-four hour results or better when we speak by faith to the mountains in our life.

Today, identify the mountains in your life. Speak what you want to happen and "on the morrow..."

Mark 11:12-14; 20-24 AMP   Mark 9:23

13

Unbroken Promises

When God has spoken something into your spirit, maybe it's a desire you have like new house or job, you can rest assured that if He said it, He'll bring it to pass.

There is a raging battle taking place between I believe and I receive, where the enemy will attack your thoughts and emotions. That's why it's imperative we feed our spirit man the Word of God every day to keep our minds renewed. We have to stay built up on what God has said as opposed to what we see, feel or think. We can't pay attention to that. We have to stay focused on the Word and remain calm.

The promise that was made to you won't come without some opposition. The last thing your enemy wants to see is you succeed. This is why you pick up your Bible daily and read out loud what God has written, so you can stay full of the Word. The Word will calm your anxiety and remove the doubt that your enemy will throw at you, just like he did Eve in the garden.

You're going to go through some things while living in this world; it's all prophecy being fulfilled. We must be confident and not full of fear since Jesus told us because He already overcame the world and because He won, we won also!

Mark 11:22-24   Romans 12:2 AMP   Genesis 3:1 AMP   John 16:33 AMP

14

The Miracle Has Already Taken Place

Your time spent in the Word and making confessions is not in vain. God said His Word will not return to Him void, it will accomplish that which pleases Him and will prosper into the thing where He sends it. Bottom line is the Word is working in your life. Could it be the answer to your prayer or the road to answered prayer doesn't look like you thought it would? Guess what! You're there. Look back to see how far you've come. Truth be told, it's better now than it was, especially when you take into account what your physician or family members have to say about your situation.

The Word was working when you didn't see it because of your current circumstances. You were looking for it one way but God worked it another way. You have a testimony and don't even recognize it. God sent you little signs of confirmation along the way. All you have to do is ask Him to open your spiritual eyes like He did Elisha's servant, then you'll see it. The leader on a prayer call shared this one-day on a call, He said "A turn around is coming to my situation and Jesus is about to confirm in the natural what I feel in my spirit."

Whatever you've believed God for, the manifestation has already been done in the spirit realm and it's on its way to this natural realm in which you live!

Isaiah 55:11 AMP   2 Kings 6:15-17 AMP

15

Dealing With Discouragement And Disappointments

One morning I began thinking about a couple of situations going on and began to feel disappointed. Immediately, the Holy Spirit reminded me of how David was at a low point in his life and he did the only thing he knew to do, seek God. David had a history with God and they enjoyed a unique relationship with one another. God said of David that He'd found a man after His own heart.

We can use David as a blueprint for our lives when we experience the many challenges life brings our way. When we get those feelings of discouragement, seek God just like David did. Increase your Word intake and if you can't get to your Bible, go off to a quiet place and pray. Ask the Holy Spirit to help you understand the lesson to be learned because there is always a lesson somewhere in there.

Don't let circumstances and situations defeat you. The Greater One lives big on the inside of you. You are *"more than a conqueror through Him that loved you!"*

1 Samuel 30:1-8   1 Samuel 13:14   Romans 8:35-39 AMP

16

Stay In Faith

While everything around you is changing, it would be hard to stay in faith if it wasn't for the Word of God. God's Word has to be the anchor in our life that keeps us headed in the right direction so that we avoid the pitfalls that may lie ahead.

The world always places before you opportunities to take shortcuts that lead to more shortcuts. The next thing you know you're all caught up and can't figure out where you went wrong. God has a plan for us. We have to let Him continue to order our steps. He knows the way. When we acknowledge Him, the Holy Spirit will lead us down the correct path. At first some of it might not make sense but if we keep putting one foot in front of the other, eventually it will.

You may encounter some delays or detours along the way. Rest assured that God knew before the foundation of the world that it would happen, and He has already made a provision for it. When they do occur keep in mind that it's not a wasted experience but rather an opportunity to learn, which will help you when you arrive at your new level.

As you go through your day, stay in faith, and be confident in knowing that God is with you. He has ordered your steps.

Mark 4:18-19   Ephesians 2:10 AMP   Proverbs 3:5-6 AMP

17

The Spirit Of Fear

Scripture tells us that fear is a spirit and God didn't give it to us. When we take an honest look at fear, it's always based on future events and never about what's happening in the here and now. I have learned over the years, to the best of my ability to try and stay inside of today. When I do, everything is all right. There is enough going on right now that requires my attention and energy. What might happen tomorrow, good or bad, will just have to wait until it gets here. When we make plans to do something or take on a life-changing event, we have to let God work out the details and trust Him or fear will creep in.

Fear can manifest itself in a variety of ways, like becoming full of doubt, or being a hoarder and afraid to throw things away "because you never can tell one day you might need it." Fear can manifest in procrastination where you're afraid to do something, so you do it at the last minute. Now you're running around like a chicken with its head cut off trying to get it done and avoid the consequences of not doing it in a timely fashion. This can cause unnecessary stress, because now you have potentially created another problem, which doesn't do anything except reinforce your fears. This is when the "negative committee" shows up and wants to play mental gymnastics with your head and emotions.

All of this can be addressed by spending time daily, renewing your mind with the Word of God. When your spirit-man hears the Word of God coming out of your mouth, your faith grows. As your faith grows your fears diminish causing fear to lose its grip.

Today, loosen the grip fear can have on your life with the Word of God. Walk in love towards everyone because there is no fear in love and "perfect love will cast out fear!"

2 Timothy 1:7 AMP   Matthew 6:34   1 John 4:18 AMP

18

Don't Quit

One of my heroes is my young cousin Aaron. What makes Aaron unique is that he was born with cerebral palsy. He walks with a slight limp and has a brace on one of his legs but the guy can out walk the average person and he loves to play football. When we go on our family vacations, he is all over the ship. We frequently bump into him on his way somewhere. I remember a time when he got a little discouraged and I shared with him how he is an inspiration to me and how he's the only one who can stop himself from doing anything. I told him to read and confess God's Word every day especially when he faces an obstacle because the Bible says you are as you think in your heart. I finished by telling him that he is one fine example of someone who doesn't know the meaning of the word "quit." Aaron graduated from high school, was accepted for admission to Ohio University, and he had aspirations to play football.

Today, I want to use this to encourage someone who might be facing some tough times. Now is not the time to quit. The closer you get to your breakthrough the more intensified the battle gets. These things are but a light affliction in comparison to what others might be experiencing.

There is an old saying "You're complaining because you don't have any shoes, but the guy across the street doesn't have any feet." Things are really not that bad are they? If you know that you're going to win when do you quit? I read the back of the Book and it says "we won!!!"

Philippians 4:13 AMP   Proverbs 23:7   2 Corinthians 4:17-18 AMP

Psalms 34:19

19

Let God Do The Talking

Periodically when we have to talk to people about something, we aren't afforded the luxury of having a script, which could cause us to fret about exactly what will be said. In the Gospel of Luke, Jesus tells us to settle it in our hearts and not to meditate on our answer because He will give us *"a mouth and wisdom."* In the Gospel of Mark, we're told that it is the Holy Ghost and not us, who will do the talking.

There are a couple of things you can do to become more effective in allowing the Holy Spirit to do the talking for you. One is spending time renewing your mind in the Word of God daily. This will allow the wisdom of God to flow freely and give you peace when you need it. Another is to practice the presence of God throughout your day. Acknowledging Him often and keeping the lines of communication open allows the Holy Spirit to have free reign when a situation comes up where you need Him to do the talking.

Today, remain sensitive to The Holy Spirit's gentle leadings and watch words of wisdom flow from your mouth. You'll say things that you never thought of saying. They will be the right words for the situation.

Luke 21:14-15 AMP   Mark 13:11 AMP   Ephesians 4:23 AMP

Proverbs 3:6; 4:5-7

20

Everybody Is Going Through Something

I picked up the newspaper one day and saw an organization where some people I know work. They were facing some serious challenges, people's lives and livelihood were at stake. Seeing this brought what I was experiencing into perspective. It also explained why the Holy Spirit had me meditating on certain verses of Psalms 91.

In my study I've come to learn that verses 3-16 of Psalms 91is solely based on meeting the conditions of verses1-2. Verse 1 talks about whoever dwells, stakes claim, in the secret place of the most High shall abide or live/reside under the shadow of El Shaddai. The safest place in the world is living under the shadow of the Almighty. That means He is covering or overshadowing us. When you speak or say that He is your refuge, your fortress (v2) and that you trust God, you will enjoy complete protection. No matter what may come your way, and things will come, you'll be safe and free from any danger or harm because angels have been dispatched to watch guard over you according to the Word of God coming out your mouth. Angels are listening and waiting. The question is what have you assigned them to do?

Today take your "something" and apply the Word of God to it. Speak to that mountain in faith and cast it into the sea where it belongs. God will deliver you and satisfy you with long life. If that's not enough, He will show you His salvation!

Psalms 91   Psalm 103:20   Mark 11:23-24

21

Gods Timing Is Perfect

One morning on the prayer call the subject was about God's timing. Some of the main points the leader covered was how God hears our prayers, answers them in His time, in His ways and not our ways. God answers them without limits. He always keeps His promise to us and if we wait on His timing the plan for our lives is even greater.

God's timing is perfect and we will see His perfect will and perfect order unfold in our lives if we trust His timing. One of the things the leader said was that the reason we feel like we do sometimes is because we have allowed the spirit of anxiousness to have space in our lives. In doing so, it has weighed us down and caused us to feel overwhelmed. We have to get back in sync with God's timing when we have stepped out of line. God allows this chaos to strengthen our patience, mature our faith, and make us complete.

One thing I've learned is to wait and not jump out in front of God, nor move in my own wisdom only to fail. Being in sync with the rhythm of God is an awesome place to be. It's a place where you get to enjoy countless manifestations from God's Word.

Today, if you're out of sync with God's timing, then let the seemingly chaotic situations you've created get you back into alignment. God allows us to be chastened because He loves us. At the end of the day, the chastening is nothing more than a course correction.

Psalms 27:14   Jeremiah 29:11-13 AMP   Hebrews 12:5-7 AMP

22

Letting Our Children Grow Up

It's hard watching your children grow up and make mistakes especially when they are grown and have left the house. Our initial response is to step in and try to fix it for them. There comes a time when you have to step aside and let them figure it out and think for themselves, while the worst-case scenario is playing through your head.

For me I am calm and steady on the outside but inside there's a storm brewing. Hoping that you covered all the bases, you ask yourself, "did I miss something"? The "negative committee" shows up and tries to assess blame along with a little guilt and some condemnation. The Holy Spirit counter-acts that by bringing back to my remembrance one of my favorite Scriptures. Once I begin speaking that Word, I begin to feel better because I believe God's Word and condemnation is not part of my life today.

The Bible tells us to train them up in the way that they should go. With the three children we recently adopted, I'm in a unique position to guide them somewhat better than I did with their older brother. Going to college, becoming a teacher and doctors, is what they've said that they want to be, and is all we talk about. The schools they will attend have already been identified along with the field of medicine for my two doctors. Most importantly, I'm teaching them to know God for themselves.

I thank God He has entrusted their care to us. I will do the best I can to guide and encourage them along the way, by celebrating their small achievements and letting them know that I am proud of them. When they make a mistake and get it wrong, I don't jump on them, but we talk about other options and if there was a better or different way it could've been done. God has a plan for their lives. Whatever He has planted in them to do it's for Him. Our responsibility is to feed and nurture the desires He has given them. When they get old and leave the house, they won't depart from it.

Yes, our children will make mistakes. When they do, hopefully they'll learn from them. It's something we all have to go through!

Romans 8:1-2 AMP   Proverbs 22:6 AMP   Ephesians 6:4 AMP

23

I Agree To Disagree

Let me preface today's message with this statement. I am not anti-gay but rather pro God. I'm like most people who have family members who are or were gay. I have lost one family member to that big disease with the little name and I loved them.

Now that pro-football has drafted their first openly gay player, players who voice an opposing point of view are punished. Why is it wrong to say you don't agree with this guy celebratory kissing his "boyfriend" on primetime television? Society has gotten to the point that they now applaud all of the "famous" people who are "coming out of the closet." This is the fallacy; we are continuing to decline morally. God became so tired of dealing with this issue He washed His hands of it and basically said: "I have told you what I want, how I designed this thing to be, yet you choose to continue on your own way, so have at it!"

Society already made it legal to kill unborn babies and made it legal for same sexes to get married. In case you haven't noticed there has been a reported increase in people being charged with bestiality. Satan has deceived the minds of people just like he did Eve. People are going for the deception hook, line and sinker! What's next? How much lower can we go?

We need to wake up and get our heads out of the sand like Ostrich's appear to do, because the enemy is after our children. They are being inundated with sexual images and as hard as we try, it's still right there in their face. That's why we have to live the God- kind of life. They have to see God's Word not only talked about in our homes, but walked out in our everyday life. If you put the Word in them, then the Word will come out and bear fruit.

If you have any questions go read the Bible, God left specific instructions.

Romans 1:24-28 AMP   Genesis 3:1-5,13 AMP

24

I've Changed

One morning I was reflecting on my past and how far I have come. It amazes me sometimes the transformative work Christ has done in me since the day I asked Him to come into my life. As the Bible says, I am truly a new creation. My old desires have been removed and the work that's been done and is still taking place in me is so that others will be drawn to Christ. I fully realize that it's not all about me anymore. The things I experience, both good and bad, are opportunities to share and to encourage others.

I am filled with the fullness of God daily. I know and understand that the Father, Son and I are together on this journey. I can't go anywhere that they don't come also. Everywhere I go they go. It's a package deal. The day I got born again God, in the person of the Holy Spirit moved in on the inside of me. I am no longer my own. My body belongs to God. Every day presents opportunities to get drawn back into the old way of doing and being but I overcome it by resisting it. I can only say this because I keep my mind renewed with and in the Word of God. In doing so I am able to sidestep the traps the enemy has set for me. The Holy Spirit is there to be my guide, and guide He does. The only time I get into trouble is when I don't follow His lead.

Today recognize that a change has taken place in you. You're not the same. This change is a lifelong process. The best is yet to come.

2 Corinthians 5:14-18   1 Corinthians 6:18-20 AMP   Ephesians 4:23 AMP

Colossians 3:10

25

You're Almost There

If the battle has intensified while you wait on the manifestation of the promises of God, then by all means stay the course. You are closer than ever, and your enemy knows it. The closer you get, the hotter the battle. This is warfare. The enemy is after your faith and his ultimate goal is to wreck your testimony. If he can get you to speak against what the Word of God says and start talking what you see, then you'll abort the process that has already been started. If you lose faith, ultimately, you'll have no testimony.

When things start going crazy, keep pushing forward. Keep speaking what the Word says. You will encounter every type of distraction imaginable. The kids will start acting crazy, symptoms will begin to show up in your body, things around the house will all of sudden fall into disrepair. It literally will be one thing after another, but you have to recognize it for what it is, it's an attack. It's nothing more than an attempt to discourage you and make you think that this faith thing just won't work and it's not worth all of the trouble. You'll experience all kinds of crazy thoughts but stay the course. When things start going topsy-turvy in my life like it's a full moon outside, I tell the devil "thanks for the heads up because you must be able to see in the spirit realm that I am closer than I know, so thanks for the confirmation!"

While you're standing amidst all that will come your way, remember that God's Word is true and the Angels are working hard behind the scenes on your behalf, to bring it to pass.

Mark 11:23-24 AMP   Galatians 6:9 AMP   2 Timothy 2:3-4 AMP

Psalms 103:20

26

I Dodged A Bullet

I remember when we went to Grandma Verna's "Home Going" service over in Mississippi. When it comes to packing the car, I usually load the suitcases in the car and make sure we have everything, but I didn't this time. When we were about twenty minutes from her house, which is an 8-hour drive from ours, I asked my wife if she grabbed the garment bag hanging on the door. It was a wonderful time for me to ask don't you think? Of course, she said no. All of the clothes we were to wear for the service were in there. We looked at each other and burst out laughing so hard we were crying. It's the fourth of July about 6 pm and Wal-Mart seemed to be our only option which made my wife laugh harder as she pictured me dressed up in clothes from there. This was a prime opportunity for both of us to get angry at each other, but we didn't. As a result, we found a clothing store that was still open and they were having a sale- BOGO from 30-50% off the already marked down price.

Because of God's grace and His favor, we recovered nicely. When the blessing and favor of God is on your life things always work out for your good. Walking in love is a lifestyle, and when you do things will always work themselves out. You've got His Word on it!

Romans 8:28 AMP   Proverbs 3:3-4   Galatians 5:6

27

Faith Is For The Middle

You've heard from God. You start on your journey with an expected end in mind. Believing God for the manifestation of something so big that you can't do it by yourself can be overwhelming, if you allow it to be. This is why we have faith and it's in the middle that we have to exercise our use of it.

You don't need as much faith to get started as you do on your way to the end. The middle is where the opposition is. This is where the enemy will throw everything that he can at you. All types of distractions like issues with your children, disagreements with your spouse, your money might start to "get funny" and then he may even throw in some symptoms of sickness for good measure. It's all an attempt to get you to abort the process. If he can get you to start talking fear instead of God's Word, then he's got you. Remember that fear is faith in what the enemy has said. Our faith is based on what God has written in His Word.

I've heard it said, "Faith in perfection is obeying God and leaving the consequences to Him." When we let God work out the details of the vision He's given, the only thing we have to do is follow the gentle leadings of the Holy Spirit. He knows which way to go and if we listen and obey that still small voice, the way will be much easier than if we did it on our own.

Mark 11:22-24 AMP   Psalms 34:19   John 16:13-14 AMP

1 Kings 19:11-13 NLT

28

The Holy Spirit Is God In The Earth

Jesus explained that the Holy Spirit will come to teach us all things and to bring the things that He (Christ) has said back to our remembrance. Holy Spirit will guide us into all truth.

God is still speaking to us today not only through His written Word but more importantly with that still small voice on the inside of you. The one I sometimes refer to as my "first mind." When I don't listen to Him when He speaks, I realize there was something down the road I could have avoided. Lately I have been enjoying the results of really following His lead, especially when it comes to getting a revelation from the written Word, applying it to my life, and getting results! It has been a real faith builder and confidence booster.

I learned a long time ago that Holy Spirit is a gentleman and won't force Himself upon me. It's up to me to follow His gentle leadings. After all, He's getting His information hot off the heavenly presses and straight from the Father Himself!

John 14:26 AMP   John 16:13 AMP   1 Kings 19:11-12

29

The Symptoms Of Fear

Fear is a spirit that did not come from God. When fear tries to "knock on your door" the best thing that you can do is open your mouth and speak against it. You can't let the enemy play those games of mental gymnastics with you. You can't fight a thought with a thought. You have to open your mouth and say something in order to interrupt the thought process to guard against fears symptoms.

Fear has a wide range of symptoms that can go from anger, procrastination and worry, to attacks on your physical body like stress, which can lead to headaches, high blood pressure and other severe maladies. When fear shows up, we have to recognize it quickly and begin defending ourselves against it with the Word of God.

Most of the time it doesn't have to be something bad to get the "fear ball" rolling. It can be a blessing that you received. Just because it's good and it came from God don't think for a minute that the enemy is going to stand idly by and watch you enjoy it without a little interference to spoil your victory. There are times when a blessing is unfolding little by little that doubt begins to creep in. Those are the times when the urge to find a way "to help God out" is the strongest. In reality the best thing to do is, stand still and continue trusting Him.

The best weapon to use against fear is the Word of God being spoken out of your mouth. It takes a renewed mind in the Word to be able to withstand the mental attacks fear brings. Don't let fear take up residence in your life. Recognize its symptoms and immediately go to work resisting it by speaking Gods Word.

As you go through your day, keep this thought in mind: Fear tolerated is faith contaminated!

2 Timothy 1:7 AMP   2 Corinthians 4:16 AMP   James 4:7 AMP

30

God Doesn't Shout

When God speaks, He doesn't shout, He whispers. How do you know when God is talking to you? One way He speaks is what I call the first mind. For example when you're driving your normal route to work and all of a sudden you get a thought to go another way. The new way will take you out of the way and is longer. You decide to keep going the way you were. All of a sudden, you're stuck in a traffic jam and the first thing you say to yourself is, "I should have listened to my first mind." That was God in the person of the Holy Spirit guiding you away from the traffic jam.

Another way He speaks to us is through His Word. It can be by hearing the Word preached or you reading it aloud. Either way that's how faith comes. When you hear the Word preached, the Spirit of God reads the Word of God to you and applies it to your heart. That's why everybody can get something different from the same sermon. It is speaking to their individual heart about their lives. Reading the Word aloud speaks to your spirit man. Your spirit man is best fed when he hears the Word coming out of your mouth. Your inner man gets stronger and the outward man gets weaker.

As you go through your day pay attention to the gentle leadings of the Holy Spirit. He's a gentleman and will not force His way on you. He speaks softly in your ear.

1 Kings 19:12 AMP   John 16:13 AMP   Romans 10:17 AMP

2 Corinthians 4:15-18 AMP

31

The Attack Is Natural First, Then Spiritual

We are at war and under serious attack. The enemy is attempting to do everything he can to prevent us from fulfilling our God-ordained destiny. We all have a call on our life and it will come to pass if we remain diligent about the things of God. The way he attacks is in the natural first which ultimately leads to our spirit. If he can get you to say or do anything that goes against what the Word of God says, eventually it will affect you spiritually. Case in point is the sexual revolution we are experiencing. I am not anti-gay. I am pro-God.

If you look at same-sex relationships from a pure physical approach it is nothing more than genocide. The ability to reproduce is not there. The more people who turn away from the natural use of their bodies in this area, the less people are born to multiply on the earth as we were instructed in the Garden of Eden. It's just another deceptive trick of the enemy. He has same sex married couples wanting to start families. They think they are "doing the normal family thing" when in actuality they have to go find someone who has done it the right way, adopt and raise their children. Or one of the couples goes and halfway does it through surrogacy and they become "parents." It's all a lie from the father of lies.

The spirit of deception has come upon the earth like never before. It is spreading like wildfire. With the technological advancements we've made, it's happening quicker and going farther than we could've imagined. The sad part is no one is paying attention that he's after our children. If he can get them while they're young, they'll grow up and infect others in their circle. We have to get back to teaching them that sex was not designed to be between two men, two women or a man and a woman but rather for a husband (male) and a wife (female). Men and women should be married. As children grow older you can delve into it on a deeper level, but you have to start now at ages 4, 5, and 6. I know some might say it's too soon but it's really not. If you don't tell them someone one else will. Do you know how many of the kids they go to school with have two mommies or two daddies? I bet you they know of at least one who does. If so, you'll find yourself explaining it to them. There is no way around it.

It's high time we put the devil on notice. Let him know that we are not ignorant of his devices. If he wants to influence them, we will counter it with the truth from God's Word and let the Word stand on its own because the truth is greater than the facts!

Romans 1:24-27 AMP   Genesis 1:27-28   2 Corinthians 2:11AMP

June

1

Two Ears

When I say that we have two ears immediately you begin thinking left and right. To a certain point you're correct. However, the two I'm talking about are the inner and outer ear. Have you ever heard your voice on a recording and noticed how it sounds different from what you're accustomed to? That's because you're used to hearing it with the inner ear and the inner ear is what's connected to and feeds your spirit man.

The Bible is very specific when it comes to speaking and hearing. We're told we can have the things that we say, and faith increases by hearing the Word of God. When we speak the Word of God as in making daily confessions, we are giving life to it and our faith is increased. I'm not discounting hearing the Word of God by other avenues, like live or recorded teaching and preaching, but hearing the Word coming out of your mouth into your inner ear on a consistent basis has a far greater impact. It makes deposits directly into your spirit man. That's why the words we speak carry so much weight and are so important. Our words should always line up with God's Word, that is how we live.

Today, be more attentive to what you say. When things seem to be going contrary to what you desire be like my brother when in the heat of the battle he says: "If God didn't write it, I'm not saying it."

Mark 11:23 NASB   Romans 10:17 AMP   Matthew 4:4

2

God's Word Works

No matter what you might face in life, all you have to do is put God's Word on it, speak it by faith and then watch it come alive. It'll work for you every time.

God's Word is not void of power. You know it's working when you start to see results manifest and you encounter rising opposition at the same time. You'll get a good report from the doctor and on your way home you'll experience car trouble. Your enemy will always try to play mental gymnastics with you by his attempts to steal your joy or saying that the Word won't work in another area of your life. Why wage such an aggressive campaign to tell me that it won't work instead of letting me try it and find out for myself that it doesn't work? That's all the proof necessary to know that what he's saying is nothing but a lie. When you get those invasive thoughts, you have to immediately capture them by speaking against it. You can't fight a thought with a thought. You have to open your mouth and speak.

Whether it's a matter concerning your finances, health or a family member, your prayer was answered the moment you prayed. You have to remain in faith and not waver. You have to take God at His Word and stand on it in the face of opposing circumstances. His Word will come to pass. If you believe it, you can receive it!

Hebrews 4:12 AMP   Isaiah 55:10-11AMP   2 Corinthians 10:5-6

Mark 11:23-24

3

Routine Or Worship?

Is the time you spend with God out of a routine or is it an act of worship? I posed this question myself recently, which culminated out of a slip-up I had. Have you ever believed for manifestation and say something against it? I did and it bothered me that it happened. I asked God how do I correct it and He said: "When you slip up, double up. You have to increase your time in my Word. Go back to where you started and do the things you were doing in the beginning and be just like a farmer, plant seeds."

We're not going to be 100% all the time. I'm grateful that God has given us a way to escape called grace! Whenever we slip-up, it's not the end of the world. We go and speak the Word because it's *"quick, powerful...."* The time I spent with God every morning somehow had turned into a routine exercise and not the worship experience it started out as. In the beginning, that time was spent because I wanted to be with God and not to just get something. The things I used to do to be with God slowly stopped. Now I realize He was trying to gently nudge me to come back for a while.

It took this little slip-up for me to reflect and notice other cracks in my foundation, like being easily distracted and irritated. Time spent with God is now a desire for me to worship and not out of obligation. It's funny how motives can change while you're busy doing the same things the same way you've always done, thinking everything is okay and it's not.

Today, I challenge you to honestly ask yourself why am I doing what I do when it comes to spending time with God. If warranted, make the necessary course corrections and get back on track!

Revelation 2:14 AMP   Hebrews 4:12 AMP   1 Chronicles 16:29

4

Lighten Your Load

The way things are going today it doesn't take much and it's not long before your plate is full. The feelings of being overwhelmed have arrived. Let's look at ways to avoid getting there.

First and foremost, go to the Word of God and feed your spirit man. The Word tells us to cast all of our cares, our anxiety on the Lord because He cares for us. Since He's caring for us there's no need for both of us doing it. This is one of those things He took care of on the Cross and when you take it to God in prayer, you'll get peace.

Another way to lighten your load is prioritize or make a list of things to do. If it has to be done today, does it have to be addressed before 9:00 a.m.? Move it to later in the day if the circumstances allow. Maybe there are some people and situations you need to politely limit your involvement with. You can do it tactfully and in love. Let the Holy Spirit be your guide. I was talking to someone recently and shared that it's okay to say "no" to people; especially to family when your welfare is at stake. Don't worry about how they'll feel. They might not like it but when it crosses the line of what's not in *your* best interest, you won't feel bad for long. They'll soon get over it. You have to learn just like I did on how to say no and not feel bad about it. If we learned how to tell our kids "no" and be all right then we can learn how when it comes to others.

As you go through your day, do a self-check. What and where can you lighten your load? It's a process. If you keep at it, God will show you how to live the carefree, good life that's been pre-arranged which can only be found In Him.

1 Peter 5:7 AMP   Philippians 4:6-7   2 Peter 1:3 AMP   Ephesians 2:10 AMP

5

When The Rubber Hits The Road

Today's title comes from a saying that the old folks used to say when you really had to experience something that you previously assumed would be a piece of cake and subsequently discovered that it wasn't. To put it another way, when it comes to faith and believing God, we can talk the talk, but when it comes to actually walking the talk that's another story.

True ministry is developed from our actual life experiences. There are some things you have to go through in order to boldly proclaim, in alignment with the Word, what God has done in you, through you and for you. This also produces an anointing. You have to crush olives in order to extract olive oil and its same way with the anointing. If you want to be anointed, that's what it takes- being crushed. Recently I talked about using your faith while in the middle, on your way to the full manifestation of a promise from God. If you want to reach the end, you have to renew your mind so you can keep the Word in your heart and mouth. That's the faith connection. Renewing your mind allows you to capture thoughts of failure and defeat. Remember this is warfare and *our weapons are not carnal but mighty through God...*

Today, continue developing your trust in God. You already possess all that He has promised. He answered your prayers the moment you prayed.

Ephesians 4:23 AMP   2 Corinthians 10:3-5 AMP   Jeremiah 17:7-8 AMP

157

6

This Is Your Time

For some time now, you've seen others get blessed and have celebrated with them. You've sown your seeds expecting a harvest. All of this done in faith and nothing seems to be happening. Then just when you think your break-through is about to happen, all types of confusion seem to break loose in your life. If this is you, then I want you to know that this is your time. The increase in challenging circumstances is only a sign to tell you that you are closer than ever. Don't stop believing.

The Bible says that "due season" is not if but when, and as long as we don't faint, we'll see the manifestation of God's promises in our lives. These are the times when you have to keep moving forward. It might be tough, but if you keep putting one foot in front of the other while speaking nothing but the Word in faith, you'll get there.

Speaking God's Word has creative power. You were created in the image of God, another speaking spirit. Just like God created the world with the words He spoke, we create our world with the words we speak. When things start to look contrary, don't let the words of your mouth be contrary also. Call those things the way you want them to be and not the way they look. You're so close. The enemy knows it and he will do whatever he can to get you to abort your destiny with negative speech.

This is your season. You have sown and now it's time to reap the harvest of the seeds you've sown. Yes, it's your time, now!

Galatians 6:9 AMP   Mark 11:22-24 AMP   Romans 4:17   John 4:35 AMP

7

Turn Down The Noise

There are times when we have to turn down the noise volume of life. As Christians we don't retreat. We just fall back, regroup, get quiet and talk with God. I've learned how to make the necessary adjustments by adding and deleting some things even some people when necessary. It can feel uncomfortable at times, but God will give you the grace to walk through it. It's all preparation for your next step into where He is taking you. God has a plan for your life and God is strategic.

The Apostle Paul prays for the churches at Ephesus and Colosse for increased wisdom and knowledge from God. I pray this for myself and for others. Pray this over your life. Where it says "you" replace it with "me" and "I." If you're praying for someone put his or her name there.

Hang in there. You're right where God wants you. Turn the noise volume down. Learn the lesson, pass the tests, keep moving forward and don't look back except to see how far you've come. Remember you're not alone. We are all in this together!

Ephesians 1:16-23   Ephesians 3:16-21   Colossians 1:9-11

8

God Is Good!

Back in the late 80's when I first started going to church, my Pastor at the time used to always say to the congregation: "God is good" and we'd say "all the time" and he would reverse it and say "and all the time" and we'd say "God is good." That kind of popped in my spirit today as I was praying.

We've come to understand it's the goodness of God that leads us to repentance. Better yet, because God's love and mercy is extended to us by not punishing us when we have missed the mark. We willfully make the necessary changes in our character that bring us into alignment with His will and purpose for our lives. It is really called grace. It's favor that we did not earn or deserve. That's what love did for us on the Cross. Jesus paid the price so that we don't have to. The Holy Ghost has poured the love of God into our hearts, and He did that just because He's good! It's not just cliché, it's a reality that we live and experience every day.

As you go through your day today, tell yourself and everyone you come in contact with that "God is good all the time and all the time God is good." When you say it, watch and see how your atmosphere changes. It's all because God is good all the time.

Romans 2:4   Romans 5:1-5 AMP   Hebrews 10:23 AMP

9

This Is A Shift and Not An Attack

One morning on the prayer call, Bishop Murphy talked about how God is shifting people around and that this is a move from God and not an attack. It might feel the same as an attack because it's uncomfortable. In reality, it's a shift that is preparation for the next level.

We all want to go to the next level in God but when it starts to happen, we start tripping! Our once familiar comfort zone has been affected by the changes God is orchestrating. Although it might feel uncomfortable, we have to trust God in spite of everything that is taking place around us. Once we recognize the shift is going on, it's going to take a daily renewing of our minds in the Word of God to help stabilize our emotions during this period of transformation.

God is bringing me to a place of maturity, a place where I now see things the way God does. He is shifting my perspective and elevating my ability to see things. I now have His perspective, and since I've changed my perspective, I can look at it as a move from God and not an attack from the enemy. My ability to see, along with my actions and my life are now based on revelation and not experience. I am walking by *faith and not by sight*, and my confessions are not lies they are prophecies.

Today mix the Word of God with faith. Let the Word come out of your mouth in faith and watch it profit you!

Romans 8:28 NASB   Romans 12:2 AMP   2 Corinthians 5:7 AMP

Hebrews 4:2 AMP

10

Watch and Pray

Now more than ever we need to watch and pray. I happened to watch a video of two ladies fighting in Wal-Mart. One got out of a handicap scooter and proceeded to fight another lady, who in turn had her little boy about six- or seven-years old help her fight off the woman. Road rage has taken a more serious tone. People are not only brandishing guns but shooting people. This is why I mention rather frequently that everybody is going through something. It has never been more evident than what we see going on not only in the world but also in our own neighborhoods.

All of this should serve as a wakeup call to us, the body of Christ, that we need to be more sensitive to the Holy Spirit as we go about our day-to-day activities. When someone cuts you off or does something crazy on the freeway, don't retaliate. Stay in Christ and remain calm. We have no idea what they might be facing. People are full of rage and they're angry. The root of all anger is fear.

This world doesn't have what we have in Christ. This is why we live to be the example of Christ. We are God in the flesh, living epistles. The only Bible some will ever see is how we conduct ourselves. This is a ministering opportunity to either win them to Christ, provide a word of comfort, and support that will help get them through something. Whatever they might be facing, know that Christ in us does the work through us.

We have to impact the world. There is no better place to start than right where you are with your circle of influence. Be the salt of the earth. Salt is no good as long as it is in the shaker!

Matthew 26:41 AMP   John 16:13 AMP   2 Corinthians 3:2-3 NIV

Hebrews 10:30 AMP

11

Believe That You Receive

One morning while making my confessions, the Holy Spirit prompted me to finish each one with this declaration "I believe that I receive."

The Bible says when you pray, to believe that you received the things you asked for in prayer and you shall have them. This is one of the fundamentals of faith. When you get right down to the nitty gritty, faith speaks to the end of the matter. You have to see it by faith before you receive it, which means you have to believe that you've already got it.

I remember a training class I had years ago called "The Seven Habits of Highly Effective People." One of the habits was that you have to begin with the end in mind. Faith is the same way. That thing or situation you're praying about must be seen with your spiritual eyes in the manifested form, in order for your faith to begin to work. Faith at its most practical level is acting on what you believe. You practice faith all day, every day without giving it a second thought. You get in your car and turn the key to start your car. Unless you've been having car problems, you have the expectation that it will start. You believe it'll start so you turn the key. That's what faith is-acting on what you believe. Take that same mind set and apply it to the Word of God when it comes to healing or whatever you're believing for. Making confessions is great. Do you see yourself healed and possessing your healing or are you just hoping it'll work?

When we make our confessions, we are calling those things that be not as if they were already manifested. It's the same process God used when He changed Abram's name to Abraham, calling him the father of a multitude while he yet had no children and a barren wife. The reality of that is it's still coming to pass today, because we are Abraham's seed and heirs according to the promise.

Exercise your faith today. Begin speaking to the end of the thing you're believing for as if it's already done. Keep speaking. You'll receive it if you believe it.

Mark 11:23-24 AMP   Romans 4:17 AMP   Galatians 3:29

12

Walking By Faith

Learning how to walk by faith at times is not easy. Once you learn the basic principles of faith, it takes a renewed mind to stay the course. The world around us is based on what we can see or feel. As Christians, we don't walk that way. Ours is a walk by faith. Let's say you're believing God for great things to happen in your life. Your faith is out there, but you haven't forgiven (place their name here). In order for our faith to work, we can't be unforgiving. Love doesn't work that way. If your love isn't right your faith won't work, because it takes love to make your faith work.

Walking by faith means walking in love. This is the most challenging part of our Christian walk. But we can do it. The things we see don't move us. Though they might be contrary to what we believe God for, our stance is "what does the Word say" and we stick with that.

Place a guard over your mouth so your words, i.e. your confessions, line up with God's Word. Develop an "It is written" attitude when it comes to your faith in God's Word. Watch the Word come alive and His promises to you get fulfilled.

It was all settled on the Cross!

Romans 12:2 AMP   2 Corinthians 5:7   Galatians 5:6 NIV

13

This Is the Answer To Your Prayer

At 5:30 this morning, I went and sat in the garage with the door raised. As I watched the lightning dance across the sky, I felt the thunder roll a few seconds later. While watching and listening to the rain fall, I began to praise God. I was having a moment.

After *fifteen yrs. of being in our home, the house is sold. We're moving. It will all be over in a couple of days. It's been an emotional rollercoaster at times because when I bought this house, God really blessed me. I had left Detroit and moved to Texas with virtually no intentions of buying a house. I wanted an apartment and a corvette, in that order. That's all. I never imagined that I would build a house from the ground up. No one had ever lived in this house before I got here. I was the first. I couldn't believe God did this for me. Now it's time to leave "Egypt" for the promise land.

When you ask God, like I did, to bless you so that you can be a blessing to others, the first thing that comes to mind is the exhilarating feeling of doing good for someone. You don't consider a road chock full of obstacles and distractions. You don't find out until you sit in the garage at 5:30 in the morning, with just you and the Lord, that this is the answer to your prayer. Every adversity was allowed to strengthen you for the next level of blessing. When God gives you the desires of your heart, you're going to have to go through some things in order for it to manifest in your life. It is well worth every bit of whatever you have to go through. I haven't gotten there yet, but my faith is greater today than it was yesterday. That's only due to the fact that I stayed in the Word and sought wise godly counsel when it got tight. I watched what words came out of my mouth. I made some mistakes and some major blunders but as soon as I realized it, I did what was necessary to correct what I could.

The greatest lesson learned so far from all of this is something I received from Charles Stanley. He said, "Obey God and leave the consequences to Him." You have to trust God that His Word is true and know that it will never fail as long as you keep sin out of your life. Keep the Word of God in your mouth, and don't doubt in your heart. Yes, it might get tight. You have the Blood, the Word and the name of Jesus on your side. How can you lose?

Psalms 37:4 AMP   Mark 11:22-24 AMP   Revelation 12:11 NLT

John 14:12-14 AMP

*1999

14

This Is A Spiritual Battle

What you're going through right now is a Spiritual battle. It is not to be fought in the flesh. This is the Lord's battle and we don't fight with carnal weapons. When we fight, we put on our armor, take out our sword which is the Word, and we go into battle.

In your Spiritual battle you will be met with all types of situations and circumstances. Be careful. Things that you thought had been laid to rest will resurface, while at the same time your new experiences will try to overwhelm you. It's almost like one of those wrestling matches where they all pile on one opponent to subdue him. That's what your enemy wants to do to you. Pile all of these things on you and start messing with your emotions. The next thing you know, somebody does something to you, and they catch the brunt of everything that has gone wrong in your life for the past six months. Now you really feel bad because have to go and apologize for "losing your cool."

I want you to stay encouraged during these times. Grab your Bible and become intimate with Psalm 91. Get to know it like you know your name, and watch your faith rise during these seemingly tough times.

2 Corinthians 10:3-5 AMP   Ephesians 6:11-17 AMP   Psalms 91

15

God Is Shifting Things Around

Recently I talked about how what might seem like an enemy attack, could really be a divine shift from God. They're both uncomfortable as they force us to deal with unexpected events and cause us to make some type of adjustment. Lately I have been feeling restless and uneasy in my spirit. This is my indicator that things are going to be changing in and around me, so hang on.

The shift could be people coming in or out of your life. It might be your children reverting to an old shortcoming that you thought was previously "nipped in the bud." All of this is going on right in the middle of you planning or maybe looking to make a major decision. I want to encourage you by letting you know that everything is in divine order! This time in life has been pre-arranged and ordained by God. We have to make consistent investments in our spirits, by spending time in the Word of God and in prayer. Your faith will grow as God allows you to be stretched to the point where you think you can't take any more, but you can. You just keep putting one foot in front of the other and keep moving forward. This is just a shift. Sometimes it takes me a couple of minutes to realize that God really does have a plan. All I have to do is stay prayerful as He allows things to be moved around.

Make this confession today, "God is working it all out for my good, to complete His plan for my life. When this phase is completed, I'm going to know God differently and that's a good thing!"

Jeremiah 29:11-13   Ephesians 4:23 AMP   Romans 8:28 AMP

16

Taking God At His Word

One of the most exciting things about the faith walk is getting to see the manifestation of God's Word come to pass. I believe God will help me do the things I can't do by myself. While I await the manifestation, I rehearse past victories. One thing I've learned is that God's Word is true. As long as I stay focused on the prize while sidestepping the distractions, I will get to His expected end for me because it's in His plan.

As I walk with God, I'm noticing a change in me. When I set aside what I want for what He wants, what He wants becomes what I want. The two wills are becoming one; His becoming mine. This all started by me simply taking God at His Word and learning how to stand when all the evidence is contrary to what His Word says. I've heard it said that God is not going to embarrass you and that is so true. He's not going to do it to Himself. As long as I don't jump in and try to help God out, I won't be embarrassed.

God lives in the eternal "now." There is no time in eternity because with God it's always now. That's why the old saying "He may not come when you want him but he's always on time" is so poignant. The right time for us is always the now time for Him.

2 Chronicles 20:5-9 AMP   Jeremiah 29:11 MSG

17

The Peace Of God

In the middle of whatever storm you might be facing today, I want you to know that God will give you peace. I'm talking about the peace that no one, not even you, can understand why you're not upset when things go awry.

Yesterday was a really busy day. It started by my having to drop the girls off at summer camp, take Ethan to daycare and meet the contractors at the house at 10:00 am so they could finish up what should have been completed two weeks ago. On the way there I received a speeding ticket, which I immediately blamed on the contractors. I get to the house and the window guy is there. He and the contractor tell me that whoever came and initially measured the glass had the wrong size and type of glass. I explained to him the importance of having it completed today because I will no longer be available. The rest of the work has to be completed so the new owners can re-inspect it prior to closing on the house. He re-measured them and said he was going back to his shop to see what he could come up with. An hour later he was back and installed the windows. That was nothing but the favor of God working on my behalf. I stayed calm and didn't go off on him. Everything worked out. The "old me" would've been "justified" with everything happening at this time in my life. My brother came to help me with a couple of repairs and to move the rest of our things into storage until our new home is finished. I am so grateful to God that I have a big brother like him. He is an inspiration to not only me, but the men from our church seek him out constantly for counsel.

When you spend time daily with God in prayer and in His Word, you'll get the God-kind of results in your life. When you speak the Word in faith, your angels go to work, while the Holy Spirit leads and guides you into all truth. Together they align the situations in your life and bring to fruition the manifestation of your expectations.

Today, you can be at peace no matter what life throws your way. God has it all worked out. You've got His Word on it.

Philippians 4:6-7 AMP   Psalms 103:20   John 16:13 AMP

Romans 8:28 NIV

18

Following The Holy Spirit

Over time I've learned that the Holy Spirit is a gentleman. He won't force Himself upon you but will speak softly into your spirit. When He does, you have to move when He says move. He's only saying what the Father tells Him to as He guides and shows you things to come.

Paying attention to Holy Spirit will save you time and money. There was a time when I was trying to get my Internet hooked up and it just wasn't working. I had been using the hot spot on my cell phone to connect. I was anxious to get it working, but it wouldn't. The phone company said there was something wrong with the modem and I needed a new one. Of course, they wanted to charge me for it. I was slightly perturbed but told them go ahead and order it. Since they installed the service that day, I had to call back in the morning and order it. While they had me on hold, the Holy Spirit was telling me I had another modem. Since we just moved, I knew right where it was. I hooked it up and all was well in my world! The Holy Spirit helped save me the expense of a new one all because I recognize His voice. That might not seem like much to some, but when you pay attention to the Holy Spirit, He will bring things back to your remembrance.

Developing a relationship with Him is one of the best things we could ever do. When you spend time in the Word, Holy Spirit will quicken a Word back to you at the right time, especially those times when you don't have a Bible handy. Spending time daily in the presence of God, in prayer and the Word pays off in ways that money can't buy. It just might save you some in the long run.

1 Kings 19:11-12 AMP   John 16:13   2 Peter 1:11-12 AMP

19

Honoring Our Parents /
Call Your Fathers

Honoring our parents is the first commandment from God that gives us a promise. The promise is one of long life if we honor our parents. I know for some that might be hard because of some unresolved childhood issues. I have been there and want to let you know that you can work through whatever the issue might be. Stop letting anger over it abort your destiny.

Forgive your parents as you want God to forgive you! I heard my pastor once say that "it's not about their performance but their position." Given everything that they probably had to work with, they were doing the best they could. Yes, mistakes were made, and we have to acknowledge it in order to begin to heal. Whether abuse or abandonment, it's in the past and can't be undone. My grandfather would say "You can't put spilled milk back into the bottle and you can't un-ring a bell that has already been rung." You have to work through it for you, so that you can get better. It's going take time and it happens in stages.

God's Word gives you permission to be angry. Yes, you have every right to be angry because you're hurt, just don't sin. Make a decision that you won't let this situation cause you to die a premature death. There are varying ways you can honor your parents if they're still alive. Pray and ask the Holy Spirit to help you find the words to say. Pick up the phone, it really doesn't weigh 100 pounds, and call. Say "hello" that's all. If you have no expectations other than to accomplish your part then you won't be disappointed. In your conversation, don't play the blame game and try to inflict the hurt you have on your parent because it'll backfire. You'll feel worse than when you started. Don't look for any acknowledgment of wrongdoing or an apology because it might not come. You have to take baby steps. In time you may get to have that conversation. You might not. Let God make that determination.

Follow the gentle leadings of the Holy Spirit as He guides you to your restoration. The love of God is your focus. Living a long life here on earth is your reward!

Exodus 20:12   Ephesians 4:26-27 AMP   John 16:13 AMP

20

Why Are You Waiting?

Looking at today's title, I want you to think about how, in the faith arena, there are times when we shouldn't be waiting. When Jesus, who is the author and finisher of our faith got results immediately, why aren't we?

Let's consider the lesson of the fig tree. Mark writes in his Gospel that Jesus spoke to the tree and the next day, when they came by, they saw that it was dead. Matthew's account tells us that it happened "immediately" and Jesus' disciples were amazed at how quick the tree died. When we think about a tree dying, automatically we know it's going to take some time. Probably up to a couple of years. This one died as soon as He spoke to it. Could the reason this isn't happening for us be because in our heads we believe, but don't expect it to in our hearts? We have to work diligently at moving away from what we see, and speak the Word of God.

Our faith grows as we go through life's challenges. The challenges won't kill us but rather like the old folks used to say, "it'll make you stronger." Always keep in mind that this is all part of the path and plan God has designed to give you the good life. As you grow, you'll begin to notice that the Word of God will manifest in your life sooner. All we have to do is believe and not doubt in our hearts.

Mark 11:12-14   Matthew 21:18-22 NLT   Ephesians 2:10 AMP

21

Turn Your Faith Switch On

I did an update to my cell phone one day, and after the update I plugged my phone into charge it. I noticed that the light didn't illuminate like it normally does. So, I plugged another device in. I thought it worked so I plugged my phone in and went to bed. Later I looked and my phone wasn't charged. I began to think everything bad about being out of town and not having my phone, none of which I could do anything about at 4:00 in the morning. The one thing that I didn't do was say anything bad. I learned that if I don't want it, don't say it. I told God "I trust you and I'm going back to sleep." When I got up, I looked for a repair shop in Detroit that I could go to after church. When I got in the car to go to church, the Holy Spirit told me to plug my phone in. When I did it began charging. After church, when I got back to my father's house, I went and looked at the plug. The cord was plugged into a power strip and the strip was turned off.

Is your faith switch turned on? You can have your faith plugged in, in your head. If we're to turn our faith on, then what we believe in our heart, either positive or negative will come out of our mouth. Keep in mind that fear is faith in the lies of the enemy. We turn on the faith switch by speaking or releasing God's Word into the atmosphere. We were created in the image of God, another speaking spirit, with the same creative power that He demonstrated when He spoke the world into existence.

Feed your spirit man the Word of God by reading it aloud daily. When you take the Word in, no matter what you might face in this life, turn on the faith switch and speak God's Word. Speaking His Word will release spirit and life into whatever situation you have, creating the world and results you desire.

Matthew 12:34 AMP   Mark 11:22-24 AMP   John 4:24   John 6:63 AMP

22

Father Of The Year

I was recognized as "Father of The Year" in honor of Father's Day at church one year. I was truly caught off guard, surprised and humbled.

For those of you who don't know the story, my wife and I became foster parents in November of 2012 to three wonderful kids who are siblings. When we took the training, we heard all the horror stories about bad kids and the revolving door, etc. They were our first placement and it was truly a God thing. I never imagined being able to love children who weren't biologically mine the way that I do. At the time they were eight, five and two years old. I had just retired from work, so I became a stay-at-home dad while my wife went to work. I took them to all of their doctor visits, got them enrolled in school, etc.

The following year God paved the way for us to adopt them. Last November, I wrote about how the stork came and visited us on the day we adopted them. Today they are thriving, well-mannered and all-around good kids. God truly has been good to my wife and I. God entrusting their care to us is really a blessing. He knew all along this would happen and He put all of us together. As I reflect back, I can now see how it was a divine set-up and when God sets you up, He sets you up BIG!

I'm thankful to my Father Charles, Carl my brother and the rest of the men who showed me by example how to be a good father. A special thanks to Pastor Sheryl Brady, my pastor and her staff and the entire Potter's House North Dallas family for recognizing God working in my life and sharing it so the world can see.

Psalms 127 AMP   Proverbs 22:6 AMP   Ephesians 6:4 AMP

23

Finding The Will Of God

There are two ways in which we can find the will of God. The first is by going to His Word and seeing what it has to say about our particular situation. When we go to His Word, we can find deliverance, healing, prosperity and peace. Everything can be found in the Word even the pathway to a specific answer not directly found in the Word.

The second way to know the will of God is using the Holy Spirit who has been given to us for a guide. Spending time fellowshipping with God in prayer and in His Word will allow you to fine tune your ear to His voice. When something comes up and you don't know exactly which way to go just ask. The answer will come. That's what King Solomon meant when he said, *"Acknowledge Him in all your ways and He'll direct your path."* God wants to be involved in every aspect of our lives especially our decision making and doesn't want to be left out.

God loves it when we make plans, because inevitably they coincide with the desires He's placed on the inside of us to carry out His plans. The key for us is to learn how to let God work out the details. That's hard because we try to cover all of the bases and we know what we want it to look like in the end with our "plans all worked out." When something unexpected comes up, this causes us to panic, get in fear and become stressed out because it's not going the way we wanted it. I remember when it used to happen to me. Not anymore. Let me rephrase that, not as intense as before. Now when things happen it might take me a minute to gather myself, and resolve that God is still in control. That reminds me of an old television show from the 60's "Father Knows Best." Our Father God really does!

Today let the Word of God and the Holy Spirit guide your thoughts and actions. You can't go wrong with that dynamic duo looking out for you. He has a plan and knows the best way to get us to where He is taking us. All we have to do is follow His lead.

John 16:13 AMP   Proverbs 3:6   Jeremiah 29:11-13 AMP

24

You Already Have Everything You'll Need

At time things might seem to be a little uncertain and you don't know exactly which way to go or what to do. Let me help put your mind at ease today by letting you know that everything we'll ever need has been made available. We just have to go get it.

God has given us everything that pertains unto life and godliness by knowing Christ who has called us to glory and virtue. We know that God has already (past tense) blessed us with all spiritual blessings, in heavenly places, in Christ. The day you were born again Christ moved in on the inside of you. Because all spiritual blessings are in heavenly places and heavenly places are in Christ and Christ is in you, then you have everything on the inside of you. The answer to problems that used to bring worry or concern like healing, prosperity or whatever you need has already been deposited in you. "God already put it in the budget" is something one of our instructors in the school of ministry used to say. We have to bring it from the spiritual into the natural. We do that by acknowledging that God has given it to us and it's in us.

So, when lack shows up simply say, "I got it, because when I go to your Word it tells me that You'll supply all of my need. So, I got it." Problems in your marriage or whatever, release your faith by acknowledging God and saying that you already have the answer on the inside of you.

You've got it, because God put it in the budget for your life!

2 Peter 1:3-4 AMP   Ephesians 1:3-4 AMP   Philemon 1:6

25

Faith and Belief - Two Sides Of The Same Coin

The Bible defines faith as the substance of things hoped for, the evidence of things not seen. If we're to look at it on a more practical level, faith is acting on what you believe. This leads me to ask-what do you believe?

When you got saved, it was your faith that Jesus died for your sins and God raised Him from the dead that lead you to act on it by accepting the free gift of salvation. You acted on what you believed. That's what faith is. Since we believe and have faith for salvation, why is it so hard to have faith and believe God's Word about everything else that concerns us? It takes the same amount of faith to get healed, delivered, and prosper that it took to get saved.

Could the reason we stumble in these other areas be due to a lack of trust? If so, it all starts with money. If you don't trust God with your money, then nothing else will work for you. Trusting God is more than lip service and is displayed by what you do. What you do in the area of finances shows your trust. Tithing and giving of your resources so others can hear the Gospel shows your trust. When you pay your bills and money is getting "funny" do you worry about how are you going to pay them or are you trusting in God to meet you at the point of your need? God rewards faithfulness and living by the Word of God produces Word results in your life. Stick to the Word and don't get moved by what you see happening around you. Let me put it to you this way: watch what you say.

Our words are in direct proportion to what we believe, and what we believe comes from what we've been depositing into our spirit. Faith comes by hearing. When you take in a steady diet of words from either God's Word or the world, it'll come out when the right amount of pressure is applied in your life. If you don't like what's coming out, then adjust what's going in. Maybe you just need to increase the amount of time spent with God in His Word. Try slowing down and meditating on it. If you take notes in church, go back over them. Let the Spirit of God speak to you so you can receive further revelation from that message.

Don't let the fear of lack prevent you from trusting God. When you give to further advance the Kingdom through tithes and offerings, it shows that you believe God to be your source. God is never trying to take anything from you. He's always trying to get more to you so He can get it through you.

My goal is to be a distribution center for God. How about you?

Hebrews 11:1 AMP   Malachi 3:10-12 AMP   Romans 10:17 AMP

Mark 11:22-24 AMP

26

It's All Good

The closer you get to your breakthrough the more you'll experience an increase in adverse situations. Since I live in Texas, I get to see the agricultural metaphors used in the Bible, especially where Jesus talks about the wheat and the tares growing up together. As I ride by the fields, I can see the weeds growing up, side by side with the wheat. All of the negative things that we experience in this Christian life are what Paul told Timothy would occur.

Recently I was telling some friends of mine that when things get better, your problems seem to increase. Personally, I have come too far to sabotage my success by falling prey to the tempting wiles of the enemy. I'm on the precipice of my breakthrough and I know it. The enemy knows what all of us like, will dress it up, and make it so appealing. Like Adam & Eve in the Garden of Eden you have to make a decision to do or not to do. Once you make the decision not to, you have to put parameters around it. If you know that the potential to get in trouble lies in going to a certain place, then don't go. You can't play the strength game, which the devil wants you to play. You're not that strong. You have to use wisdom and do like the Word says, submit to God and resist the devil. That means you just have to say "no" to some things in order to protect yourself. Sin is fun and exciting, but it's only for a moment. I heard it said, "Sin will take you further than you planned on going, keep you longer than you planned on staying and cost you more than you planned on paying."

God has prearranged and ordained the good life for all of us. When we spend time with Him in His Word and in prayer, we'll receive directions on what path to take. Make no mistake about it, it's all God and it's all good!

Matthew 13:24-30 NLT   2 Timothy 3:12 AMP   James 4:7 AMP

Ephesians 2:10 AMP

27

The Love Commandment

When I was back in Detroit helping my father with the funeral arrangements for my mother, I discovered that he was being mistreated. When I got involved, things began to turn themselves around. Eventually I had the opportunity to address the individual involved, and expressed my concerns. They partially got the message, but either way I moved on.

As I was preparing to leave and catch my flight home, I was told this same person took his level of disrespect of my father to another level. The old me wanted to stop by and have a discussion with them on the way to the airport, so that we could come to "an understanding," but I didn't. Love was not the first emotion rising up within me. I don't like to see things like this happen to my dad, especially at this time in his life. It angered me. I know and understand that loving others is a commandment straight from Jesus and that forgiveness coupled with walking in love is a decision that sometimes has to be repeated over and over again with the same transgressor.

Total forgiveness is a process that requires work and time. The work requires you to first stop saying anything bad about it and them. Quit giving it fuel. The more you do-give it fuel-the more intense it gets. Align your thoughts with the Word. The person who wronged you could be a Christian brother or sister, which makes the process even more painstaking. There is a reward and it's called freedom. You have to remain diligent throughout the process. That means keep the Word in your eyes, ears and mouth.

When people do me wrong, I pray for them. I ask God to do specific things in their life. All of the things I want Him to do in my life I ask that it manifest in theirs. It takes me a minute to get there but eventually I do. When I do I feel better about the whole thing, because love has kicked in and taken charge.

Today, no matter who or what, work at letting the love of Christ come through you onto others. There's a payoff and it's worth all the effort it takes to get there.

Matthew 22:36-40   2 Peter 3:13-14 AMP   Luke 6:27-28 AMP

28

You've Already Won!

In the heat of the battle, if you stick with His Word then you've won! Although the fight might continue until your enemy is finally subdued, keep the faith and do not get emotional. It takes work and you have to keep confessing the Word of God. This is all Spiritual warfare.

A recent battle that hit me right between the eyes, really caught me off guard. Because of the people involved it was totally unexpected. The Holy Spirit reminded me that we're not perfect-none of us, and good people do bad things. Everyone one of us is susceptible to making bad decisions without regard to whoever might be adversely affected. Once you become aware of the fact that you might've wronged someone, don't let it linger. As soon as possible go make it right. The old folks used to say,"Crow goes down better when it's warm", so deal with it quickly and don't worry about the results. If they forgive you great; if not, all you really want to do is keep your side of the street clean. Keep in mind that your being forgiven is tied directly to how you forgive others. When you see your brother or sister caught up, remember that one day it could be you, so how would you want to be approached?

God loves you so much that everything you'll ever need, whether it is grace, mercy or provision of any type, He's already made it available. No matter what opposition you might be facing today, know that you've already won!

Hebrews 10:23 AMP   *Luke 6:38*   *Galatians 6:1 AMP*   *2 Peter 1:3-4 AMP*

29

Praying For Those In Authority

When you look at the state of the world today, our leaders need our prayers. Everything that is unfolding around us is nothing more than prophecy being fulfilled. It's legal in the United States for members of the same sex to get married and seemingly enjoy the same rights and privileges as a husband and wife. There is one twist: now there are two husbands or two wives and not husband and wife as God designed it. When you look at it honestly, this all traces back to our elected officials and their positions on these issues.

The Apostle Paul admonishes us to pray for all those in authority. We pray for the peace of Jerusalem, our church leadership, elected officials on the national level: president, vice president and their staffs, foreign heads of state, joint chiefs, members of the supreme court, national legislators. Then the state: The Governor and his staff, state legislators and then our entire local elected officials as well our local law enforcement and fire officials and then we pray for our employers. I always ask that they get godly counsel and wisdom, then I begin praying the perfect prayer by praying in the spirit. The ensuing result of this is that we will lead a quiet and peaceable life in all godliness and honesty. I've noticed that once I was disciplined in praying like this, although the situations might not immediately change there is a certain level of peace that comes over me.

Remember, the things that are happening today are nothing but prophecy coming to pass. The stage is being set for the end time conflict. That's why today we must pray for ALL those in authority.

Matthew 24:4-14   Romans 1:24-32 AMP   1 Timothy 2:1-4

30

Let Your Wounds Heal

When you get a scrape or cut, as soon as it began to heal a scab was formed. When you were young your mother probably told you, as many others did when you got caught picking at it, to leave it alone and let the wound heal.

In order for us to heal emotionally, we have to first stop "picking at the scab." By that I mean quit talking about whatever it is. Nothing you say or do will turn back the hands of time to undo what has already been done, so let it go. The more you talk about it, the longer you stay wounded and you miss the joy that this day has to offer.

Your body was designed to live forever. When a physical injury occurs, it has all the capabilities to heal itself as long as things are functioning properly. When we get wounded emotionally it takes the Word of God deposited into our spirit, along with some natural things. This is the "Band-Aid" that can heal our wounds.

Let the Word of God be the "band aid" that binds up your wounds. Begin the healing process of being made whole and receive full restoration not only in your body but emotions also.

Proverbs 18:21 NLT   Psalms 107:20 NLT   Matthew 6:8-13 AMP

July

1

The Mountain Test

I wrote about mountains recently and the last thing I expected that day was a test on the subject. The test started that evening while we were on vacation. The first mountain threw me for a loop and caught me totally off guard but once I got a hold of my emotions and spoke to it, things began to work themselves out. The last mountain was like Mt. Everest. After we checked out of the resort and were at the airport about to go through security, I realized I forgot to empty the safe in our room where I put my wife's passport, some cash and the car keys. I was going to try and go back and fetch our belongings, but it might mean my missing the flight, which would've been another "mountain." Through the whole process I was fairly calm and had peace even with the lady in line who "attempted" to advise me where the line started and that I couldn't just walk up to the counter and ask a question. Long-story short, we caught our flight. I called my sister and she gave us a ride home, where I got the other set of keys and she took me back to get the car. The resort mailed our things to us and all was well!

Because I keep renewing my mind in the Word of God, peace acted like an umpire in me. I kept my cool when all the evidence supported my "losing it" which wouldn't have made the situation any better. I was telling my brother that I am fully persuaded God's Word is active in my life, and I confess daily that His commanded blessing is on my life and favor surrounds me like a shield. When you know and walk in the blessing and favor of God all things work out for your good!

Colossians 3:15 AMP   Psalms 5:12 AMP   Romans 8:28

2

Expectation

One morning I had a flashback to when I was a child when Christmas was approaching, I would be filled with anticipation because I expected to receive some gifts. I began thinking this is the way we should be all the time when it comes to the Word of God. There should always be an expectation for a manifestation from the Word of God that we've sown.

In Jesus' Parable of Soils, He talks about the type of ground seeds are sown into and their subsequent yield. He tells us the sower is sowing the Word of God. Just as a farmer sows corn seed into the ground and expects a harvest or manifestation of corn, when we sow, whether it is the Word of God by speaking it into the ground of our hearts, or sowing financial seed into a ministry, we must have the expectation of receiving in order for it to come to pass.

I used to give without *"maintaining the expectation"* of receiving until I heard a message on this subject and now it's always in the forefront of my mind when I give. Whenever a situation comes up I immediately refer to my covenant. I speak what my covenant says and boldly proclaim that I have seed in the ground and God's got me covered.

If you've been sowing and have yet to see manifestation, don't lose heart. Your seed just has some deep roots and it is going to produce more than a 100-fold return. Keep in mind that 100-fold is not God's best. He can do far more than you could ever ask or think because He is a God who has no limits.

Mark 4:3-14 AMP   Malachi 3:10-11 AMP   Ephesians 3: 20 AMP

3

My Son

I am so proud of my son Matthew who I have to take a praise break and give God the glory....

God is a good God!! One morning I started scrolling through Twitter catching up on some of the people I follow, and I ran across a Tweet my son sent. He said: "It's funny that teens say a real relationship fights all the time. That's why I never heard my parents have one while I was in TX." I shared it with my wife and we both said virtually at the same time that unbeknown to us, he was watching. I'm grateful we showed him a better way: God's way. When I talked to him, I let him know I was proud of him and he said he remembers me telling him that the woman is always right. I said "Yep and it's the man's responsibility to make and keep it right. It doesn't take all of that hooping and hollering, getting all worked up and saying things you really shouldn't." I learned all of that from the men God placed in my life to be an example: my dad, brother, and my former Pastor Bishop Keith Butler. Maintaining this stance just makes things so much better.

Bishop Butler used to quote this frequently, "It is better to dwell in a corner of the housetop, than with a brawling woman in a wide house." There's a lot of validity in that Scripture. So much so, that to expound on it here, I wouldn't do it justice. Suffice it to say brothers we have to "man up." Even if you felt that you were right, you're wrong if you let disagreements go unchecked. You have to give honor to your wife, if not your prayers will be hindered.

The Bible tells us to love our wives as Christ loved the church. When you do, it makes your house a home and you'll like coming home to a peaceful house.

Proverbs 21:9   1 Peter 3:7 AMP   Ephesians 5:23-25 AMP

4

Thanksgiving

As I encounter the vicissitudes of life (how about that for a $3 word and spell check), the one thing that keeps me grounded is being thankful. One morning my reading touched on it and the one point that stuck out said, "See how many times you can thank me daily; this will awaken your awareness to a multitude of blessings. It will also cushion the impact of trials when they come against you. Practice my Presence by practicing the discipline of thankfulness."

The Apostle Paul tells us to pray without ceasing. One way to accomplish that is to just say "thanks." Prayer is communicating with God and not bombarding Him with a boatload of requests. Just saying a simple thank you for no reason keeps you God-centered. You begin to see things differently. It will cause you to move from being reactionary to responsive while enjoying a peace that only comes from a thankful heart to a loving God.

Thanksgiving is the key to gaining access into the presence of God and is the most powerful weapon we have to fight the "woe is me" of life when they crop up.

Psalms 100:4 AMP   1 Thessalonians 5:17-18 AMP   Ephesians 5:20

5

Don't Hit The Override Button

Let me tell you about a situation where I could have let anger override common sense, but I didn't. I was driving home one night in the rain. Just me and the Lord minding our own business, having a good time. All of a sudden the driver of the car behind me decides I am not going fast enough, so he attempts to encourage me to pick it up some and began tailgating in the rain. My conversation with the Lord abruptly stopped and the old Brett got behind the wheel. The first thing the old me did was slow down with the intent to begin tapping the brakes for a little extra-added effect.

Then this thought came to me, "Look at you, now how is this going to end. If he hits your car then you'll be standing in the rain and then this'll end in ways that won't be pretty. All because you want to try and prove a point that doesn't have to be made." So at my first chance I changed lanes and let him and another car go past. He sped off into the dark of the rain soaked night. I made it home safely because I didn't hit the override button.

We all know the difference between right and wrong. From little Johnny who all of a sudden decides he is going to smack his sister, to each of us when we do what we do sometimes-knowing good and well that it's wrong and do it anyway. Written or unwritten, we know better because God said that He would write His laws in our hearts.

To keep us on track when we were younger, God gave us parents for mentors. Our parents, because of their love for us provided discipline when we did wrong. Now that we're older and much wiser, the Holy Spirit provides that subtle little gut check that says, "don't do it." When we make the conscious split-second decision to do wrong and do it, we have hit "the override button" and now our inner man doesn't feel so good. That's when we go to God, repent and move on. Remember God loves you and knew up front this would happen and has made provisions for it through Christ.

So the next time you find yourself in one of those situations that might cause regret, listen to the Holy Spirit. He's your guide. Don't hit the override button.

Hebrews 12:14 NLT   Jeremiah 31:33 AMP   Proverbs 22:15

6

Forgiveness

One morning I woke up with this one word rolling around in my spirit: "Forgiveness."

We all at some point in this journey are going to be or we have been in need of forgiveness. There's no way around it. The beauty of this is that Christ has paid the price in advance for our forgiveness.

You ever notice how sometimes we can walk around with the love of God in our hearts and in a moment's notice will act as judge, jury and if need be executioner to someone? It's done by the words that come out of our mouth. I myself am guilty of this. Not as much today as yesterday, but every now and then a remnant will resurface, and I have to remember all that God has forgiven me of. If I want it then I must give it, because the exact way I give it out will be the way it comes back to me.

As you go through your day, give yourself a break and forgive you first. Be good to you, and then forgive them as God has forgiven you. Remember, forgiveness is not a feeling it's a decision!

Matthew 18:23-35 AMP   Luke 6:38 AMP

7

Unanswered Prayer: Do You Doubt?

There are times while we are waiting on the full manifestation of our prayers that we might start to doubt whether or not it's going to happen. We don't have to say anything to cause us to doubt because it will happen right between your ears and get into your heart. We have to always remember that we are walking by faith and not by sight. If we fail to be vigilant about this area of our walk, doubt will creep in.

Jesus cautions us not to doubt in our hearts. As long as we don't doubt, we can have the things we've said. One thing that will help us to stay free from doubt is to keep our minds renewed in and on the Word of God. Having a renewed mind keeps the Word of God fresh in our minds and our hearts. This keeps us in constant agreement with what the Word has to say about our situation no matter how it may look right now.

Always remember the closer you get to your manifestation, things will arise and make it seem like you're the farthest away with no hope in sight. Trust God to work out the details. Our faith is built on His Word and nothing else. Just don't faint. Due season is not if, but when!

2 Corinthians 5:7 AMP   Mark 11:23 AMP   Ephesians 4:23 AMP

Galatians 6:9 AMP

8

Listening To Those Around You

Today let's talk about listening to those around us, saved or not. You can tell where people are and what's going on in their lives if you just listen to what they're saying. In doing so the Holy Spirit will reveal to you areas or things that you can pray with them or for them. You have to use some wisdom in this area because you don't want to be intrusive or thought of as eve's dropping and being nosey.

Should they mention sickness of some type, God's Word says that as believers there are signs that follow us. If we lay hands on the sick, they shall recover. If you can hold their hand and quietly pray with them the prayer of faith, then do it. If not, simply do what the Word says and touch them. You don't have to be flamboyant about it. You can do it in a very subtle way by shaking their hands or touching them, then go on your way and confess they are healed in Jesus' name. Either way, the process of their healing has begun because you are fulfilling the requirement of the laying on of hands, using the name of Jesus, and making a confession.

Remember no matter what their situation might be, healing or praying for a loved one who might be lost, if you can't pray with them you definitely can pray for them.

Mark 16:17-18   Mark 11:23-24 AMP   John 14:13-14   James 5:13-16 AMP

9

Your Debt's Paid In Full

If you were told today "your debt is paid in full" when you go to pay a bill how would you react? You'd be ecstatic, probably shout and give God all kinds of praise, especially if it was your mortgage or student loans. What Christ did for us should evoke the same type of response.

The events that transpired on the way to the Cross are just as important as to what occurred on the Cross. There were five (the number of grace) places Christ shed His blood and what we received as a result.

1. We were healed because of the beating / stripes He received on His back.
2. We have authority because of the crown of thorns that was placed His head.
3. We have dominion because of the spikes that went into His feet.
4. We have prosperity because of the spikes they put in His hands.
5. Our sins were washed away because they pierced Him in His side, and He shed blood and water.

When He finally died and went to Hades, He did that so we wouldn't have to. Yes, He died for our sins, but I want you to look at it from a slightly different perspective: **He paid the penalty for our sins.** The penalty was a death where we would have been separated from the Father like Jesus Christ temporarily was. Our separation would have been for eternity.

I heard this description of eternity recently and it paints a very vivid picture. Imagine you're in the Sahara Desert, and every thousand of years you pick up a grain of sand until you completely removed all of the sand. That's an extremely long time. Imagine having to endure the agony Christ did forever and ever and ever. Thank God we don't have to because we were bought with a price. We should glorify God in our body and spirit because they are His!

As you go through your day today, meditate on the truth that you've been redeemed, and the price paid wasn't a cheap one. Christ laid down His life just for you!

Your account has been paid in full!

Galatians 3:13   1 Corinthians 6:20 AMP   Hebrews 10:9-13 AMP

10

Conversations About God

On the last day of our cruise I was sitting on my balcony in the early morning darkness listening to the waves crash below as we head towards Miami. I was thanking God for blessing us like He did. My kids thoroughly enjoyed themselves. This was the first time they had been on a cruise. Jamaica was great. "No problem mon, it was irie." They got a chance to swim with the turtles when we stopped at the Cayman Islands. As we cruised, I got a chance to talk with my cousin Aaron, the one I refer to as my hero. He stopped by my cabin a couple of times and we just chatted. He was about to enter college and I shared with him how he has to maintain his relationship with Christ if he wants to have any success. He is pursuing his passion for sports journalism. As we were talking, another one of my younger cousins was sitting on the balcony next door. She heard us talking and joined our conversation. I shared with both of them that you have to get God involved in your decision-making process. In doing so, He will show you which way to go. You just have to fine tune the voice of God when He speaks. I shared with them the "I should've followed my first mind" concept of when He is speaking to you and told them to learn and follow it.

We talked about how every step is preparation for the next level and even if you mess up it's not a waste of time. There are lessons to be learned in everything we do. Most of the time you'll have one big lesson and inside of it will be a host of little ones. Learn from them.

As I look back over my life and how far the Lord has brought me, I am forever grateful. I know and continue to thank Him and acknowledge that it's all about Him. I was sharing with some people on the cruise with us how when you serve God, He will bless you beyond what you could've ever expected. I don't do what I do just to receive a blessing. When I do as the Spirit leads, I get blessed.

The bottom line is that when God blesses us, we should be a distribution center for what He has given us. Blessings should flow through us freely like water through a pipe into the lives of others. I heard it said one time that even the inside of the pipe gets wet, which means there will be some left over for you to enjoy.

Proverbs 3:5-6   Psalms 5:12   Genesis 12:2 AMP

11

Don't Let Up

In your corner of the world, things are going really good for you right now. You've got some money in your pocket and you feel better physically than you have in a long time. Let me caution you that now is not the time to let up. Don't start slacking off on your reading, praying and confessing God's Word. You have to remain diligent in your pursuit of the things you desire from the Word of God. That means keeping your mind renewed in the Word. This is the best way to prevent the enemy from sowing seeds of deception, by having you think that you can take a day off or it doesn't take all that. Recognize it for what it is-a lie.

If you want to keep what you have, then it's going to take maintaining your spiritual condition daily. Keep the Word of God in front of your eyes and speaking it out of your mouth. You have to stick to it. By that I mean if the Word is working in your life, then don't fall away from the very thing that got you to where you are just because things got better. If you do, before you know it symptoms of sickness in your body, financial lack or some other type of circumstance that you had been standing against will surely come to visit you again.

God said in His Word that we can have what we say, "if we don't doubt in our hearts." If we want the things that the Word promises us, then we have to keep our hearts full of the Word. There is life in the Word. As long as we don't let up on our daily maintenance, then we can have and enjoy the good life Christ died for that His Word promises us.

Ephesians 4:23 AMP   Mark 11:23 MSG   John 6:63   Titus 2:14 AMP

12

We Are The Example

One day when my wife came home, she wasn't feeling good. She continually kept sneezing and coughing. After a while our oldest daughter told her she was going to pray for her. She and her younger sister came, laid hands on my wife and prayed for her (according to God's Word) like I do when they're sick or get hurt. That was a confirming sign that our children watch what we do and will emulate that behavior, good or bad.

We are the examples of Christ not only our to children, which is a good thing but to all of the people around us. Are you living the kind of life that can lead others to Him or are you an undercover Christian afraid to share your faith? When was the last time you invited others to your church? Sometimes we can be afraid of being rejected or coming off "preachy." If you keep a couple of things in mind all will be well.

First, if you meet rejection like I did, and have shared it with you before how God told me on a plane after attempting to minister healing to someone, that the person didn't reject Brett but rejected Him. That was a very liberating moment for me because I learned it's not about me but Him. Secondly, let the Holy Spirit guide you. He will give you the words to say or a subject to start a conversation that eventually will lead to introducing them to Christ or just share a comforting word with them.

We have been commissioned to carry this good news into the world, so that others can have the same opportunity to receive eternal life just like we did. At the end of the day, all we have to do is like Pastor Sheryl Brady says and that is: "Clear the path and point them to Jesus." Just point them in His direction and then the decision is theirs to make.

Mark 16:17-18 AMP   Matthew 28:19-20 NLT   Philippians 4:9 AMP

13

It's Not By Accident There Is A God

How can you reasonably deny the existence of God with all of the evidence we have at our disposal? Just look around. All of creation didn't just come from nowhere as some would have you believe. It takes more faith to believe there isn't a God than to just simply believe and accept that there is one. You have to work really hard to maintain a stance like that. As I sit on my balcony cruising the ocean, I enjoy the beauty of His creation. Looking at the ocean and hearing the sound of the waves, the wind blowing and seeing Cuba in the distance. I think of all that He has done for my family and me. I have to say "thank you" because I am truly grateful.

The world in which we live in is forever changing. The line where you stand with biblical principles keeps moving. But God and His Word has not and will not change no matter what the world does or says. Every encounter we have with someone has been orchestrated or allowed by God. It is an opportunity to share the love of God freely without hesitation or reservation. You can brag on Him, His mercy, and grace without being "preachy" just share as the Holy Spirit leads. Your role might be to either plant a seed or water it. Make no mistake about it, God will get the increase.

Just do your part and watch God do His!

Genesis 1:1 AMP   Isaiah 45:22   Hebrews 13:8 AMP   1 Corinthians 3:6

14

God's Word Gives Hope

Back in 1984 there was a time when I didn't have hope and wanted to commit suicide. I was in the valley between the mountains of yesterday and tomorrow. I was twenty-six years old with my whole life in front of me. Yet I didn't see a way out of the things that were happening in my life. There was a voice speaking to me saying "Don't do it" that was louder than the one telling me to go ahead. I know today that was the voice of God, and had I not listened to it, I would've missed today.

Today I get my hope from God's Word. When I read how Abraham, who against hope believed in hope that he would be who God said he would be, it gives me hope. God gave him a Word and that Word is still being fulfilled today.

Faith gives substance to our hope. Faith and belief are two sides of the same coin and are linked together with hope. It's almost like the buddy system, where they all go together. You need one to fuel or support the other two. If one is missing the others won't function.

Today keep yourself built up in the Word of God by speaking the Word. It keeps faith coming and gives substance to your hope.

1 Kings 19:11-12 AMP   Romans 4:17-18 AMP   Hebrews 11:1 AMP

15

Your Own Personal Measure Of Faith

When it comes to faith, God has given all of us a certain amount to get started. We all have an equal amount to begin with according to His purposes for our life. If that measure or level is to increase, then the onus is upon us to do the work necessary in order to bring it to pass. This whole faith walk rests on what do you believe. It seems that we have enough faith to believe God for eternity but not enough to deal with our day-to-day issues. When it comes to eternity, we exercise blind faith, but to handle the issues of today could it be that our senses get in the way?

Our healing, prosperity and redemption was accomplished on the way to and on the Cross. When Jesus said "It is finished" it was. His work was done. When He died, our old man died with Him, and on the third day when He rose, we rose also. We're a new creature created in Christ. Everything we'll ever need has already been provided. If we're to really enjoy all that Christ died for, then we have to reinforce our beliefs and that means spending time in His Word. Read aloud what the Word says about you and receive it into your heart (spirit man).

We believe, because of the finished works of Christ, that we have passed from death to life. Keep in mind that you don't enter into eternal life when you die. You entered into it the moment you accepted Jesus as your Lord and Saviour.

Romans 12:3 AMP   2 Corinthians 5:17 AMP   Isaiah 53:4-6 MSG

2 Peter 1:3-4 AMP

16

Who Moved?

Have you ever had those moments when things are happening all around you and you don't really feel close to God as you used to? The question I want to pose to you is-who moved you or God?

One of my favorite personality names of God is Jehovah Shammah, which means "The Lord is there." Since we know that He is Omnipresent (He is everywhere at all times), why are there times when I feel distant from Him? As it is with any relationship, it's a two-way street where both parties have to be engaged with one another in dialogue. One of the questions I ask myself is have I maintained my part of the deal? Did I spend time with Him today just to be in His presence or was I like a needy kid with some sort of demand or need that I feel He has to take care of ASAP?

God wants to enjoy fellowship with us just like He did in the garden with Adam and his wife. For us to spend time with Him just for who He is, and not for what He can do for us. Always keep in mind that the Greater One lives big on the inside of all of us and has not moved. Could the real answer be that we have moved away from doing the things we used to do and now feel the distance it brought? All we have to do is start where we are right now and begin practicing the presence of God. When you draw close to Him, He will draw close to you.

Ezekiel 48:35 Jeremiah 29:12-13   1 John 4:4 AMP   James 4:8 AMP

17

An Attitude Of Praise

While we await the manifestation of the things we have been praying for, one key to our receiving is to praise God in advance for those things, as if we already have them. I've learned the difference between praise and worship.

We praise God for what He's done and worship Him for who He is. A thankful, heartfelt praise given when the "hour is the darkest" will not only keep you calm but will confuse the enemy, because that's when he expects us to be on pins and needles, full of doubt and fear.

One thing to keep in mind is that praise is a weapon to be used against our enemy. In 2 Chronicles 20, the story of Jehoshaphat and the men of Judah and Jerusalem is my favorite example of what praise can do. Jehoshaphat was outnumbered and defeat was certain. He had a problem (v1-4). He gave a testimony (v6-9). Jehoshaphat prayed (v10-13), and received his answer (v14-17). In v18-22 they got themselves together and began to sing and give praises unto the Lord. Then in v23-24 they saw what the Lord meant when He said they wouldn't have to fight, but just stand still and see His salvation. Their enemies killed each other, and in v25 when it was all said and done, it took them three days to get the spoils from a battle they didn't even fight. Finally, in v26-30 they blessed the Lord, rejoiced in their victory and had peace.

God wants you to have the same results. It's available when you praise Him in advance for what He is about to do in your life.

So today, give Him Praise!

2 Chronicles 20:1-30

18

Petty Annoyances Means Having To Make Adjustments

As I was going along early one morning, today's title was a thought I had rolling around in my spirit.

Since we've been temporarily living in this apartment until our home is finished (three more Wednesdays to go thank you Jesus), I have had the luxury of taking the dog out every morning for her walk. Since we live on the third floor, I take the elevator to get downstairs. Right next to the elevator are diagonal yellow stripes to indicate no parking. Every day the same two vehicles are parked there. I have to walk around them, and I get seriously irritated. The old me, wants to leave a sarcastic note on their cars but recognize it would be futile if I can't experience their reaction also. That's when the Holy Spirit told me it was a petty annoyance don't get distracted, just make the adjustments and move on.

What's happening in your world that quite possibly could be something so minor, that if allowed could turn into something major in your mind? It's little things that the enemy uses to distract us and take our focus off of the bigger picture. I have so many more important things that require my attention right now, that where someone whom I don't know and have no knowledge of their situation parks, doesn't even make the top 100.

Sometimes we can allow ourselves to get distracted by things like this due to what's going on in our lives at the particular moment. I know for me it's probably all of these changes I'm going through that makes me want to exert control over others. I have the entire negative committee of what "ifs" periodically coming by to visit adding their two cents to the pot. As soon as they do, they're summarily dismissed. Could I quite possibly be afraid of what future unknowns hold for me?

When God blesses, sometimes there is a certain amount of tension that comes along with it. The best way to handle it is to keep the main thing, the main thing. Don't get waylaid by minor distractions. Stay prayed up and in His Word, all while putting one foot in front of the other. Just keep making whatever adjustments are needed along the way because it's going to work out for your good in the end.

Song of Solomon 2:15   Proverbs 3:6 AMP   Psalms 63:1 AMP

Romans 8:26-28 AMP

19

God's Working In You

God is at work in all of us to will and to do His good pleasure. When I think of Him working in me, immediately I think of Him not only working things out of me but also depositing more of His Spirit in me so that I can become more like Him. If it's for His good pleasure, then that explains why sometimes I feel like I'm in a constant makeover where minor character adjustments are seemingly always taking place. At times this can feel rather uncomfortable. God working through my brother always reminds me to ask, "What is the lesson I'm to learn in this"? The answer is usually my being shown that He's fine tuning me for what's to come. There are things in my makeup that need to either be reshaped or discarded during this phase of my development.

I know and trust God has a plan. It is a good plan with a better than I could've expected, doing it on my own outcome. The thing that hooks me is how He unfolds it a little at a time, step by step. If He showed me the final product, I invariably would mess it up trying to "help God out" to get there.

Today I trust the work He's doing in me. I am on God's mind and He wants to bless me. He's in me working out His plan for my life. All I have to do is trust and obey. *Do you?*

Philippians 2:12-13 AMP   Jeremiah 29:11-13   Psalm 115:12-15 AMP

20

Praying For Others

Have you ever had people just pop into your head and you wonder how they are or someone comes across your mind repeatedly? When it happens that's a prime opportunity for you to pray for them. The Holy Spirit is seeking someone like you to stand in the gap for them.

In the Book of James, he talks about the unceasing, fervent (boiling hot) prayer of a righteous man avails much. When the Holy Spirit prompts you like this, know that you are well able and equipped to go in and do battle. We're engaged in a spiritual battle. It's on us to be sensitive to the Holy Spirit's leadings when one of our comrades might be in trouble or about to face something that our prayers can divert.

When I was living in Detroit, I remember a testimony I heard about the wife of one of the security members in our church. She came home one night after Bible study and was prompted by the Holy Spirit to pray. She prayed for a while, not knowing what she was praying about as she prayed in the spirit. Her husband came home from work that night. At the time he was a Sergeant on the gang squad for the Detroit Police Department. He relayed to her an incident that almost cost him his life but God...

Our prayers are effective when we pray one for another. Daily cover your family, your pastor and those in authority over us. When we do, Scripture tells us that we can lead a quiet, peaceable life in all godliness and honesty. They might not change, but we have!

Ezekiel 22:30   James 5:16 AMP   1 Timothy 2:1-4 AMP

21

Same Faith

One morning during my prayer time, the Lord began to show me once again that it takes the same amount of faith to receive what has already been provided for us (i.e. healing, prosperity and deliverance) as it does to receive the free gift of salvation.

Everything was made available to us through the death, burial and resurrection of Jesus. What hinders us might be directly related to how we think, what we see and feel. The best way to remove anything that might impede us from receiving what's already ours is to renew our mind daily in the Word, so that the Word of God becomes your final authority. The process of renewing the mind is not a onetime event but rather a lifestyle. It should be a part of our daily routine so that when things come up your first thought is "What does the Word say?" and that only comes from spending time in the Word.

Getting to know how God thinks about things so that we can align our thinking with His is a sure-fire way to receive what's already been given to you. Learning how to release your faith is done by speaking what you believe.

Just as easy as it was to believe Christ died for your sins, it takes the same amount of faith to appropriate healing, deliverance and prosperity in your life. All it takes is a renewed mind.

Romans 10:8-13 AMP   2 Peter 1:2-4 AMP   Luke 17:5-6 AMP

Romans 12:2 AMP

22

Prayerfully Reading God's Word

I've learned that when I prayerfully approach God's Word, I always receive wisdom and revelation from what I read.

There is life in the Word, and the Word gives life when we read it aloud /give voice to it. Reading aloud is a good habit to get into. Your spirit man is fed better when he can hear the life that is in the Word spoken out of your mouth as opposed to you reading silently. Your Bible is a living instrument, and the Words written on the pages come to life when you speak them.

Take your time to digest what you read. After you've read a couple of sentences meditate on it asking yourself what does this really mean and how can I apply it to my life? Use a dictionary to look up the meaning of words that might be familiar. Along with looking up the reference Scriptures your Bible has noted for some words will help you to gain a deeper understanding of exactly what the Spirit is saying.

These are just some things that I've learned to do and wanted to share them with you to help you like it's helped me get more from the Word.

John 6:63 AMP   Romans 10:17 AMP   1 Timothy 4:15 AMP

2 Timothy 2:15 AMP

23

The Measure Of Faith

The Apostle Paul tells us that God has apportioned to every man a measure of faith. That means we all have been given an equal starting point when it comes to having faith. The responsibility to develop our faith further is ours. We have to set aside time daily to spend with God praying in the Holy Spirit to build ourselves up in faith.

I don't want you to get the act of how faith comes confused with building your faith because there is a difference. We get faith by hearing and we build ourselves up by praying in the Spirit.

With faith as our foundation, we are to build ourselves to progress continually in the things of God. Praying in the Spirit or in tongues, helps with our prayers as we don't know what to pray, but the Spirit knows.

Today allow the Holy Spirit to guide you in your prayers. You'll be amazed at the results!

Romans 12:3 AMP   Jude 20 AMP   Romans 8:26 AMP

24

Getting God Involved

There are times when we all make moves without God. This is where we do something like make a purchase, and don't seek God about it. You wanted it. It wasn't expensive but it's going to cost you something like responsibility, and now you're in it for the long haul. If we seek Him first and not in the middle after we've gotten started, we can avoid trouble and delays.

God wants to be involved in all of our decisions. It's really in our best interest to seek Him out. Most of the time when we have some major decision or life changing event about to take place, we're real quick to seek the Lord about it, but what about the little things of life? The ones that you "can handle on your own." We don't think about asking God what He thinks, or should we even do it because in our minds it might be a little thing.

There is nothing too small. As a matter of fact, that's the best place to start. It's the little things that'll teach you how to recognize the voice of God. Start by asking what clothes you should wear, what to eat for lunch. It's all about practicing the presence of God. It takes time and practice to get it right (trial and error), but eventually you get the point where it happens automatically, without giving it a second thought.

The end result of putting this principle to use is that you'll begin to live a life directed by the guidance of the Holy Spirit, and that life brings promise and rewards.

Proverbs 3:5-6   Psalms 37:23 AMP   1 Kings 19:11-12   John 16:13 AMP

25

Don't Be Deceived

There is a level of deception taking place right now in the body of Christ like we have never experienced before, and it goes deep. People are falling away or rather being led away under the guise of having heard from the Lord. On the other hand, we have church leaders taking their own lives because somehow they lost hope and it became all about them and not relying on God for the work that has to be done. Don't be deceived folks. Satan is out here sifting people like wheat.

The purpose of sifting wheat is to separate the wheat from the chaff. "In the OT days sifting was a vigorous process that was accomplished by forcefully shaking the wheat with both hands from side to side, in a seesaw motion, where the lighter chaff would come to the surface and would then be blown away with the mouth." Satan is out here shaking people's lives and sometimes turning them upside down in an attempt to separate them from God.

You have to keep in mind that the battlefield is your mind and your soul is the spoils. Man is a tri-part being. We are spirit beings that possess a soul and live in a body. The enemy wants your soul, that's where your mind, will and emotions are kept. If he can get you to think and feel contrary to the Word of God, then he's on his way to getting you. He might start out real subtle by giving you an idea that you think is from the Father but it's not. In the long run it'll cost you your anointing, family and relationships. Yes, those who you were close with will separate themselves from you. It reminds me of when my grandfather used to say, "birds of a feather flock together." You'll never see chickens and eagles together because they have nothing in common. One can't fly and never leaves the ground while the other soars gracefully through the skies.

You might know someone who this message has brought to mind. You've talked and tried to reason with them, but they seem dug in. You know what, they probably are. The only thing we can do now is pray that the eyes of their understanding be enlightened. Ask God to send a labourer across their path. Somebody they'll listen to. I have someone that the Holy Spirit keeps prompting me to pray for. I know it because they periodically will come to mind and then the thought of them hangs around for a while. That's how I know that I'm to pray for them. I ask you once again, how about you? Who is it? That's the one He wants you to pray for. When we take the time to pray for one another a healing takes place.

Deuteronomy 11:16 AMP   Luke 22:31   Ephesians 1:15-23 MSG   James 5:16 AMP

26

You're Being Set Up

Periodically I've had the opportunity to share the Word of God with various strangers that have been placed across my path. I want to share what happened one Sunday when we were staying in the apartment temporarily.

The car parked next to ours was vandalized late Saturday night or early Sunday morning and we noticed the broken window while we were leaving for church. When we returned, I was outside talking to one of my neighbors and the lady whose car it was came out and said they stole her purse. We began talking and since I had a captive audience, I began sharing with her about the goodness of God and how this didn't take Him by surprise. He had it already figured out from the foundation of the earth; all you have to do is trust Him. I went on to tell her "it wasn't by accident that we met. God knew this day was coming and He arranged for me to be here to tell you to trust Him. All you have to do is just keep moving forward, do what you have to do and let God deal with the rest. Just trust Him."

Sharing the Word and being able to minister to people at the point of their need is a real blessing and isn't something to be taken lightly. These pre-arranged encounters like the one I shared are not by chance but are strategically designed by God. It's all in His plan and He needs people (yielded vessels) to do His work here in the earth.

When God uses situations like this to get a Word through you, know that you were in the right place at the right time to carry this out and because of your faithfulness, He can trust you. Every day I understand more what was meant when I was told that the call He has placed on my life is not about me. It's about others. It doesn't necessarily mean that they are lost; maybe they're just in need of an encouraging word during a rough time.

Today be sensitive to the leadings of the Holy Spirit. You're the messenger and there is someone out there that God has a placed in your path that you have a word for.

Psalm 37:23 AMP   Proverbs 15:23 AMP   John 16:13 AMP

27

God Can Heal Your Marriage

One morning the thought of marriages being healed came to mind. God can heal your marriage if you allow Him. All it takes is the willingness to confront the issues and not the person. Whenever things go wrong in a relationship, the first thing we tend to do is play the blame game without looking at our part in it. No matter what the issue or problem, we all have a part. The question is can you accept responsibility for yours?

All relationships whether it is marriage, friends or family are a two-way street, and they take effort from both parties to make it work. In marriage it's never going to be 50/50, at the best you might get 80/20 and you're the 80 giving or 20 receiving. There is going to be conflict, disagreements, and disappointments, but all of these can be overcome if you let love have its way. When we look at what the Apostle Paul wrote in the book of love, we have the perfect roadmap for a journey with love. These are basically the does and don'ts of love. If you follow them there is nothing that you can't overcome. Relief / restoration might not happen overnight, but it will come. Due season is not if but when.

I want to share with husbands and wives something I've picked up along the way. #1 Don't keep score – Love doesn't keep an account of suffered wrongs. #2 The most important one: DON'T have "serious" discussions in the bedroom. Go to the kitchen; sit down at the table and talk but not in your bedroom. Your bedroom is for sleeping and sex.

The Bible tells both husband and wife to submit one to the other. Husbands are to love our wives and wives are to submit and honor us Husbands. It is our responsibility to keep it together and if necessary "fall on the sword" just to keep the peace, even when we feel as if we've done no wrong. Love ALWAYS takes the high road. ALWAYS!

A friend of mine once told me something that helps govern my actions. He said that God shows His love for you through your wife, while He shows His love for her through you! There are time when I have to ask myself, is this how God wants to show His love for her?

1 Corinthians 13:4-8 AMP   Galatians 6:8-9 AMP   Ephesians 5:21-33 AMP

28

He's Still Able

One morning when I awoke, the song by James Fortune and FIYA "He's Still Able" was playing in my heart. I just kept singing the chorus (the only part I knew) "God reminded me, that He's still able" over and over.

It's an exciting thing to watch the promises of God unfold and begin to manifest in your life. Sometimes I feel like a kid on Christmas Eve, full of expectation and joyful anticipation to see what's going to happen next. God has been exceeding my expectations and moving in ways that non-believers can't understand or explain, while the saints say "Praise God." Manifestation of God's Word has become an increasing reality in my life and I now see the fruit of trusting in God after you've done all you could. God working through people like my Pastor and my brother are always providing words of encouragement, and for that I'm grateful.

Today as you go through your day, know that God is able no matter where you are and His promises are yes and amen.

Ephesians 3:20 AMP   Psalm 37:5 AMP   2 Corinthians 1:20 AMP

29

The Goodness Of God

The goodness of God makes us want to change our ways and accept God's will. I now see how my relationship with God has and continues to evolve. The closer I come to Him, the closer He comes to me. The more time I spend in His Word, the greater is the revelation I receive. This causes me to make adjustments in my character so that I begin to look and act like His Word.

I remember a situation I once had with someone who needed to be addressed. It was somewhat overdue, but the time just wasn't right. All while on the inside I was like an oven keeping the food warm. Which is better because the old me would have been on high boil ready to strike at a moment's notice... but God. When I had the opportunity to confront them I was uncharacteristically calm. My tone was as if I was asking you to please pass me the salt, at the same time getting my point across. It was appreciatively received which was my goal, and we were able to talk more about it later. This helped reinforce something I had become acutely aware of: there's a payoff for not jumping in front of God. If I had, the timing wouldn't have been right and it quite possibly wouldn't have been received like it was.

So often I want to get in there and "fix it" by helping God out, only to later realize He didn't need my help, but now I need additional help from Him to straighten it out. Him being the God that He is steps in, makes the necessary corrections and then treats me like nothing ever happened in the first place. This causes me to love Him just that much more. That's the goodness of God: loving us in our faults. God loves us and we have to be an expression of His love to all of those around us. We can't afford any longer to be an undercover Christian. We have to be bold and courageous when it comes to not only telling, but also showing people that yes, we really do stand for something, and we won't fall for anything!

As you go through your day, can you be the example of love to others that drew you to Christ? After all, if it weren't for His goodness where would you be?

Romans 2:4 AMP   James 4:8 AMP   Ecclesiastes 12:13

30

God Can't Change

The *Book of Hebrews* says Jesus is the "same, yesterday, today and forever." That means God won't change. If He's the same back then, now and tomorrow, then everything He accomplished back then is still going to be in effect today. It's all because of the Blood of Jesus. What happened on the way to the cross bears the same significance as what happened on the cross.

The reason we're healed is because of the beating they laid on Christ.

The reason we have our authority is because of the crown of thorns that was placed His head.

The reason we have our dominion is because of the nails that went into His feet.

The reason we have prosperity is because of the nails they put in His hands.

The reason our sins are washed away came when they pierced Him in His side, where He shed blood and water.

Everything you'll ever need has already been provided. Being God inside minded will help reinforce all Christ has done for you. The day you were born again, God moved in and took up residence on the inside of you. You're no longer alone. The greater one lives big in us and is there to help us overcome the evil one. When we get fully developed in this, our confidence hits a new level. It's a mindset that slowly brings about a change in character and beliefs. Knowing that God is on the inside of you will make you think twice about saying and doing a lot of things you were accustomed to. This is why we have to spend time in his Word to keep our minds renewed.

When situations arise, know that God, who is in you, has already equipped you to handle it. He cannot change. You've got His Word on it.

Hebrews 13:8   2 Peter 1:3 AMP   Colossians 1:27 AMP   1 John 4:4

31

Making Adjustments

As we travel along in our walk with Christ, we must remain sensitive to the gentle leadings of the Holy Spirit. He guides us in making necessary adjustments along our path.

You've been predestinated to be conformed into the image of God's Son. That is the process God has you engaged in. He is constantly molding you like clay on the potter's wheel, into vessels that will, in time, bring forth His Glory. What we have to do is trust the process. I can only speak for myself, how sometimes when the process begins I feel uncomfortable. Nowadays, I get to the point of recognizing it as a shift pretty quickly.

I don't trip as hard or as long as I used to. The Holy Spirit will quicken an on-time Word to me that will help settle me down. I then take that Word and begin confessing it, which helps build my faith and boost my confidence.

We all are in the process of becoming more Christ like which means we have to become more God centered and less self-centered. As you go through your day today, remember that God loves you. He had this all worked out for you from the foundation of the world and He has given you everything that you'll need to make it.

John 16:13 AMP   Romans 8:29   John 14:26 AMP

August

1

The Answers for Today's Test

From Genesis to Revelation the Bible tells about the love God has for His man. It shows us various aspects of that love as it relates to being hurt, forgiveness, restoration and most important redemption. When I look at the love God has for me and how it is expressed throughout the entire Bible, I walk away knowing that there is no way I could ever love Him as much as He loves me. I've learned that there is no "fear in love" and if I become fearful, I can regroup and get back to love.

All though I might fall short at times, I have been given the perfect example of how to love others. It takes a lot of work but the rewards, when you get it right, far outweigh the feelings when you miss it.

Here are the answers for today's test. Take the time to study the material as testing will begin shortly. The teacher has given you the answers before the test. He will not be talking once the testing has begun. ***This is an open book test***!

1 John 4:10-21

2

He's Working It Out

Every morning I have a basic routine that I follow when it comes to spending time with the Lord and then preparing to write this message. Yesterday I was meditating on being flexible and sure enough that was what I wound up doing. I wasn't thrown into disarray as much as I was a little uncomfortable because I had this strong urge to do things differently. I felt like I was putting Him on the back burner to do something else, needless to say I did it.

At this stage of my journey I really trust God more and more every day. I have learned and I am still learning how to be flexible enough to allow Him to change the way He wants things done, in order to work out the details of the things I'm expecting to be manifested in my life. I believe that He changes our routines so that He can change our perspective, then we can begin to think and see things in a different light.

There's a purpose to everything God allows to happen not only with us but everybody He allows to come across our path. We might not fully understand the "why" and "what for" immediately, but like my grandfather used to say, "hindsight is 20/20 vision." The Holy Spirit will reveal it to you at an appointed time. One day you'll be washing dishes, and something from years ago will all of a sudden makes sense. You'll begin to understand why this person had to come and why another had to leave or why you didn't get that job you really wanted.

By now we've come to trust God as He takes care of the minute details of our wants and desires. As long as we stay prayerfully attentive and stay in His Word, in the end everything works out for our good.

Jeremiah 17:7-8 NLT   Psalm 37:3-4 AMP   Romans 8:24-28 AMP

3

Prayers That Avail Much

The Bible talks about how *"the effectual, fervent prayer of the righteous avails much."* The moment you accepted Jesus as your Savior not only were you born again, you also became righteous or in right standing with God. No more sin-consciousness but righteousness-consciousness. The Old Testament law was replaced by New Testament grace. Under the law it took the priest and high priest to perform yearly ordinances and sacrifices to cover the sins of the people. But when Christ died, He became both the priest and sacrifice. Our sins stopped being covered but were remitted, done away with once and for all. In our new position we can come boldly to the throne of grace not only for ourselves but on behalf of others as well and get desired results.

One of the best ways to get results when we pray is to pray the Word. When we pray the Word, in essence we are communicating back to God what He has already said to us, about us, and affirming to Him that we are in agreement with it. Because we know of our new position In Him, we have full confidence that as long as we pray the Word of God, we're praying the will of God and He not only hears but answers our prayers as well.

As you go through your day, continually keep in mind that God answers the prayers of the righteous and that means you. You're in right standing with God. Your past wrongs and anything that you have yet to do wrong has already been forgiven. By faith you have accessed this grace where you now stand.

James 5:16 AMP   Hebrews 9:12-15 AMP   1 John 5:14-15

4

This Is Not a Loss, It's a Gain

As we are continually being molded and shaped, one of the things God does is remove things or situations that we've had for a long time which are no longer useful. They might have started out as good but wound up becoming a bad habit or an unhealthy practice. Whatever it is, allow it to be removed because it's not a loss but a gain.

I've come to learn from my own personal experiences, that whatever God is trying to give me is far better than what He is trying to relieve me of if I just let it go. Letting go doesn't hurt. It's the holding on that causes us pain. Whether it's an old relationship, a past hurt or an old habit that we have to be rid of, just let it go. It won't be of any use to where He's taking you.

These days all of us have a lot on our plates. If we are truly going to follow Christ, and be His example in the earth, then we have to allow God to work out of us anything that isn't like Him. Trusting God is an ongoing process that takes us through a myriad of emotions eventually striping us of the old man, as we put on the new.

As we continue on this walk, be mindful of this one thing, the Holy Spirit has already told you where you're going. He just didn't tell you how you'd get there.

Ephesians 4:22-24 AMP   1 Thessalonians 1:5-8 AMP   John 16:13 AMP

5

Healed and Made Whole

On a prayer call one morning, the topic was "being made whole." This got me to thinking how getting healed, delivered and set free from something is wonderful. It's a good start, but completion of recovery doesn't happen unless you've been made whole. I'm talking total restoration.

If we look at the account of how the children of Israel came out from Egypt after 400 years of slavery with the entire wealth of the land and none of them were feeble. Basically, they were made whole. When Jesus healed the lepers not only was their skin cleansed, but they were restored back to a position where they could be seen amongst the people and were no longer treated as an outcast by society. If God did it for them, He'll do it for you. Whatever your situation or circumstance might be, there is only one thing that could be preventing God from making you whole and it's you. I heard it said, "Your feet can't take you where your thinking hasn't been." Do you see yourself whole in every area of your life? If not, all you have to do is renew your mind in the Word and expect to be made hole in order to receive it.

Plant the Word (seed) by faith into the ground (your heart) and expect a harvest. Give God something to work with. He will restore you to a position of wholeness.

Psalms 105:37   Mark 1:40-45 AMP   Mark 4:20 AMP

6

The Blessing

When we think of the blessing, there is a tendency to confuse the results of the blessing with the actual blessing itself (i.e. new car, home or maybe you got a promotion on your job). All of those are the results of the blessing. If we're to define the blessing, we could say that it is an empowerment to succeed or prosper from God. When I look at the life of Abram, God said that He would bless him, and He did. Abram was very rich in cattle, silver, and gold.

Following the gentle leadings of the Holy Spirit and confessing daily that "God's commanded blessing is on my life", will activate the blessing in your life. God said in His Word that He will bless the righteous and favor will surround him (the one who is righteous) like a shield. Since I'm righteous, both the blessing and favor are active on me. This has to be our mind set. Blessing and favor are connected and inseparable. The blessing and favor of God are here to make us superior to all of our circumstances. It allows us to rise above all of the negativity that's surely to come against us as we walk this thing out.

Today, make the declaration that God's commanded blessing is on your life and you have favor with both God and man.

Genesis 12:2; 13:2   Proverbs 10:22 AMP   Psalms 5:12 AMP

7

Being Guided By Faith Not Facts

In paraphrasing what I got from a prayer call one day, we have to be guided by faith and not facts. Our faith is in God's Word and what He has promised us in His Word. No matter what the situation looks like right now, all of the test and trials you've experienced are doing nothing but positioning you for destiny. That's what this is all about. The vision He gave you. That thing He spoke to you in His Word, this is what He's preparing you for. God is strengthening you for this final push.

Whenever you receive a factual report (i.e. medical diagnosis) don't repeat it, instead go to the Word and get some faith. Replace the fact with faith because facts can change on you. The Bible says to have faith in God, or the Godkind of faith and we can have whatever we say. Why not say what God has already said in His Word. Search the Scriptures and create a list of confessions. As people of faith, everything we do hangs on the Word, that's why it's advantageous for you to build yourself up in the Word, so you can be armed and ready at a moment's notice.

Make this confession: Today I walk in the strength of God's Word. I walk in complete joy!

Mark 11:22-23 AMP   1 Peter 2:24 AMP   2 Corinthians 9:6-8 AMP

8

It's Time To Share

Now more than ever it's time for us to share the Gospel of Jesus Christ to all of those around us. I've mentioned before about being set up by God to minister to people. It seems like it's happening more and more where God is pre-arranging encounters with people who are in need of a Word. People are searching for peace. It doesn't matter whether they're saved or not, they've exhausted every avenue they know looking for peace, yet it remains out of their grasp. Then at the right time, in the right place along comes one of us with a Word designed specifically for them.

You can be passionate about what's in your heart without being pushy, especially if you have someone who isn't saved and they have a misconception about something. Just *"lovingly"* share what God's done for you, where you were and where you are now. Notice I put an emphasis on love. When we get these chances, be sensitive to not only where they might be spiritually but also to the Holy Spirit, as you let Him guide the whole conversation. We don't want to beat them over the head with what we know to be true. Your tone and demeanor, if coming from a stance of love and grace, will leave them refreshed, and your words will have pricked their hearts.

We have a lot of work to do and not much time left. Jesus told us when the end would be near and according to His Word it's fast approaching. With Churches being able to broadcast their services on the Internet, along with Facebook and Twitter, the Gospel is quickly being spread around the world. So I ask "Are you doing your part?" Just hold down your corner, let the Word do the work and you'll make a mark that can't be erased.

Colossians 4:5-6 MSG   John 16:13 AMP   Matthew 24:6-14 AMP

9

Are You Listening?

One aspect of our walk with Christ is that we become better people, which means improving our listening skills. Have you ever thought about a Scripture on your way to Church only to have the sermon touch on it? When God talks to us through His Word, we have to allow it to correct us. By that I mean let the Word shine in the areas of your life that could use some light. Is there an area where the light has been turned on and you are brushing it off? Maybe it's a reoccurring thought about your diet or the need to exercise, and everywhere you go somehow it inadvertently comes to your consciousness.

I remember years ago my doctor suggested I have a colonoscopy. I cringed at the thought because I heard the "horror stories" of the process so I rejected it. Then I heard how a prominent pastor's wife harassed him into going, they found cancer early and it saved his life. Yet I still dismissed the thought. Then as I was driving to Church one day there was a billboard off of the freeway with big bold, you couldn't miss it print that said, "Go and have a colonoscopy done today." I surrendered and went. They found and removed some polyps that came back clear. What if I had continued to ignore the Holy Spirit and they caught it too late? I would have had to use my faith and fight for my life, or I might not be here today.

The point is this; God is always talking to us as He tries to lead us to or away from something. It can be either through His Word, a gentle leading, prompting from the Holy Spirit, an intuitive thought, a conversation with someone or a billboard sign on the freeway. Either way God chooses to do it, we have to be swift to hear and obedient to do what He says when He says it. Delayed obedience is nothing more than disobedience under cover.

So my question to you today is: are you listening?

Revelation 2:7   2 Timothy 3:16-17 NLT   James 1:19-24 MSG

Exodus 23:20-22 NLT

10

The Voice Of God

Do you know what the voice of God sounds like? Many times throughout our day God is trying to talk to us, but do you hear Him?

It's a shame how God has to compete with Facebook or our "busy schedules" with all of its demands at work and home. Amongst the clamor of this world, the Holy Spirit is still trying to speak to us. Gentleman that He is, He quietly steps out of the way and awaits His turn, allowing that "other stuff" to take cuts. Yet, He never complains, all the while knowing that if we just listen to Him things would go easier.

He's that gentle nudge telling you to take a different route to work and you blow it off because that would take you longer. Five minutes later, when you're stuck in traffic, going nowhere real fast you say to yourself, "I should've listened to my first mind!" That was God talking. He knew there was a traffic jam and out of love didn't want you caught in it. What could have been a "minor" inconvenience turned into extreme frustration with no one to blame but yourself. Had you gone another way God could've given you green light favor and you might've been on time or earlier! It's exercises like this that teach us valuable lessons. We learn through trial and error how to pay attention to that still small voice. Paying attention is another term for being obedient. You must do what He says, when He says to do it, because delayed obedience is disobedience. There is a payoff for doing things God's way instead of our own. When we hear and obey, we don't get stuck in traffic, people's lives can be changed for the better and we are protected from dangers both seen and unseen.

It takes time and getting in a couple of traffic jams to learn and appreciate God talking to you. He might tell you some things that seem at the time to be unorthodox but know this one rule; God will never go against His written Word. Let me put it another way. If God tells you to build a boat and you don't have the means, I'm pretty sure that doesn't mean go rob or steal from Home Depot because God hates robbery. Getting what you need is His problem not yours. Just listen, He'll show you where to go.

John 16:13 AMP   1 Kings 19:11-12   Exodus 20:15 AMP

11

The Simplicity In Christ

I'm still amazed at how God has inexplicably woven all of our paths to cross. Every encounter we have has been pre-arranged by God, to fulfill a divine purpose. One day I had a chance to minister to a young man who is a friend of a family member. He's someone whom I haven't met in person but have talked with on the phone several times. He called with several things on his mind. The most important one we talked about was salvation.

As we talked, he was concerned about going to heaven and not getting there because of sin. I knew he had accepted Christ as his Savior, but he said he didn't feel God like he once did and thought he would miss heaven. I told him that people don't go to Hades because of sin; they go because they've rejected Christ and His plan for salvation. We all make mistakes and miss the mark. If everyone who accepted Christ and still committed a sin went there, what's the use in getting saved? No matter what you've done wrong in the past and have yet to do in the future, Christ paid the price for it all. You've been forgiven. Our relationship with Christ is not based on feelings but on the faith of whether or not you believe that He died and paid the penalty for your sins. I told my family friend if you want to feel differently about God, then you have to do things differently and that means spending some time with Him. If you don't live a Christian life here on earth you won't miss going to heaven, but you will miss the good life He planned for you to have right here on earth. All you have to do is make the decision that the Holy Spirit is pushing you to make. He said, "it couldn't be that simple." I told him, "yes it is" and that the devil wants him to think that he'll never get there so what's the use in living right. That's when I shared with him how just like Eve was deceived in the garden, Satan will subtlety deceive our minds from the simplicity that is found in Christ. I reminded him that it's not by accident we're talking on the phone today about this; especially with us living on opposite sides of the country. This is God's way of showing you that He loves you and wants nothing but the best for you. When we got finished talking, I prayed with him and he felt better.

I've come to realize more and more that I have to slowdown and start paying more attention to what's going on around me. People are hurting and the enemy is having a field day in the lives of those around us. Given the number of suicides of some pastors, those in leadership at our churches also need prayer.

Take time today to show the love of God to all you meet. You never know what they might be facing. Coming in contact with you may give them hope and make all the difference in the world!

Acts 4:12 AMP   Romans 10:9-10 AMP   Ephesians 2:10 AMP

2 Corinthians 11:3 AMP

12

Relationships

I forward the "Uplift" text messages I receive from @Hart Ramsey daily and the list of recipients keeps growing. Through a series of events, there's a young man who's been receiving them. Seems the person who I thought was getting them has a new cell and he got his old number. He began texting me and asked, "Who are you that say such good things to me?" I told him who I was and every now and then he would ask me things about God, prayer and ask me to pray for him. I got a message from him one night asking is there really a God and some other challenges he is facing. I replied and it really got me to thinking how my brother always says, "we're all in this together and iron sharpens iron." Although he was reaching out to me for help, he doesn't realize how much he helped me.

When anyone reaches out to us, we have to be mindful that God has strategically arranged this encounter and we are well equipped to handle it. There is a mutual benefit that will be realized because this is all in His plan. We are all part of the Body of Christ, fitly joined together in love.

Remember God can only work through people. Take all of your relationships and encounters with people seriously. You can never tell when you might be called upon and you want people to be comfortable enough to feel they can approach you.

Proverbs 27:17 AMP   Jeremiah 29:11-12   Ephesians 4:16 AMP

13

Forgiveness Is A Decision

I was talking to a friend one day and we got on the subject of unforgiveness and how toxic it can be. He related to me how a family member of his had become so angry and unforgiving that he became downright hateful, which eventually led to him acquiring bad health and dying prematurely. One morning as I was in my time with the Lord, He was telling me that forgiveness is a decision. Getting to the decision point can come in stages depending on the severity of the hurt, but it can be achieved. Eventually you'll get to a place where forgiving people becomes automatic, without giving it a second thought.

Faith works by love. Walking in love means walking in forgiveness. If your faith is out there, and you want your prayers answered then you have to be forgiving. Our forgiveness from the Father is in direct proportion to how we forgive others. Christ hung, bled and died so that we could be forgiven upfront for any and everything we would ever even think about doing wrong-let alone do it.

Make this confession today "As God has forgiven me, I have forgiven (insert their name). and today I walk in total forgiveness towards everyone." I saw this posted on Facebook: Forgive others not because they deserve forgiveness, but because you deserve peace.

Galatians 5:6   Matthew 6:12 AMP   Ephesians 4:32 AMP

14

Time and Money

How much of your time and money is given to the Word of God? Some people don't do it at all, or they start out with a bang and little by little slack off with a myriad of reasons why they can't do it (i.e. I'll do it later or I had to pay this or that because _____ fill in the blank). Yet when people get sick or get into some legal issues, they have the time and money to seek out a doctor or lawyer. All of this could have been averted had they first chosen to honor God with their time and money.

Spending time in the Word of God produces the necessary wisdom you'll need to navigate through this life. I'm not saying that things won't happen, but you might be able to avoid some serious pitfalls along your journey. The best decision one could ever make in the area of finances is to get God involved. It shows that you trust Him. My wife and I tithe. There was time not long ago that I gave an offering every week to our spiritual leader Pastor Sheryl Brady. At the time I was reading a book on this subject called *The Cup, The Cake and The Coin* by Dr. I.V. Hilliard, and it really blessed me. As a result of my faithfulness in sowing into the life of the one who God has assigned as my shepherd, we received three unexpected checks in the mail one day. Let me be clear about this. I don't give just to get, but when I give to further advance the Kingdom and to honor my shepherd then I receive. You can say what you want to about the Church, preachers and money but the "proof is in the pudding."

The question is do you trust your money more than you trust God? It really all boils down to this one truth: Your present circumstances clearly reflect the value you place on God, His Word and money. I keep learning over and over that God is faithful and you can't beat God giving.

Proverbs 4:20-23   Malachi 3:10-12

15

Changing Perspectives

One day I had some work done on my car, and while it was in the shop I rented a vehicle. The only thing they had was a pickup truck, so I took it. While driving I noticed how traveling along familiar routes looked different. Because I was sitting up higher than normal, my view, my perspective had changed. Which got me to thinking about how the inspired Word of God will change the way we see things when we put it to work in our life.

God's Word will breathe life into any challenging situation you might encounter. As you spend time reading and meditating in the Word, what once could've been an overwhelming occurrence in your life is now filled with hope. If you take your mind off of what's bothering you and put the focus on God you'll have peace.

One of the reasons I reference different versions of the Bible is because they give a different perspective and sometimes a deeper understanding of what God is trying to convey through His Word. Also, when you read a certain Scripture in your Bible, you know those verses that are noted at the bottom or in the center margin, take the time and look them up. They will add some clarity to the verse you initially were reading or maybe add light to something that is totally unrelated and all of a sudden you get the revelation.

Take time today to let the Word of God become engrafted into your life: If you do, you'll start to see the things in your life in an entirely different and better light.

2 Timothy 3:16 AMP   Isaiah 26:3 AMP   James 1:21

16

Pray and Don't Be Afraid

Praying for the peace of Jerusalem coupled with all of the things we see happening around the globe today is simply the Scriptures being fulfilled. That's how the prayer call started one morning.

There are people God has in place to fulfill the Scriptures. We need to pray for them. There are saints in the Ukraine, Russia and Jerusalem who need our prayers. We need to be praying for all of our leaders not only on the national, but state and local levels as well. These are some challenging times. Leaders need to be surrounded by wise counsel that can provide wisdom and strength to make the right decisions.

All of the violence happening not just over in Europe, but right here on American soil demands that we intercede. Bullets are flying with no regard for human life on the streets of Chicago as they have been turned into a virtual war zone. Innocent children, if they make it outside, go out to play and don't come back home alive. Let that thought marinate with you for a moment.

When it comes to pestilences, a mosquito bite can infect you and either kill you with virus' like West Nile, Zika or a new disease that'll make you "sick as a dog" called Chikungunya fever. All of this and more is once again nothing but the fulfilling of the Scriptures. The enemy has stepped up his game and it is time we do the same.

Now more than ever we need to be praying and reading our Bible. When we do, our spirit man is renewed and we get filled with hope and peace, so that we'll be armed with the very tools needed to keep fear in check.

Psalm 122:6 AMP   1 Timothy 2:1-4 MSG   Matthew 24:6-8

17

Choices

Where you are in life right now is a direct result of the choices you've made. On the surface you're probably agreeing with me, but when you really think about it we all make choices throughout the day basically on autopilot. The majority of our decisions we don't even give a second thought because we're on automatic. Training and /or re-training your spirit helps you make better choices.

When you put the Word of God into your life on a consistent basis, you are more apt to make choices and decisions that are in line with the Word. As the church world says, you'll be "walking in the Spirit and not the flesh." Walking in the Spirit or the flesh is nothing more than a mindset that is either in line with the Word of God or it isn't. When you're in the Spirit there is a certain amount of freedom that comes along with it as opposed to the bondage and fear that comes with the flesh.

If you don't like what you're getting out of life today, then start putting something different in. There is no better place to start than with the Word of God. When you prayerfully read the Word of God and speak it out loud, it goes in and feeds your spirit man. As he is continually being fed, you'll begin to notice subtle changes, which will lead to better choices and subsequently better results that are based on the Word of God.

Today take the Word in and watch the Word come alive in every area of your life!

Romans 8:1-8 MSG   Hebrews 4:12 AMP

18

Word First

Making the Word of God first priority can have a profound effect on your life. When things happen, and you know that in this life they will, you'll immediately know where it's coming from; whether or not it's an enemy attack or some self-induced situation, and how to appropriately handle it. God wants us to be equipped with the Word. I firmly believe that every believer should have a toolkit of Scriptures. Ones they are familiarized with so that at a moment's notice, with no Bible handy they can be recalled. You might not know exactly where it can be found, but you know what it says and how to use it.

Something I've done that assists me is write key words of certain verses and where they can be found on the inside cover of my Bible, along with highlighting and marking up my Bible. This helps me immensely during my reading and study time.

Take time today to make what God has said in His Word first in your life, then your first response will always be "What does the Word say?"

2 Timothy 3:16-17   Proverbs 4:20-23   2 Timothy 2:15 AMP

19

How Do You Treat God?

Maybe I should ask what type of relationship do you have with the Father?

Over time I've witnessed people going about their life, making decisions and not getting anywhere real fast. You can't treat God like He's your spiritual Santa Claus or a genie in a bottle awaiting you to come and make a request to be fulfilled. Nor can you come to Him when you need to make a decision about something and expect to hear from Him when you haven't been spending time daily with Him and in His Word. It's not that He won't speak, you just won't be able to distinguish His voice from what your feelings want in order to make a quality decision.

God is like any parent. He wants to enjoy a relationship with His children. That means spending time daily with Him in His Word and prayer. This is the only way I've found that allows me to keep the noise volume of life down so I can hear from Him and be in position to be of maximum use for the Kingdom. Keeping the lines of communication open is paramount to a successful relationship. God has a plan and purpose for all of us. We have to discover what it is and allow God to work through us so we can eventually reach our pre-arranged destiny.

If things are not lining up the way you want them to be, then increase your time spent with the Father, watch how the Word will come alive and go to work on your behalf.

Psalms 40:1-2   Ephesians 2:10 AMP   Hebrews 4:12 AMP

20

Let God's Word Do The Work

God's Word is alive and full of power. The Word of God contains everything that you will need for this life. No matter what situation life throws your way, when you speak the Word, you're speaking life into it. The more Word you put on it just that much more life is inserted into it, especially when things get tight or start to look sideways. You might not readily feel like it, but you have to push past those negative feelings and put the Word to work. You put pressure on the Word when you speak it by faith.

Sometimes I have to get off by myself, maybe go for a ride in the car with no radio on, to pray and just fellowship with the Lord. It's during times like these the Holy Spirit will quicken a Word that speaks life to me. This is a perfect time for me to hear from the Lord, get direction, wisdom and if warranted correction. Remember that prayer is a two-way street. You have to receive as well as transmit.

Today be sensitive to the Holy Spirit as He guides you to share a life-giving Word with someone. There are people who are hurting. They need a Word from the Lord. Remember, "One Word from God can change your life forever."

Hebrews 4:12 AMP   2 Timothy 3:16-17 NLT   1 Kings 19:11-13 NLT

21

Don't Get Caught Compromising

It's very easy to compromise or take short cuts when we're performing certain tasks, the one thing you can't afford to do is compromise when it comes to obeying God. If you do, it will cost you your anointing. Saul was king and he chose to obey the voice of the people rather than the voice of God. He compromised and the ensuing result was God rejected him from being king over Israel.

There are a lot of factors that go into causing one to compromise. The main one for us is fear. When fearful thoughts begin to invade our mind, we have to shut it down immediately. We do that by speaking God's Word. Whatever it is you're facing, there is a Word to cover you and combat the doubt in your heart. The enemy will use everything he can to find and exploit a weakness. It could be a good-looking member of the opposite sex during a tough time in your marriage, or when you've made a vow of celibacy as a single. How about buying a lottery ticket to take a chance on winning half of a billion dollars because you're experiencing some financial challenges. If you were to win, it would only make your life worse because you don't have the discipline to manage the funds you have at your disposal today, which is why you are in this position in the first place.

The bottom line is somewhere along the way, you started believing that God won't take care of you as He promised. The best way to avoid compromising situations is to stay full of the Word. Feed your faith the Word of God on a consistent basis and when attacked, you won't fall for his deceitful suggestions. At the end of the day that's all the devil has is the power of suggestion.

1 Samuel 15:24-26   Mark 11:23-24 AMP   1 John 5:14-15 AMP

22

Everything You Have Is A Seed

In the church world, when we hear the term "seed to be sown" immediately we begin to think of money, and that is so far from the truth. Everything we have at our disposal is seed to be sown. So I ask, what are you sowing back into the Kingdom?

When it comes to our time, we can spend it volunteering. There are a plethora of opportunities available in your local church, where just an hour or two a couple of Sundays a month would help your pastor as they continue to give themselves over to prayer and ministering the Word. Your fellow church members also could get a well-deserved break. This is especially true for larger churches because you always see somebody doing the work or the work has already been done, so the need tends to get overlooked. What some fail to realize is that if you take a closer look, it's the same folks every Sunday doing the work. They show up faithfully before service while you are still in the bed. Most work through the service while you get fed the Word and are probably there after church is over as you are on your way home. All while never complaining about being of service to God.

Has God blessed you with a car or home? Are you willing to share what He's given you and help someone with a ride to church, go visit the sick in the hospital, or maybe invite some people to come by your house and share the "good news" over a light meal or snack? Ask the Holy Spirit to show you what He would have you to do.

Personally, I don't do it to get something from God. I just want to bless others with what He's given me. I've learned that when I make my resources or myself available to God, He always without fail, blesses the seed I have sown with a harvest. You never can tell when the time comes that we are the only Bible some people will ever see.

2 Corinthians 9:10 NLT   Acts 6:1-4 AMP   Matthew 25:35-36 AMP

2 Corinthians 3:2-3

23

Life Balances It All Out

I remember a conversation that I once had with my Grandmother. As we shared updates on family members, she began telling me of the issues someone was facing. As our conversations generally went, we started talking about life and how God allows certain events and people to come across our paths. I shared with her how God has designed life so that it all balances out.

We don't have to concern ourselves with trying to "get back" when people mistreat or take advantage of us, God said that He's the one that'll set the record straight. By the same token if you're out here mistreating and "dogging people", it is with love I can tell you: your day is coming! The Kingdom of God is built on the agricultural system where you reap what you sow. If you plant an apple seed into the ground, you're not going to get tomatoes, you're going to get an apple tree. This principle holds true for everything in life.

You can be on either the receiving or giving end of good and bad but make no mistake about it, what goes around comes around. All of life's events eventually come full circle. You've got His Word on it!

Romans 12:19 NLT   Galatians 6:7 AMP   Job 4:8 AMP   Isaiah 55:11 AMP

24

Sending Our Children Off To School

With the beginning of a new school year, it's time to speak the Word of God in prayer not only over our children but also with them. To cover them with our prayers is definitely our responsibility, but to teach them how to pray for themselves puts them in a better position to ward off the attacks from the enemy that is sure to come their way.

When they see us maintaining our relationship with the Father, they can't help but take notice and follow. I remember my pastor in Detroit saying how it was his responsibility to teach us how to know God for ourselves. As parents, grandparents or whatever role you play in a young child's life, when they see us consistently doing anything good or bad it'll make an impression. Since we are in this unique position, let's "milk it" for all it's worth and use this opportunity for further advancing God's Kingdom. They need to see the Word of God in action. Armed with the knowledge that when they pray in faith, they are protected from all harm and danger.

Our children are growing up. As they grow, they'll be bombarded with all types of images and things that when we were their ages it was unheard of. All we can do is guide, cover them as best we can, and trust God with the results.

Ephesians 6:1-4   2 Corinthians 5:7 AMP   Mark 11:23-24 AMP

25

The Tricks Of The Enemy

When you look around it seems like every day Satan seems to hit a new stride with his deceptive tactics. People everywhere are now "coming out of the closet" by disclosing their sexual preferences, while people we hold "in high regard" applaud them. This seems to add an overwhelming sense of acceptance for having illegal and immoral sex. All of this is being done little by little, inch by inch.

If he can deceive us while lulling us into a sense of complacency then his next move is to go after our children, grandchildren, nieces and nephews. If he can get to them while they are in their formative stages, then he has them. Nowadays there are children under the age of ten, some as young as six years old now declaring they are gay or want to be identified as a member of the opposite sex. The Scripture that tells us to "train up a child in the way he should go." This can cut both ways either in the Word or the world.

This is why it's imperative that as born-again believers, we are to watch, guard and stand in the gap for our children. We can pray for them, which is good and something we should be doing daily. More importantly, they need to see God's Word walked out in front of them on a daily basis. Your children or people in your extended family ought to know without a shadow of a doubt, what you believe and where you stand. It's not hard if it's what you truly believe and are walking the talk. Don't worry about being too deep and going over their heads. You can reach them. Kids today are smarter than we were at that age.

We've reached a point where we have to reject and refuse to accept the things that the world is now calling normal. Yes, it will make you unpopular amongst some folks when you make your stance known. At the end of day, will you hear "well done...?"

Leviticus 18: 22 MSG   Proverbs 22:6 AMP   Matthew 25:21

26

Uptight

I remember once when I had a minor issue to deal with. On the days leading up to it I had rehearsed several different, non-essential scenarios between my ears, and not a one of them was remotely valid. By the time I had to deal with it I had become a "tad bit" anxious. That's when the Holy Spirit gently nudged me with a reminder not to be anxious and if I've given it over to God in prayer, make my confessions and then let peace take over.

As I started speaking God's Word my outlook changed. I evicted those thoughts that were living rent free in my head. Gradually I began to feel better and became more God focused. When the situation was dealt with, it was nothing like the non-sense I had tried to manufacture in my head. Afterwards, I was laughing to myself about it. I remembered when I was a young boy there was a song by Little Stevie Wonder called "Uptight." I just kept hearing part of the chorus: "Baby, everything is all right, uptight, clean out of sight." I went and dug it out of my collection and played it. I'm here to tell you everything is all right, whatever it is you might be facing, don't get uptight. Trust God and His Word. He'll remove it clean out of sight.

Philippians 4:6-7 NLT   Mark 11:23-24 AMP   Psalm 37:3-5 AMP

27

Keep It Flowing

If God were to ask what do you want, what would your answer be? What's in your heart? Could you answer like Solomon and not ask for material things for yourself?

Once the flow of blessings begins, you can dare to believe and ask God for bigger and better. At this level, our focus has changed. Our thoughts and desires should be geared more toward others rather than self. We have to keep it flowing, and the best way to do it is be led by the Spirit and not guided by our emotions. They might cause you some regret down the road, even if your intentions were in the right place. Let me give you an example. There are people who have either heard or seen others get blessed in certain areas because of a seed they have sown. They might have given a car away and got blessed by a new and better car debt-free. Then when some see the fruit of their harvest they go and give theirs away looking to get the same harvest. When it doesn't manifest, they get angry with God and fall away. What they failed to realize is God prepared them to be in a position to give on that level, which led to that subsequent level of manifestation. To get to that level, you have to be led by the Spirit and not the flesh.

The blessing is perpetual, and we have been called to be distribution centers. If God gets it to you, His intent is to get it through you. When you bless others keep God in the mix. By that I mean always talk and brag on Him. Squeeze in a partial testimony about something He's done for you.

If your desire is to bless others on the level I described above, then let God prepare. You can start right where you are. What about the clothes in your closets? As long as they're in better than good condition, ask the Lord to show you who can you bless. Take them to the cleaners and then sow them. Remember, your capacity to receive is predicated on your level of giving.

I heard it said once that there is no way water can go through a pipe and the insides not get wet. When you give, God is going to make sure you get a return on your giving; you have His Word on it.

2 Chronicles 1:7-12 NLT   Romans 8:1 AMP   Luke 6:38 NLT

28

You Can Make It

Now that we have attained this new level with God, in order for us to be successful we are going to need a total mental makeover. We have to adjust our thinking. We can no longer do things the old way or take things for granted like we used to.

Little-by-little God is tweaking us by revealing what changes we need to make in our lives. One of the ways He accomplishes this is by allowing us to be stretched in ways we previously didn't expect to endure. Now that we are armed with the knowledge that this is all purposed by design, to bring us into alignment with His plan for our life-we can make it.

Time now to step up your game and take the blinders off because you need to see what's taking place around you. You're going to make some mistakes; there is no way around it. The key is to make new ones and when you do, just make the necessary adjustments and move forward. It's almost like the game of golf. You can only play the hole in front of you and not worry about the one you just completed. Learn from it and go on to the next one.

There is so much at stake now that the plan can only be revealed to you bit-by-bit. You have been pre-selected for this time. Yes, you're going to make it. God crafted you to be who you are. He knows "everything" about you. Nothing that you can do will take Him by surprise. He put it all in the budget for your life.

Romans 12:2 NLT   2 Timothy 1:9 AMP   2 Peter 1:3-4 AMP

29

Stay Focused

With all of the moving parts involved with change, I sometimes catch myself mentally having fights with people when I'm suffering from a perceived wrongdoing. I know it's nothing but the enemy trying to get me into strife and take the focus off of my current assignment.

The other day I allowed one of those mental ones to manifest into a real one with someone from a company that owes me money. After I got off the phone with them, I didn't feel quite right and I called back and apologized because I could've handled it better and that deep down inside if I trust God, He'll work it all out. I have to keep my sights on the Word and not the situation.

Strife, when in full effect, will hinder your prayer life and cause you not to hear from God clearly. You can't hear from God who speaks softly, when you have all of that other noise clamoring for your attention. It'll drown Him out every time. I have to go back to my roots and remember that I have a short list of people, places, and things that I allow to shift my focus. The majority of them that I know aren't on it. There are times when I have to resolve it within myself and say "not right now" with whatever it is that might be trying to invade my space, just so that I can have some peace of mind and still hear when the Holy Spirit is speaking.

We have an awesome responsibility that comes with this walk. In the beginning, keeping the peace and walking in love is easier said than done. It is doable and gets easier the more you put it into practice. At this stage it's not enough that we talk the talk, but that we ***walk the talk*** also.

Psalm 37:3 AMP   Proverbs 20:3 NLT   Ephesians 4:1-3 AMP

30

Hurry Up And Wait

This is a fast-paced world that we live in. There is one thing that's noticeably lacking that we could use more of and that's patience.

You have to practice patience. It takes time to develop in you. We have to learn to wait and that requires a certain amount of self-discipline. There are times when out shopping you have to tell yourself, "No, not right now", or ask yourself, "Is this something that I really need or just want?" I'm preaching to the choir here because I see a lot of "things" that look nice or I could use, but I have to ask myself the same questions and I have to work at it, but in the long run if I just wait, God will have something better come my way.

One of the dangers of not being patient is jumping out in front of God, especially when a decision has to be made. That's when you have to really listen for His voice and make sure you've heard from Him. It's easy to step out believing that finally an opportunity you've long desired is here and that it came from God. You realize later that maybe you've should've waited. It's a tough lesson to learn but once you get it, you know that if you can just wait, He'll bring it all together. You've got to wait.

If God has allowed doors to close in your life, wait on Him to open another one. Until then, get your hand off the doorknob.

James 1:3-4 AMP   Romans 5:1-5 NLT   Psalm 27:13-14 AMP

31

Trusting God Today

Given the way things are evolving in the world today, if you don't have a relationship with the Father then you are up the proverbial "creek without a paddle." Obeying and trusting God's commands are paramount to advancing toward fulfilling our destiny. When He says do something now, we can't mentally debate whether or not it fits into our mold and design of what we're supposed to do on the way to where we're going. We have to move now. A lot of times God has prepared a small window of opportunity that's designed just for us and we have to move now. We have to trust His timing and get into the flow of His rhythm. I've learned sometimes the answer to our prayers doesn't always look like what we thought it would. That's why we have to trust Him.

God orders our steps because He can see our future in the now. Those steps sometime land onto a path of misfortune, but don't get discouraged. God didn't do it. If He allows it then there is some good that's going to come out of it. You just have to trust Him through the process and keep a prayerful attitude.

One thing that helps me are the tools in my toolbox, Scriptures hidden in my heart. I have an arsenal available to me on a moment's notice, because I've spent consistent time meditating on the Word. I'm not going to sugar coat it. There are times when I feel off balance and when I do, I go to the Word, speak the Word and eventually get back to the center. I have a lot of favorites in my toolbox, Isaiah 26:3 is one of them. When I keep my mind on Him, there is a certain amount of peace the envelopes me. I know, like some friends of mine always say when things are going sideways "This too shall pass."

I have peace as long as I stay inside of today. Everything is okay today. Tomorrow will take care of itself and the past is the past. I just have to keep putting one foot in front of the other trusting God every step of the way.

Psalms 37:23 AMP   Romans 8:28-29 AMP   Isaiah 26:3 AMP

September

1

Keeping Your Faith Switch Turned On

Faith at its most basic definition is acting on what you believe. Faith comes by hearing and hearing by the Word of God. The things you hear and then acting on develops your faith. You can either get developed in the things of God or the things of the world. It all depends on what you're taking in. One thing I do and you can too, is begin listening to one recorded message repeatedly. You'd be surprised at how you can hear the same sermon repeatedly and then one day you'll hear something for the first time that is applicable currently to your life. It will have you saying, "As many times as I've listened to this message this is the first time I heard that." Maybe you'll hear a testimony about what someone did and at a certain time, try it and discover it works for you also.

Hearing it preached is not enough. You have to put some action behind it and one way we do this is by speaking the Word of God from our mouth. This carries a far greater weight for your spirit man than to just hear it being spoken by someone else. Do you really believe what you're hearing? If you do, then it should be coming out of your mouth so that your spirit man can hear you giving voice to God's Word. Remember, you and I were created in the image of God (another speaking spirit). We have the same creative power He has when it comes to the words coming out of our mouth. Just as He framed the universe with the Words He spoke, we frame our world by the words we speak.

Today keep your faith switch turned on by listening to the Word not only being preached, but also have it coming out of your mouth. Your spirit man gets developed and your faith grows.

Romans 10:17 AMP   *Genesis 1:26 AMP*   *John 4:24 AMP*   *Hebrews 11:3 AMP*

2

Sabotaging Success

I remember once when I was in a phase of transition that was chock full of events. Little life lessons had been learned where sometimes I felt like I was on one of those big exercise balls about to fall off and then roll to the other side only to have the same experience from a different perspective. The emotional kitchen sink was even thrown and almost hit me in the head.

As I travel along this journey (and that's just what this is a journey) I can see how God has me in a state of perpetual preparedness. Every step taken has a purpose even though I might not readily see it. I trust God and from where I sit it's the best choice. My track record before I answered His call leaves no room for doubt that this is the best course of action. If I remain diligent in doing the basics: reading my Bible daily and praying, it seems like God is leading me with nuggets from His Word and I'm following like the kids had *ET* in the movie doing with candy. Every time I get one nugget it's revelatory. Messages from the pulpit bring comfort through confirmation that this journey is in direct alignment with His Word.

One nugget I received said that God would only show me step by step, one step at a time. If He were to show me the end right then, I couldn't handle it without experiencing my current phase of preparation and then the next and the next one.... I'm doing the best I can, and God knows it.

There is a part of the old me I learned couldn't go with me any further and it made me somewhat sad. The old me was kicking and screaming "No! I want to go!" You ought to see him throwing temper tantrums, wanting to really act out and sabotage my success. The only thing is, I've been there, done that and all I got was a t-shirt? No thank you, I have enough of those t-shirts already!

So as I continue on in this journey I'm learning how to stop, smell the roses along the way and enjoy the trip without sabotaging my success!

Romans 8:28-29 AMP   Jeremiah 29:11-12 AMP

3

Who Is God To You?

In the Old Testament days God was known through several different character names. Our fathers Abraham, Isaac and Jacob knew Him as Elohim: The Creator. At times David knew Him as simply Jehovah: the self-existing One. He has also been known as Jehovah Rophe: God our healer. Jesus became all of those different character names rolled into one. As an example, today when we need provisions, we don't have to call on Jehovah Jireh, we simply call on the name Jesus. Yes, Jesus at certain times in our life will be manifested to us in different ways, but He is still the great I AM. He is all that we will ever need Him to be, when we need Him.

Jesus gave us specific instructions on how to use His name. We are to ask the Father in His name and when we do, He will do whatever we've asked so that the Father may be glorified. As we continue to grow and develop in the things of God, we get to know Him on a deeper level. As our faith grows, so does our confidence. We eventually get to the point, that when we use the name of Jesus, it's not done casually but rather intentionally, with the full expectation of getting results.

As you think about who God is to you today, remember He's whoever you need Him to be and when you need Him. Just use the name of Jesus!

Exodus 3:14-15 AMP   John 14:13-14 AMP   1 John 5:14-15 AMP

4

Being Restored

You're valuable to God and He wants to restore you. In the natural, people don't restore things if they have no value and it's the same with God. You are important and valuable to Him. He loves you and that's why He wants to restore you back to the place where you were and recover what you lost.

Could be you've made some bad decisions in the past. Maybe you took a wrong turn that has taken years from your life and you still haven't fully recovered from it. If so, I want you to rest assured that God is a restorer and He will allow you to recover all that you've lost.

Being restored is a process. You have to trust God in and through the process. Sometimes it might not feel or seem like things are going your way, but they are. We don't base the things of God on how we feel because our feelings can change just like the weather here in Texas. God's Word is our final authority, and when challenges come the first words that come from our heart and out of our mouth should be "What does the Word say?" You can only get like that when you make an investment of your time in the Word. That old saying of "no deposit, no return" is true. If you don't put it in, you can't get it out. The only thing that will come out is what you've been spending time with.

We have to be Kingdom minded and that takes a constant renewing of the mind if we're to get to a point where we think of others more than ourselves. When God restores you, please keep in mind that it's not all about you, but for the Kingdom. On the prayer call one morning, the Elder talked about how God is restoring us for the real harvest that is out there: The souls of the lost.

God is not against us having nice things but there is something out there more precious to Him than us having a new house or car. He wants us to go out, claim the lost and lead others to Jesus. Pastor Sheryl Brady put it best when she said, "we should clear the path and point them to Jesus."

My question to you is, What have you been spending time with and are you clearing and pointing?

Joel 2:25 AMP   1 Samuel 30:8   Ephesians 4:23 AMP   Luke 10:2

5

My Comfort Zone Has Changed

For the past couple of days this thought has been rolling around in my spirit and don't you know this past Sunday it was one of the points of the sermon that was being preached, couple that with how I read about it the day before and I said "Ok Lord this is confirmation, I get the message."

I am so far out of my comfort zone that I keep hearing the chorus from a song that says "I won't go back, can't go back to the way it used to be, for your presence came and changed me." I'm reminded of when God delivered Israel out of Egypt, once they crossed the Red Sea, He closed it up making it impossible for them to return to the comfortableness of the old and familiar, especially when the new things He had placed before them seemed overwhelming. As I journey on this new level, I realize that I couldn't go back if I wanted to regardless of how I may feel, as that door has been shut.

You might find yourself like Israel at times but know that getting adjusted takes time. Although it might take some time we have to keep moving. It's no excuse to get stagnated and let fear paralyze you. The challenges are the same they just look different. The playbook of your enemy has not changed. They will always either involve money, health, relationships or emotions. One or the other, or even a combination of them will be used against you. Recognize them for what they are; a distraction, so keep moving.

Keeping the lines of communication open is the best thing we can do. Staying connected and constantly drawing from the spirit realm by reading the Word and praying in the Spirit is paramount to helping you stay encouraged as you navigate through these uncharted waters of your new life.

Exodus 14:26-30 AMP   Mark 4:19 AMP   John 15:5   Romans 8:26-27 AMP

6

Tough Times

The phrase "Everybody is going thru something" is true and heard so often today that it has almost become cliché. Don't get me wrong, people are facing challenges like never before. Things we would hear or read about happening to others have now parked on our front porches.

Due to the advancements of modern technology, more than ever before the Word of God is being preached around the world. While at the same time issues with our children, spouses and money are increasing as the enemy tries to find an effective wedge that he can use to drive between God and us. Good and bad are growing together. Jesus talked about this and said that the wheat (good / Word of God) and the tares (evil) would grow up together. The reapers wanted to gather up the tares, but the owner of the field told them to let it be until harvest time because he didn't want to destroy any wheat. Then at harvest time gather the tares first and bundle them up to be burned and put the wheat in the barn. With everything that is happening I want you to relax and know if it's good then God designed it and if it's bad He's allowed it.

By the 7th day of creation God knew what would happen today and He has already made preparations for your victory. Don't lose sight of the Word. Everything you need He has already provided. Stay in the Word and you'll be okay. Live in the here and now, leave yesterday alone and stay out of tomorrow. Everything is ok today. And above all don't make a permanent decision over a temporary situation! I'm telling you it will change just like the weather in Texas!!

Just know that God loves you and rest in that.

Matthew 13:24-30 AMP   2 Peter 1:3 AMP   1 John 4:9-10

7

Prayers Of The Righteous

I was listening to a song about prayer and this one verse "The prayers of the righteous avail much" stuck in my head.

This should serve as a reminder to us all that God answers prayer. Let's break it down: **Prayer**: *a petition or request made to God.* **Righteous**: *right standing with God because I accept the work that Christ has done for me.* **Avail**: *produces results.* **Much**: *to a great extent or degree; greatly.* Take each word and meditate on them. **Meditate**: *chew on it, think constantly about, mutter, speaking to yourself.* Then put it all together and meditate some more. When you do this, I promise that faith will rise up on the inside of you and you'll be reenergized.

Whatever curve ball life has thrown your way, knowing in your "knower" that God answers your prayers will produce an attitude in-line with what Paul talked about in Romans 5. We don't glory or rejoice because we have tribulations; we glory in them, and we don't get all bent out of shape when they come. Why? Because of Who we know and What we know about Whom we know.

Armed with the knowledge of this, how can we have an attitude or disposition of anything other than "everything's going to be ok," because it will!!

James 5:13-18 NLT   Romans 5:3-9 AMP

8

What Goes Around Comes Around

What you do to and for others, either good or bad, will invariably come back into your life. This is why you should always try and do good. I've learned from own personal experiences over the years that blessings are perpetual. Which leads me to our topic for today.

When we go out to eat, frequently the Holy Spirit will place it on my heart to anonymously pay for someone sitting at another table's meal. When I do my wife always hurries out to the car so they won't know that it was us, but I get a kick out of it because I can just imagine how they must feel when they ask for their check and are told that it's already been paid for and they don't know who it was.

The other day all five of us, my wife, the kids and I took my mother-in-law out to dinner for her birthday. When it came time to get the check it was already paid for! Seems some friends of ours that were also in the restaurant paid it before they left. My mother-in-law was shocked to say the least. She had never seen anyone do something like that and for it to occur on her birthday really made it special.

The next day I thanked our benefactors for their generosity and told them about my mother-in-law's experience. They were even more blessed by hearing that they were a part of her birthday blessing. It all goes back to the Word where it says God will reward openly what you do secretly, and when you give, men will give back to you. We definitely reaped from the seeds we've sown into the lives of people that we don't know and have never seen again.

We are blessed to be a blessing. They definitely are perpetual and that's a good thing.

Matthew 6:1-4 AMP   Luke 6:38 AMP   Galatians 6:7-10 AMP

9

It's A Package Deal

The relationship we have with the Father and Son is a package deal. You can't have one without the other. If we're to maintain it, that's going to require spending time in the Word of God on a consistent basis. A steady diet of God's Word will produce fruit in our lives, especially when challenges arise.

Rightly dividing God's Word removes doubt, helps avoid confusion and prevents you from going off on a spiritual tangent. I've witnessed firsthand people who I've ministered with and family members, take and twist the Word of God just enough to make it palatable and sound like truth. It's the same trick the enemy used back in the garden on the woman and it's still in his playbook. Why would he change from something that has been so effective in the past? If he can get one to buy into what he's saying, then have that one recruit another and so on, then he gets a perverted version of the Word distributed, while those who have bought into it believe they've gained a "new revelation" from God. In all actuality that couldn't be further from the truth. It's a lie. To confront them is a waste of time, because they won't hear you and quite possibly will turn on you.

The Elect of God know better and do better. His sheep know His voice and another's voice they will not follow. It might sound good, but you have to ask yourself does it line up with the Word of God as it is already written. The bottom line is this: the enemy is trying to get people thinking that they can change the Word of God to fit their life or dismiss it, instead of changing their life to fit His Word. Gods' Word won't change. Any change that is to be made has to happen in us!

John 14:20   2 Timothy 2:15 AMP   Genesis 3:1-5 AMP   John 10:1-5

10

We're All In This Together

Don't think for a moment that you're all alone and like the old song says, "Nobody knows the troubles you have but Jesus", because it's not true. The things you are facing today somebody, somewhere has already been there and if you're trusting God in the middle of your go through, He will strategically send someone across your path to help encourage you.

I remember when I had the opportunity to share with a dear friend that was dealing with working in a hostile environment, which is something I had to deal with frequently when I was working. While I was going through one particular time, a pastor friend of mine told me that this was all a character-building exercise, and nobody likes to exercise because sometimes it hurts. That was so true. When I look back on it, I dealt with that situation for two years and for the life of me it seemed much longer. God gave me the grace to go through it with dignity. God gave me a different revelation of what "working all things together for my good" means because it's in His plan.

I learned a lot about what I could and couldn't handle. The most important thing I learned was how to walk on a daily basis in love toward people who don't mean you any good. I'm talking about your employers / boss' and not co-workers. This requires a different level of everything. I've mentioned this before and it bears repeating, whenever you get faced with a situation like this no matter whom or where, we have to pray for them. It's what I had to do. Everything I'm expecting God to do in my life I want to happen in theirs. That their marriage and children be blessed. That they prosper at work, and that God will bless and give them favor in all they do. I pray that they walk in divine health, and the peace of God that passes all understanding will mount guard over their hearts and mind. You can do the same. Just pray. It takes doing it for a while before it really becomes sincere, but it's a start. Before long you'll be on automatic!

Remember we're all in this together. The thing you're dealing with today is not for you but for someone else so you can share with them how God got you through it!

Romans 8:28 AMP   John 14:13-14   Philippians 4:6-9 AMP

11

We Walk By Faith...

We are to walk by faith and not by sight. Learning how to or rather getting developed in walking by faith takes a lot of work, which means you have to exercise it daily.

As an example, you're waiting for the manifestation of something from the Kingdom in your life. You've got your faith out there. You're walking in love and making your confessions daily, yet it seems like everything around you is contrary to what you want to happen. That's when you have to say to yourself "I'm walking by faith and not by sight." Recognize this is a battle between the internal you (your spirit man) and external circumstances. Ours is a walk by faith. That's why we have to stay in faith and keep listening to the Holy Spirit. Messages from the pulpit will come sprinkled with little nuggets of confirmation, so you have to pay attention.

We can't get caught up in the things of the devil (i.e. the sensory). We know that senses are his realm. If he can get our focus off of the Word and onto what we see, feel and think, then he will begin to offer us compromising solutions. They always come in the form of immediate gratification, which means that we pay for it on the back end or down the road. Rest assured, he wouldn't tell you that upfront because his solutions look to be the best thing for right now, but as the old folks used to say; eventually you will have to pay the piper.

It doesn't take much to get caught up in the affairs of this world but if you keep renewing your mind by speaking the Word, then your faith will grow. As your faith grows, so does your confidence. In the end you'll be walking more by faith than by sight.

My question to you is, How are you walking?

2 Corinthians 5:7 AMP   Ephesians 4:23 AMP   Romans 10:17 AMP

12

Accepting What God Allows

One of the greatest weapons we have is the Word of God. Spending time with God in His Word is never a waste of time. Whether it's reading your Bible, listening to a recorded sermon, or going to church, it pays off.

God speaks to me about these messages sometimes when I first get up and I'm shaving. That's when the Holy Spirit really ministers to me. He'll bring back to my remembrance certain Scriptures or tell me about something I'm dealing with and how God has it all worked out. This whole journey is about my destiny. God knows how to get me where He wants me to be. I accept what God allows and don't fight it. I was sharing with someone recently about dealing with opposition and I told them at times there are some things that you'll have to do in the natural, but the key is to respond and not react. When changes happen that you have no immediate control over, do what you can to protect yourself. Trust God and go with the flow.

I tell people all the time that I have been walking with God just a little too long now to turn back. ***I've learned and am still learning*** how to trust Him. When I glance back over my past, if it had not been for His love, mercy and grace I could be anywhere. Instead I'm here writing to you. Nobody but God could do this work in my life and for that I am grateful.

When "stuff" comes up, "be still and know that He is God." The sooner you accept what He allows, the sooner you'll start to feel better.

Ephesians 6:17   Romans 8:28-30 AMP   Psalm 46:10

13

Wait A Minute

There are times when you just have to say to yourself wait a minute, and it's okay to do it. No matter what might be going on or decisions that have to be made, if you have to say "stop, not right now" do it and don't feel bad about it.

I know firsthand the ramifications that come with not doing so when your instincts are telling you to. If you ignore it and "hit the override button" you'll wind up with a bunch of regret that far outweighs the hurt someone might feel if you do. If you have to step back, catch your breath and let things settle down then do it. Self-preservation is the first law of nature and I've adopted a saying by William Shakespeare that I use from time to time, "To thine own self be true." You have to be true to you or else all bets are off. There are times when you sacrifice for others, and then there are times when there is the absence of peace. That's when you have to trust God and wait on His timing.

If you happen to be in waiting mode, wait patiently and let the Holy Spirit be your guide. God has a plan and purpose for all of our lives. Everyday He's revealing it to us little-by- little.

Psalms 27:14 AMP   Isaiah 40:29-31 AMP   Colossians 3:15 AMP

14

Jesus Got Results Immediately And At Once

In the Gospels of both Matthew and Mark we read the account of the fig tree being cursed. Mark's version says they saw it dried up in the morning i.e. the next day; however, Matthew says it happened presently or immediately. The Amplified Bible says at once.

If we look throughout the four gospels, there are numerous accounts of provisions being met, people being healed and made whole by Jesus immediately. Since we are created in His image and He lives in us, why are we not getting the same results when we pray? We should be getting results at once. The problem is we never thought about it so we didn't have the expectation to get immediate results. For some of us, myself included, it's always been an "I'm waiting on the manifestation" expectation. I'm fully aware that both immediately and waiting are valid, but why should I expect to wait when God lives in the eternal now. There is no time where God lives because it's always now. There is no past or future with God. It's always now. We live in a world where we measure time. We have beginnings and ends, as if we're in a box with limits. With God there are no limits. Keep in mind the first two words in Hebrews 11 are "Now faith."

In order to change our perception or transform our thinking, it's going to take renewing the mind. Read the Gospels where Jesus got those results and then see yourself when you pray, getting the same. Begin today thinking, saying and believing in the now of God.

Expect it to happen NOW!

Mark 11:20   Matthew 21:19-20 AMP   Hebrews 11:1   Romans 12:2 AMP

15

The God Kind Of Faith

Jesus tells us to have the faith of God or rather the Godkind of faith. It's the kind of faith that exercises its authority by speaking, and whatever is spoken to or about comes to pass. We know that the world was framed by the words God spoke. We were created in the image of God (another speaking spirit) and we have the same faith power available to us. Jesus tells us a couple of times that if we speak to things and believed what we said, then those things would obey us. He even challenged His disciples as to where their faith was after they awoke Him thinking they were going to die while in the middle of a hurricane. Jesus calmly rose, rebuked the wind and told the sea peace, be still, and the wind ceased and there was calm. They knew He could do something about it, which is why they awoke Him from His sleep in the first place, but He was telling them that they could've done the very same thing. If you listen to the words that others around you speak, you can tell where they are in the faith process, especially if they are facing some type of challenge.

My question to you is what does your faith say? Faith speaks to the end of a matter and not the beginning or middle. No matter where you are or whatever it is you might be facing, what do you want the end to look like? Are your words or faith lining up with it? We create it by speaking it. So today let your faith speak to it and not your emotions!

Hebrews 11:3 AMP   Mark 4:37-40 AMP   Luke 17:6 AMP

16

Entering Into The Rest Of God

Initially when you think of rest or resting, you picture yourself relaxing by the pool or being a couch potato. Maybe even catching up on some much-needed sleep, but the rest of God that the Bible references means that we have ceased from doing our own works and are doing the work God has planned for us. Jesus tells us to come to Him and He will give us rest, put on His yoke and learn of Him.

When we follow after the plans God has for us and are diligent about our task, the work He has is far easier for us to complete if we do it His way and not ours. Spending time with Him daily in prayer and in His Word gives us our assignment for the day. When we lay aside our agenda and pick up His, our day seems to go much smoother. Those little irritants that come along during the day don't seem to be as significant when we have the yoke of Christ on us.

Enter into the rest of God just like He did on the 7th day. Stop doing your work. Begin to do more of His work because His yoke is easy, and His burden is light!

Hebrews 4:9-11 AMP   Matthew 11:28-30 AMP   Jeremiah 29:11-13

17

Overcoming Life's Irritations

When those little things of life crop up they can be what we call irritants. You know those times when something, not a major thing doesn't seem to go your way or someone does that "one more thing" that you don't like, but you're trying to be cool and not go off so you hold it in. When they come up, not dealing with them immediately and correctly can cause undue stress and anxiety, when all we have to do is roll the care of that thing onto the Lord.

Now more than ever, we have to let God care for us because your enemy is well aware that his lease is about to expire so he sends them, and they are solely meant to distract you from what God has called you to do. Giving our cares to Him relieves us from the burden of having to carry them around ourselves. It's one of those "God already put it in the budget" things that Christ paid for on the cross. If when Christ died, He took them, it makes no sense for us to keep them. Let Him have ALL of them.

As you go through your day and you start to feel yourself getting irritated, cast the care of that thing onto the Lord. Tell God that you give to Him the whole thing and then let it go. It takes some practice so just keep confessing it and eventually you'll get there. If forgiveness is in order then give it, because at some point we all stand in need of it. Remember, as we give it to others we receive the same measure back.

1 Peter 5:7-8 AMP   Colossians 2:14 AMP   Luke 6:38

18

The Currency Of The Kingdom

I got this nugget "Faith is the currency of the Kingdom" from a message I heard one day. As I began to meditate on this, the Holy Spirit began ministering to me on how the more faith you have, the more you can get from the Kingdom and the quicker it will come. Jesus got results immediately. He was able to do it because He had that amount of faith and we can too. All we have to do is make the same type of investment He did by spending time with the Father in prayer. He never said or did anything unless the Father told Him to.

Jesus said "have faith in God" or the God kind of faith. That's a faith that believes what you speak you create. You were created in the image of God (another speaking spirit) with the same creative power in your words that He has. If we mimic Jesus' example by spending time with the Father in prayer, in His Word, and follow the gentle leadings of the Holy Spirit we can grow our faith getting the same results.

Have you made a deposit and spoken the Word of God today? Remember, faith is your currency in the Kingdom. The more you have, the more you can get and the quicker it will come.

Mark 11:22-24 AMP   Luke 6:12 AMP   John 8:26-30 AMP   John 16:13 AMP

19

Pursuing Gods Presence

If you're reading this, I want you to know that there is a call on your life and the job is not done. You have work to do, and the best way to find out what it is that you should be doing is to continually seek God.

We all have a destiny and an assignment to fulfill. Do you know what yours is? Is it a place or achievement to accomplish this feat and move onto the next? I beg to differ. According to the Bible if you've been called then you've been predestined to be conformed into the image of His Son. Predestinated. Your whole life has been pre-determined, fore-ordained, and appointed beforehand by an unchangeable purpose. God knew from the foundation of the world that today would come and you'd be reading at this particular moment about being predestined.

As we pursue Him, we are constantly being conformed (changed, reformed, molded and shaped) into the image of Christ. Every day we should become more Christ-like in everything that we do. Seeking the presence of God either through His Word, praise and worship or the fruit of our lips, invites Him into our lives. God rewards those who are diligent about seeking Him with an increase in wisdom and knowledge-things that money can't buy. The people whose lives we touch should be better after an encounter with us, no matter how brief it might be. There should be something about you that leaves a smile on their face and a pleasant thought whenever they think about you or hears your name mentioned.

We are being changed from the inside out. Jesus is the Word. Take the Word (Christ) in and watch the Word (Christ) come out of you in all that you do.

Romans 8:29-30 AMP   Ephesians 1:4-5 AMP   2 Timothy 1:9 AMP

Colossians 3:9-11 AMP

20

Keeping The Momentum

Whatever it took to get you to the place in God that you now enjoy, it's going to take the same, if not more of what you did to stay here. There is never a day off or time to rest on our laurels in the spirit realm. The enemy wants to lull us into a sense of complacency by thinking we've arrived, when we actually haven't but are on our way to the next level because there is always more to come. I want you to meditate on that for a minute; **THERE'S ALWAYS MORE TO COME,** and that's a good thing.

There is always more to come when you're actively pursuing the things of God. Every new experience that we have shows us another facet of God we hadn't seen before. One time He might be Jehovah Jireh-your provider, and then at other times He'll be Jehovah Rophe-your healer. It's all based on the station you're at in life at the time, which is why we can't stop advancing forward. This is warfare and we are taking back our territory. When we fail to keep moving, before you know it the things that we've achieved will erode little by little and be gone.

Perhaps you haven't gotten your breakthrough yet, just stay the course and don't let up. Faith comes by hearing the Word of God, and your faith grows stronger when your spirit man hears the Word of God spoken out of your mouth as opposed to listening to someone else speak it. Don't get me wrong both of them work. The one that works the best and will have a greater impact is when your inner ear is hearing you speak the Word and let that feed your spirit man.

You're on the way to fulfilling the plan God has for your life. Don't stop now, keep moving. The best is yet to come.

2 Peter 1:3-10 AMP   Romans 10:17 AMP

21

Starve Your Doubt To Death

Are you contemplating needing to make a faith move, but in the back of your mind you have a Plan B? In the faith arena there is no Plan B. Sometimes faith can feel like you're jumping off of a cliff and you can't see the net that's supposed to catch you, but you have to believe it's there and that it'll catch you.

The best way to starve your doubts is to grow or feed your faith. Feeding your faith is going to require that you increase your Word intake daily. When you put the Word to work, it will overtake and starve your doubt. Read the Scriptures out loud that talk about faith, especially where Jesus said, "and shall not doubt in his heart." Rehearse and memorize them. Get them so ingrained into your spirit man that if doubt should ever arise in your mind, your heart will be so full of the Word that you begin to speak it and the Word will choke the life out of your doubt.

We have to always keep in mind that faith speaks to the end of a thing. Do you see the thing that your faith is working on? You have to see it through the eyes of faith. If by faith you don't see it clearly, just keep speaking the Word by faith and it will get clearer. Paul tells us that "in due season" we'll get our manifestation as long as we don't faint. Remember due season is not if, but when.

Mark 11:22-24 AMP   Luke 17:5-6 AMP   Galatians 6:8-9 AMP

22

Put All Of Your Trust In God

I heard Dr. Charles Stanley make a really profound statement one day. He said, "God never told us to understand Him, only to trust Him." This is so true. When we look at the Scriptures, they talk about trusting Him, and when you do you will be blessed and taken care of in every area of your life.

When things seemingly aren't going our way, that's when we have to trust God the most. No matter what it looks like in the middle of your go through, we have to reach a point in this walk where we know and trust that He is working it out for our good. To grow in our trust means sometimes we might have to rehearse past victories. That's where we enjoy those I remember when moments. If He did it before He will surely do it again.

We serve a God who sees the big picture when it comes to our lives and when we put Him first, trust comes a whole lot easier. That requires being diligent in your pursuit of Him through His Word. We have to continually seek God in all that we do. It can be just as simple as asking the Holy Spirit what do I do or which way am I supposed to go about this. He is an ever-present help, ready, willing and able to assist and guide us at a moment's notice. He'll answer your request, just be patient in the waiting and don't let the flesh try to push past the spirit and override the process. There is always going to be a battle between the spirit and flesh, but the spirit man can win if we stay on top of our daily maintenance.

Keep your mind renewed. Mount guard over your gates, your eyes and ears. The Word will come alive. Your trust is sure to grow.

Psalms 37:3   Romans 8:28 AMP   John 16:13-14 AMP   Ephesians 4:23 AMP

23

Jesus Is The Word

One morning as I was in the Word and meditating on it, I couldn't stop thinking about how Jesus is the always the same, yesterday, today and forever. One of the reasons He can't change is because God lives in the eternal now. If it's always now, then there is no time for Him to change. He will not and cannot change. Since God can't change; God and Jesus are one, and Jesus is the Word, then His Word can't change either. The things spoken to the people back in the Old Testament days are still relevant today because God never changes and the Word (Jesus) is the same. As an example, the promises and instructions found in the books of Psalms and Proverbs are just as valid today as the promises to the tither found in Malachi. Remember our foundation God and Jesus are one, Jesus is the Word and He never changes. Just about all of life's issues and concerns can be dealt with specifically in the Word, and if you can't find a Word then we're told to follow the Holy Spirit and let peace be your guide. If you have peace about it then do it, if not standstill. Something I always caution people on and that is not to confuse the absence of peace with fear. On the surface they might resemble one another but you can tell fear because he always brings along his "cousin torment" and that's not how love works.

As you go through your day today always keep this in mind, Jesus is the Word, God and Jesus are One, and Jesus never changes.

Hebrews 13:8   Malachi 3:10-12   Colossians 3:15 AMP   1 John 4:18 AMP

24

God Honors His Men And Keeps His Word

One morning I was reading one of my favorite Scriptures on healing. It's the account of Hezekiah's prayer being answered with a Word from God through the Prophet Isaiah that he would be healed. Not only would he receive healing but also there would be fifteen years added to his life. He and the city would be delivered out of the hands of the King of Assyria. God said that He would do this for His own sake, and for His servant David. This prompted me to think why David? By this time, he has been dead for almost 400 years. Then I saw that the text references David as his father.

David was a man after God's own heart who struggled in his personal life, but he never compromised his relationship with the Lord. He was a king who never allowed idolatry to be a problem while he reigned. After all this time God is still honoring him. This led me to think about another man that was dear to God by the name of Abraham, and how he was given a promise that is still being fulfilled to this day. He was told just as he couldn't number the stars in the sky, the number of his seed would be that great. The Word God spoke back then is still coming to pass today: "If you're in Christ, then you're Abraham's seed and an heir according to the promise."

God honors those who honor him. When you keep God and His Word in your heart, great things will happen in and through you. What has God specifically promised to you from His Word? We have to trust the timing of God and remember He lives in the eternal now but we live in a world where there is time. Whatever it is, just know that He is not slack on fulfilling His promises. God keeps His Word. It's coming. He promised it!

2 Kings 20:1-6 AMP   Genesis 15:1-5   Galatians 3:28-29 AMP

25

Forgiveness Means Forgetting

True forgiveness means forgetting what someone has done to you. We all have said at some point "I might forgive them but I won't forget it." Jesus said that getting our prayers answered and receiving our own forgiveness is tied to the level forgiveness we give others. With that in mind, ask yourself who haven't I forgiven like I've asked God to forgive me? You know the person that when their name is mentioned, you get a bad taste in your mouth or those nasty little thoughts start running through your mind like a hamster on one of those wheels in a cage, and you call yourself forgiving them but did you forget it also? Everything you've asked God to forgive is still hanging around as unforgiveness until you deal with it. When we mess up, we fully expect God to forgive us as we "confess our sins" to him don't we? Still you say, "but I don't feel like forgiving them, you don't know what they did." I'm going to let you in on a little secret: forgiveness is not a feeling it's a decision.

It takes work to walk in love, forgive people and forget what they did. It's a process but you can do it, all you have to do is repent and start anew. You're not going to always get it right at first but keep trying. God cares more about persistence than He does perfection. The end result is you will be so in tune with the love of God that you will start forgiving people before they do anything. You never can tell, one day God might put you in a position where those very same people come to you for prayer and how can God hear you with all of that stuff in the way. It's all about the love of Christ flowing through us onto others.

Today make the decision to let it go and talk to God about it. One thing I've learned is that just because I have forgiven someone doesn't mean that I have to invite them over for dinner.

Mark 11:24-26 AMP   1 John 1:9 AMP   1 John 4:15-21

26

Why Are You So Angry?

I pose this question to you as this thought has been rolling around in my spirit for a couple of days now. On the surface it seems to be a legitimate question but maybe the correct one is *what* are you angry about?

The Bible talks about being angry and it cautions not let it manifest into sin. That means don't let yourself get to the point where you say or do something that you'll wind up later regretting. I heard someone say that you have to push back on anger when it appears. Do whatever it takes but don't let yourself "go there." You have to know you, so examine yourself. Ask the Holy Spirit to reveal your triggers, and in time He will. Look at what sets you off and avoid it when possible and if you can't, then learn how to respond and not react.

Anger is based on fear, which is a spirit God didn't give you. It is usually coming from a loss perspective, either perceived or real. For example, you have the fear of not having enough money. End of the month and the bills are coming in. You begin dwelling on how to make ends meet. Your spouse goes out and buys something and then the one kid want this and it cost money, the other child wants to go somewhere and needs some money, and on the way home from the grocery store, you noticed that gas went up another 15 cents a gallon. So you start tripping on the entire family and they don't know what in the world is wrong with you. No wonder you're in fear, you've failed to put God into the equation. You can't do it by yourself. You need the Word of God. Whether it's financial, relational or physical, what does His Word say about it? Spending time renewing your mind in the Word of God makes thoughts of failure and defeat dissipate as faith takes over.

It's written that you can have what you say. Prosperity in every area of your life (i.e. your health, finances or relationships) is all predicated on what's coming out of your mouth. Speaking the Word of God in faith will create the God type of world that you desire to live in. A world that is free from fear and full of love.

Ephesians 4:26 NLT   2 Corinthians 13:5-8 AMP   2 Timothy 1:7 AMP

Mark 11:23

270

27

God Delivers And Restores

We all at some point have or will make some mistakes and bad choices that result in time lost and missed opportunities. Not only will God deliver you from whatever it was you might have gotten caught up in, but He will restore you also.

Anything lost because of it you can get it back and more; all you have to do is give Him something to work with. What are you doing with your time and money right now? Are you sowing toward the Kingdom or are you trying to figure things out on your own? You have to get God involved, which means seeking His way of doing things and then submitting to them. Once you start this process, you'll be amazed at how He will restore you and go beyond what you could've ever imagined. What you once considered lost has returned. New opportunities that arise from seemingly nowhere, will ignite and revitalize dormant desires and dreams. One day you'll look up and wonder how you got here, and when you reflect back, you'll see the hand of God all along the way.

Every misstep has been taken into account. It wasn't a waste of time; they were all lessons to be learned. At the time you were unaware of the experience you'd gain, but down the road it'll make sense because God will place someone across your path to benefit from what you went through and make it all worthwhile.

If your desire is to walk in total deliverance and restoration, then do the best you can today and don't allow your past to hold you hostage. We only look back to see how far we came and are no longer bitter toward anybody or anything that brought us to where we are today.

Joel 2:23-26 NLT   Matthew 6:33 AMP   Ephesians 3:20 AMP

Philippians 3:13

28

The Finisher Is On The Scene

This was the message given to us one morning on the prayer call as were nearing the end of a 21 day fast: The finisher is on the scene and we're almost there.

This started me to thinking how when you look back over your life, others might have been running a race similar to yours and have finished, beating you to the finish line. That's not what your race is about. God never said you would be first but that He would make sure you finished. That's all. He said He would abundantly exceed whatever you could ask or think according to the power that lies within you. He is that power. He will complete the work that He started in you. Whatever held you back has to let you go, just keep moving.

The route God put you on was designed specifically for you. It might not have been the quickest route according to our standards but it was the best. He strategically placed everything you'd need along the way. All the connections and resources you needed were there. He gave you this opportunity and He had this person there when you needed them. He gave you favor over here, provided supernaturally there, maybe even performed a miracle or two. Everything you needed was provided. You never went without. It might have seemed like it at the time but step back and look at it again. Look how far you've come. Every obstacle that could've prevented you from finishing has been removed.

You will cross the finish line because the finisher is here. God is here to help you. Don't look at someone else's race, run yours and stay in your lane. There has been a specific path carved out just for you. You will finish and finish strong.

Philippians 1:6 AMP   Ephesians 3:20 AMP   Ecclesiastes 9:11

29

The 9th Month

One morning on the prayer call, Bishop Murphy talked about how we survived all of the things that we went through. Even if it meant we lost some things, because if it had not been for the Lord on our side we would have been in jail or maybe dead, but God. If you had to live in your car at least you had a car to sleep in. He went on to talk about how we have moved on to a new chapter in our life and the things we went through, we will never have to deal with again and for that reason alone we ought to give God praise.

Our enemy understood that if we would make it through this 9th month, this birthing season, this messy painful season and get into the 10th month, that God's bringing those things to a close and He is perfecting those things that concern us. Stay the course. He's getting rid of people in your life and is dealing a swift deadly blow to them. Stop complaining. It may not be like we want it, but our attitude should be that we will bless the Lord at all times. This is the last time you'll deal with this enemy so stand still and see the salvation of the Lord. Place a demand on today with this declaration: "This is the last day I'll have to deal with this Pharaoh and wherever God leads I will follow."

Psalms 138:7-8   Psalms 34:1-4   Exodus 14:13-14 AMP

30

It's An Inside Job

God deals with us internally where both He and the real you coexist. God is a Spirit and we were made in His image, which by default makes us spirit beings also. We are a spirit who possess' a soul and we live in a body. We're spirits having a human experience and when it comes to us, God works from the inside out.

What He has deposited in us has to come out in order for us to do the work He has planned. When we spend time daily reading and meditating on the Word, God downloads updated information into our spirit man. The Holy Spirit has been sent to guide us to that place He has prepared for us right here on earth. That place is the good life. It's a life filled with promise, hope, and full of joy. That's not to say there won't be difficulties because there will, but whatever God allows to cross your path, know He has already prearranged enough grace for you to get through it. Notice I said get and not go through. I want you to start thinking past tense. Get means you got or better yet, you have made it through. We can only reach this point when we take the Word and deposit it on a daily basis into our spirit man. We have to put the Word in, in order to get Word results out. Becoming God inside minded allows His love to be expressed in everything we do, no matter where we go or who we encounter.

The greater One lives big on the inside of each and every one of us waiting to be expressed to the world. Today, let the love of God be expressed to others in all that you do. Remember it's an inside job!

John 4:24 AMP   John 16:13   Ephesians 2:10 AMP   1 John 4:4; 15-16 AMP

October

1

When Your Enough Is Not Enough

As I walk this thing out, every now and then I get to a point where I've learned to trust God on a different level. God said in His Word that He'd supply all our need according to His riches in glory by Christ Jesus.

When I look at the word "all", it means in every area of life my needs will be met. Not just money as is usually associated with this verse. I want you to think about trusting God with your children after they have left the house, as you watch them make the mistakes you're familiar with. You have to trust God, just like I did, that what you put in them will bear fruit down the road, and it will.

Maybe you're dealing with symptoms of sickness in your body. You know and believe God is a healer, but you've opted to go for the "miraculous" and ignore the obvious. Are you trying to get Him to do it your way or are you letting Him do it His way? God can miraculously heal you by taking the prescribed advice of your physician. It might take you having surgery if that's the way God wants to eradicate it. When it comes to taking medication, medicine won't heal you, but it can keep the symptoms down until your faith catches up. Let's say you feel led by the Spirit to give some money but you start looking at your need and begin fearing lack. Change your focus by looking at what the Word says. Just like He provided for Abraham, He'll provide for you.

Today, meditate on the name El- Shaddai (Almighty God). This is the Name of God who is more than enough. He is able to meet you at the point of your every need.

Philippians 4:19 AMP   Genesis 22:8-14 AMP   Genesis 28:3-4 AMP

2

Praying For Protection

I was involved in a car accident one day, and a couple of days later I saw the aftermath of two separate accidents along with receiving a text from one of my cousins on the same day that someone ran into his vehicle. These events prompted me to begin praying in the Spirit for a hedge of protection.

When we witness or hear about these types of situations or others, as believers our spirits should be quickened to immediately begin praying against these attacks. We should be praying with and for our children every morning before they walk out the door on their way to school. There are too many designs out there garnering for their attention and lives, and we have to remain diligent in our opposition against the enemy through prayer and cover our children.

If we're to build our confidence in God, to know that He will answer our prayers, then we have to spend time in His Word. When you find His promises on certain Scriptures, underline, highlight or circle them. Do something so that when you go back for review, they'll stand out, and then meditate and chew on it or a while. Let it marinate in your mind and when you speak His Word it'll become rooted in your spirit.

When you do these simple things, your confidence grows. As you begin to exercise your faith muscle, you'll see or hear answers to the things you've been praying about. Someone you know will tell about how they narrowly escaped something that only God could've saved them from, and the Holy Spirit will gently whisper to you that it was your prayers that protected them.

Today begin praying for protection against whatever the enemy throws at you. Plead the Blood of Jesus over your family, home, job and all of your possessions. The Blood of Jesus is still in effect. It is working on our behalf when we activate it by proclaiming what the Blood has done for us.

1 John 5:14-15 AMP   James 5:16 AMP   Revelation 12:11 AMP   Philemon 6

3

Rising Opposition

By now you are completely aware that you pose a threat to the enemy's camp. He is on assignment and will do anything that he can to prevent you from being successful.

He'll throw everything at you including the kitchen sink to dissuade you. Please recognize the things that'll come up won't always be some type of major catastrophe, but rather little irritants sent to bug you. When they arise you have to mount guard over your mouth (i.e. watch what you say), because you'll have to make a split second decision whether to speak or not and if you do say something then let it be in alignment with the Word of God. We don't want our words to trip us up. They can if we're not careful because our words have creative power.

We speak against the enemy and put him in his place with the Word of God. The attacks won't stop, but if we keep our Word tank full, then we can successfully deflect whatever he throws our way. He's always trying so be aware that if something didn't work, he'll just change tactics and look for another way in. Although you'll be told differently, there is no shame in making a mistake. If he trips you up, then get up, dust yourself off, and get back into the fight. It's only shameful if you stay down and let him walk all over you.

Every now and then you're going to take a hit, this is warfare, but I looked at the back of the book and it says we won!

Song of Solomon 2:15   Mark 11:23 AMP   2 Corinthians 2:10-11 AMP

Revelation 22:14 AMP

4

From Faith To Faith

As we go from one level of faith to another it can be somewhat unstable, but once you've reached the next level it is a sign that our faith has increased.

Living by faith from one level to the next, we replace our old ways of thinking and doing by learning how to respond to those familiar situations in a totally new and different way. There will be challenges to your faith and it comes with the territory, and when they happen don't let fear in. Whatever faith is calling for remember it is not a loss, just go to the Word. When God promises you something in His Word He didn't lie and no matter what it may look like right now, it will come to pass. God is our source and He will always meet His own need. All He needs is a man or woman like you who's yielded to Him and willing to do the work and be His hands here in the earth.

Your level of faith is determined by how much time you consistently spend in the Word. If your desire is to operate on a higher level of faith, then you'll have to maintain a high level of His Word deposited in your heart. Today make an investment in His Word. If you keep at it and don't quit, it'll pay off!

Habakkuk 2:4 AMP   Numbers 23:19 AMP   Luke 22:31-32 AMP

Galatians 6:9 AMP

5

Standing In The Gap

Has someone recently crossed your mind, either friend or foe that you haven't thought about or seen in long time and then you wind up thinking about them again later in the day? It's not by accident or coincidence that it's happening. That's the Holy Spirit gently nudging you to pray for them. They could be experiencing some type of difficulty in their life or the Lord wants to use you to avert some calamity that might be coming their way. It doesn't matter what it could be, the bottom line is God has called upon you to pray for them.

There are going to be times when God prompts us to stand in the gap for others because of our relationship with Him. He knows that when called on we'll step up. All you have to do is look around or turn on the news to see that people everywhere are going through something and it's on us as born again, Spirit filled believers to go before the throne for others in prayer. We might not be privy to their exact circumstance but if we use our prayer language (tongues) or pray the Word as the Holy Spirit leads, we will be effective. We are the righteous and when we pray effectually and fervently, our prayers "make tremendous power available and it is dynamic in its working."

Today don't let your standing in the gap opportunity pass you by. You don't know who or when God called on someone to stand in the gap for you. He does and they did!

John 16:13 AMP   Ezekiel 22:29-30 AMP   James 5:16 AMP

6

You Were Born To Win

Your whole life has been designed to not only make you a winner, but to succeed at whatever you do. Losing is not in your DNA.

The moment you accepted Christ as your Savior you received a DNA transfer. You now have His death-defeating, devil-overcoming DNA down on the inside of you. It's flowing through your entire being. You're now programmed or pre-wired to live the victorious life, which is found in Christ. Don't let anyone or anything impress upon you something different; you're an over comer.

Make no mistake about it, winning comes with a price tag. You'll be met with some of the most intense opposition you've ever seen. If you want to thoroughly embrace all that God has planned for you and win consistently, then you have to keep your mind renewed in the Word of God. The Spirit of God reads the Word of God to your heart and will strengthen your faith. That's a mind in constant communication with God, enabling you to receive timely updates and instructions to help navigate around the distractions that are sure to come your way. Don't get emotional in the heat of the battle. If you stick to the Word you've already won and your feelings will eventually fall in line with the Word.

I want you to know that no matter what it might look like, you can make it. God has fixed this day for you to win. Everything God promised in His Word is just waiting for you to receive it. Keep speaking the Word. This is your time to be blessed.

Joshua 1:8 AMP   Ephesians 2:10 AMP   Psalms 34:19   Romans 12:2 AMP

7

Do You Have A Set Time To Pray?

I remember back in Detroit when I first started going to church, my pastor at the time Bishop Keith Butler said, "It is better to ask for guidance in the morning, than to ask for a whole lot of forgiveness at the end of the day." That statement has stayed with me all of these years and is the reason I still get up early while the rest of the house is quiet and spend time in worship with God in prayer and the Word.

David said, "Early will I seek thee" and that's something I've incorporated into my daily life. When I first started it was a struggle, that's when I got the five-minute concept. When I dedicated to spend the first five minutes of my day with God in prayer and His Word, five minutes wasn't enough and before long the time evolved into an hour and I began looking forward to getting up early and spending time with the Lord.

There is a payoff to spending quiet time with God every day. As you read His Word while it's quiet, God's thoughts from the Word flow freely. You're able to establish a dialogue through prayer between you and the Father where the lines of communication are wide open. He prompts you every morning to get up and "let's get together" because He has so much He wants to share with you. It's gotten to the point with me that I don't have an alarm clock. I haven't used one in years. My internal clock is so in tune with Him that I instinctively know just about what time it is every morning when I wake up. Still today, there are some mornings that are not as easy as others to get up. I've noticed that when I don't, I become "rushed" in my time with Him because the rest of the house is up moving and there's too much going on that interferes with us quietly enjoying each other's company, unhurried and free from distraction.

God rewards those who are diligent about seeking Him. If you aren't already doing so, do whatever it takes and create that early morning worship experience between you and the Father. When you do, you'll start getting the early edition of your Holy Ghost news "hot off the presses."

Psalms 63   NKJV John 4:23-24 AMP   Hebrews 11:6 AMP

8

Do You Pray In Faith Or Fear?

There are times when prayers can be motivated out of fear and not faith. For example, you get a bad report from the doctor and you are told you only have 2 months to live. Is your prayer going to be out of fear because you're afraid to die or is it in faith because you know in your "knower" that your job isn't done, and that the enemy is trying to short circuit your work? It's the same act of praying for healing, but what is the drive? There's no doubting that immediately all kinds of thoughts will run through your mind and your emotions will be all over the place when you get a report like that, but you have to let the initial wave of emotions subside. Go get your Bible, find all of the healing Scriptures and begin to confess them in faith. The more you speak the Word of God concerning the matter the more your faith will increase. Before long, your confidence has become what some might say is arrogance and that's okay because you know what the Word says and that trumps what the doctor said. I'm not saying don't take your medicine. Medicine can't heal you but it'll help keep the symptoms down until your faith reaches the level where God's Word has kicked in and medicine is no longer needed. A clear sign that you might be in fear is that fear brings torment, and that's not of God because God is love and perfect love cast out fear.

Speaking the Word of faith in faith, leaves very little room for fear. Remember, that your enemy can only suggest thoughts that generate fear. One thing I tell people all the time is that we can't be scared of death. How can the enemy scare you with the very thing that will usher you into the presence of the Lord? We are not ignorant of the games he plays and the tools he uses to trip us up. We have the Word of God and when we speak it by faith then we have the very things that we desired when we pray. No matter what it might look like along the way, the angels are on assignment to see that it's eventually fulfilled.

Romans 10:17 AMP   1 John 4:18 AMP   2 Corinthians 5:8 AMP

1 John 5:14-15 AMP

9

Inside Job

I had been meditating on how God works in our lives. Everything He does is always on the inside; basically it's an inside job. Jeremiah 31 tells us that He will put His law in our inward parts and write it in our hearts. In doing so He doesn't want to concern us with teaching them to anyone because they'll already know. If you think about it, you know right from wrong. Even if no one tells you, you know. That's when you get that gut check in your spirit right when you're about to do or say something and it says; "now you know that wasn't right."

God deals with us on the inside because we were created in His image, another talking Spirit just like Him, only difference is we also have a soul and live in a body. Simply put we are Spirit beings having a human experience. God deals with us Spirit to spirit, His bearing witness with ours. When reading your Bible, you'll see in the New Testament how God uses the word "in" rather frequently. Paul tells us in the Book of Acts that it is "in Him we live and move and have our being." Whenever you hear the word "spirit" that should trigger you to think: "inside job." Keep in mind the enemy tries to gain access to you through the spirit. He needs a body just like God does and gains access through the images we expose ourselves to. It can be music, pictures or words. What goes in must come out! When you deal with people whose "spirit" isn't right, know where it's coming from: your enemy. The Bible tells us "we wrestle not against flesh and blood." The world is full of people who get hung up on the color or shapes of our houses, but we strive to rise above that.

Remember it's an inside job. God is working in you to bring out all that He has planted for the world to see, so they'll know that there is a God who has filled us with hope, and He loves us all unconditionally!!

Jeremiah 31:33-34 AMP   Acts 17:26-28 AMP   Ephesians 6:12 AMP

10

The Peace That Passes All Understanding

There is a certain level of peace that comes in your relationship with Christ. When things around you seem to be chaotic and you're having one of those "if it ain't one thing it's another" kind of days, God's Word offers you a level of peace that voids all understanding.

In his letter to the church at Philippi, the Apostle Paul lays out the roadmap to the peace that passes all understanding. He tells us not to be worried or anxious about anything, but that our approach to God should be prayerful, coupled with thanksgiving, and in doing so we will receive peace and it will keep our hearts (spirit man) and minds through Christ (the anointed one and His anointing). This is the peace that when you're in the middle of not so pleasant circumstances and situations, you and others are amazed at how calm you are.

I'm reminded of how in the middle of the storm that Jesus' disciples thought they were about to die. Jesus spoke to the storm saying, "Peace, be still", and the storm obeyed Him. We can have the same results in our personal life by speaking to our storms when they arise and by faith simply say, "Peace, be still." They will calm down and we then can enjoy a peace that only comes from God!

Philippians 4:6-7 AMP   Mark 4:38-40

11

Your Personal Google-The Holy Spirit

Today, whenever we want to know something, one of the first things we'll say is "Google it!" As born-again believers we have our own personal Google in the person of the Holy Spirit, and when we want to know anything, we should go to Him because the answer's in us. We've got all of our answers down on the inside and it's up to us to access them. Whether you call it intuition or instinct, the Holy Spirit is talking to you about you, and the path and direction He wants you to take.

The connection has been deposited in us and now the responsibility is ours to bring it into our consciousness. When you get the information or answer that you need, I implore you to please pay attention because He won't lead you wrong. There are times when you'll have to do something that probably won't make sense, or you'll get catapulted into a situation that changes the direction you were comfortable going in. That's when you have to step out on faith and move when He says move. Remember, this all part of His plan for your life. Stay focused and flexible. I've seen it happen over and over again not only in my life but in the lives of others. God strategically places people along the way to assist you towards the next phase of development.

Everything you'll ever need has already been provided for. The day you were born again, God deposited on the inside of you His Spirit. Our born-again spirit and His are now the only way He communicates with us, whether it be praying in the Spirit, through the Word being read, preached or being sung in a song. If we stay sensitive to His gentle leadings more will constantly be revealed to us.

Stop looking around outside for what you have on the inside of you. The Spirit of God in you is your own personal "Google." You have 24/7 access to all of the information you'll ever need from the one who created everything there is. If you don't have an answer, have you asked Him the question?

Ephesians 2:10 AMP   1 John 4:4 AMP   2 Peter 1:3-4 AMP   John 16:13 AMP

12

Spiritual Turbulence

Have you ever been on a plane when the flight attendant comes on and says: "Ok ladies and gentlemen if you would please return to your seats, the captain has turned on the fasten seat belt sign?" The captain then comes on and explains that we are experiencing a little turbulence and he is going to take the aircraft up higher to get out of it. This is exactly how my morning started one day with turbulence, some of which was self-induced. One thing after another began to irritate me like a pebble in my shoe. I could feel myself getting closer and closer to hitting the "override button." This is where I start saying and doing things that I don't want to, while the other side of me knows that I want to do the right things, which would have really made for a spectacular start of the day. Instead I saw it for what it is - spiritual warfare on the inside me. I needed to go higher. I took a deep breath, got off to a spot all by myself, prayed, and then started my day all over again.

Whenever you encounter some turbulence throughout your day, go to your arsenal and pull out your sword, which is the Word of God. Take the Word in and ***make the decision*** that today you choose to seek and pursue peace while enjoying the good life God has pre-arranged for you to walk in.

Romans 7:19-23 AMP   Ephesians 6:17-18   Psalms 34:14   Psalms 37:37 AMP

13

Letting Peace Be Your Guide

Have you ever been faced with having to make a decision and you didn't know exactly which way to go? You searched the Scriptures yet couldn't find a specific Word that dealt with your situation. If so, that's when you have to let peace or the absence of it be your guide. It could be a career opportunity that requires having to move out of state and you just don't know what to do. The first thing not to do is ask people what they think or what would they do if they were in this situation. Instead start praying, especially in tongues. That's how we get God involved by seeking direction and instructions straight from the Holy Spirit. When we pray in the Spirit we get wisdom and peace.

Peace has to act like an umpire in times like this. You'll know it when you get it. I always caution people not to mistake the absence of peace with fear. Although they might seem similar there is a clear distinction between the two because fear brings tormenting thoughts. The ones that won't let you sleep at night telling you if you do it, this or that could happen. They are all a bunch of lies sent to do nothing but instill fear in you, attempting to prevent you from entering your God ordained destiny. While on the other hand the absence of peace is that subtle "I don't feel quite right about this in my spirit" kind of thought, without all of the drama fearful thoughts bring.

Once you get peace about it, then you seek counsel from either your pastor or spiritual mentor. They should do nothing but confirm what you have already sought God about and have the corresponding peace concerning it.

Colossians 3:15 AMP   Romans 8:26-27 AMP   1 John 4:18   Psalms 1:1 AMP

14

Trust God And Look In The Mirror

With the way things are changing if we're not careful fear will creep in. You know the Word and see your circumstances all while trying to believe God, but it doesn't make sense how it will work out.

There is something that has been placed before you that is bigger than you and it has to be God at work. You've done all that you could do. Now it's up to Him. Yet in the back of your mind you're thinking about the people who are counting on you and how you don't want to fail them. That's when you have to go and look into the mirror of God's Word and see how you're supposed to look, with your attitude and disposition, because you're changing.

When Peter took his eyes off of Jesus and started looking at his circumstances he began to sink. The same thing can happen to us. This is why we have to always keep in mind that ours is a walk by faith and not by sight. We keep putting one foot in front of the other, with our eyes on His Word and maintain a forward motion as we continue to trust Him, because in the end we know that everything will be all right.

Today look into the mirror of His Word. Take it and speak it over your situation because there is life in the Word, and we give it life when we speak it!

2 Corinthians 3:18 AMP   Matthew 14:28-31   2 Corinthians 5:7 AMP

15

Are You Ready?

Today's title poses a legitimate question. With all of the events that are happening around us, what have you been doing to prepare to protect your house and family? Let me share with you something I do. I have a list of healing confessions that come from a book by Charles Capps titled *God's Creative Power for Healing*. I say them every morning. I speak God's Word over my entire body before the enemy uses symptoms of anything to attack me. I speak the spirit and life of His Word against tumors and growths, my blood pressure, immune system, heart and arteries...etc. I do what I can to prevent ever having any issues in those areas of my body. I started using this book back in 2012, at the time I was taking medicine for high blood pressure and other symptoms, but by my speaking God's Word over it, it lowered and I have been medicine and symptom free for over two years.

It's easier to build a house before the storm comes than to try and erect one in the middle of one. Let's call it preventive maintenance. There are a lot of resources out there to utilize if you don't already have something in place. Before you read your Bible ask the Holy Spirit to show you where to go and then write them down. Let them become an integral part of your daily time with the Lord and watch how He will lead you to other Scriptures that'll speak to different areas of your life. God is always speaking to us either through His Word, His still small voice or even this book. Are you listening? If so, what are you doing with what He told you?

You hear all of the news reports about what's happening around the world and even here at home. Are you ready?

Isaiah 53:5 AMP   Mark 11:23-24   Romans 10:17 AMP

16

Peace With And From God

There is a lot going on in the world today that either directly or indirectly affects all of us. If we are going to be the calmness in the middle of everything else then we need to exercise and be an example of the peace of God. We can only be like that because of our faith. When you know that you know, deep down in your "knower" that everything is going to be all right, then you don't sweat the mundane. Why, because we have been justified by faith in the finished works of Christ. This causes us to have peace with God. If we have peace with God, then a certain level of confidence and boldness ought to rise up within us. This peace removes all anxiety and worry. When life's events happen, we are the ones who go boldly and proclaim the Word of the Lord and get the manifested results from that Word.

Today let the God-kind of peace rule throughout your day. Christ paid for it. Take advantage of it.

Romans 5:1 AMP   Philippians 4:6-7 AMP   Acts 10:36-38

17

The Tithe-Part1

I remember once when I took my car in to get the brakes worked on, the mechanic told me I also needed my wheel bearings worked on. When I went in later to pick it up, he told me that it was too dangerous for me to have been driving. If I hadn't gotten it repaired, he wasn't going to let me drive off the lot. I thanked him for what he had done because I was truly grateful.

When I got home the Holy Spirit began ministering to me saying that it was my tithe that protected me. God said in His Word that He would rebuke the devourer for my sake. The timing was just right. When the repairs needed to be fixed the money showed up. The best thing to take away from this is seeing once again that God is faithful. Like the old folks used to say He kept me from dangers seen and unseen.

There are factions of people who have fallen into serious error on this subject. Some of them have even gone so far as to write books and bad mouth certain pastors and high-profile church leaders over this subject. What amazes me is how easily the devil has deceived people into thinking that they are on "the right side of this issue" when in all actuality they couldn't be further from the truth. They operate under the guise of "shedding light and educating the church" when the bottom line is money and no faith in God and His Word.

Let me be clear, I don't give my money to the church. I give my money to God through my local church, to help finance the work we are doing for God. That's where my tithes go. I see the evidence of it every time I go to church and the doors are open, the lights are on, I can hear the musicians doing their sound check etc. It takes money to finance these things and more. If Jesus were here today, He would have a sound system, lights, cameras, internet capabilities and the folks required to make it all come together. All of these things take money. You can't find enough experienced volunteers to run an operation like this every week. It takes paid professionals to get the job done and put out a message that draws people to Christ. At our church the gospel goes out all over the world via the internet, CD & DVD's. When souls are saved because I'm a tither, they are credited to my account as if I actually led them to Jesus myself.

Malachi 3:10-12   Deuteronomy 7:9 AMP

18

The Tithe-Part2

I don't believe for one moment that when I give to God through my local church that it's a Sunday morning stick up. It's my opportunity to prove to myself that I trust God. I wave it in the devil's face to show him and say, "look at what God has done for me, and that He is faithful to His Word that's working in my life."

There are some churches that don't do right by the monies they receive from their congregation. More often than not they quickly fall by the wayside, never to be heard from again. I learned a couple of things early on. One is to trust the Holy Spirit to guide me to the correct ministry as He has in the past. They will bear fruit of what they do and that's something that cannot be denied, disputed or debated. I give to God through them. If they abuse it or do wrong, I trust God to be the judge in the end. The other is not to get involved in giving emotionally but to be led by the Spirit. If people are sowing a special offering during a service, most of the time the Holy Spirit will impress upon me ahead of time an amount to give. I listen to that still small voice and not my feelings, because you can do a faith action out of fear and when the harvest never manifest, the first thing we tend to do is question God as to why, when He never told us to do it in the first place.

When you tithe, it is not only a worship experience, it is the opportunity to get into covenant agreement with God. That covenant has promises for provisions, protection and a harvest for those who get involved and are willing to put their faith in God's Word and not in their money or what others have to say about it. It has to be done by faith. You can faithfully give God 10% and not tithe. You can do it out of the fear of being cursed if you don't and that's not love. Either Christ redeemed us from the curse of the law or not. It can't be both ways. Otherwise we neglect the chance to worship God.

When it comes to tithing, I can't afford not to! I don't think that a dime on a dollar is too much to give back to God for what He has already given me and add to that the blessing and promises that come from being in covenant with Him. I am grateful!

Malachi 3:10-12   Proverbs 3:9-10 AMP   Galatians 3:13-14

1 Kings 19:11-12.

19

When God Says No

If you truly know the voice of God when He speaks to you, then sometimes He says "No." When He says "No" its not to try and keep something good from you but just the opposite, He is trying to get something better than thing that you want right now to you.

Let me share an experience with you that I had. In 2005 I was looking for a new car. My sister had a Lincoln Navigator that I loved. It was too much vehicle for just me, so I shifted my focus to what I thought was the next best thing, the Lincoln Aviator. I went out and began looking and after a couple of ventures I heard the Holy Spirit say "No, I've got something better for you." So, I waited. While I was waiting, I encountered a few people who owned them and they weren't satisfied with the gas mileage and other things. This was right around time gas prices began to rise and I began to adjust my desire for it.

In the fall of 2005 after the 2006's vehicles came out, I got an email from one of the dealers I had visited. They were having a sale on the 2005 Lincoln LS', I asked the Lord if it was okay and He said yes. I was able to get a new car and save thousands of dollars because of the timing. The model year had changed over, and it was at the end of the month when they make a big push to get their inventory numbers down and sales numbers up.

This is just an example of two very important points of which the most important one is knowing the voice of God. Secondly learning how to be okay when God says "No." He is never trying to keep anything good from you. He is like any good father and wants nothing but the best for His children. All we have to do is follow His lead.

1 Kings 19:11-13   Jeremiah 29:11-13 John 14:26 AMP

20

God Or Guns

On the prayer call one morning, Pastor talked about praying for our children, teaching them to pray without ceasing and we should be praying for godly teachers to come into the school systems.

It is on us blood-bought believers to stand in the gap for our children and pray for the school leaders. A while ago they announced one of the school districts here in North Texas voted, passed and trained two staff members to carry guns. In the event anything happened they would be the first responders. They have replaced prayer and God in our schools with guns. Now tell me, what is wrong with this picture? There had been talk going around about the idea for some time, but now they have actually gone ahead and done it. I bet if you tried to get them to think about adding prayer back, you would be met with so much resistance your head would spin. There are too many variables involved that if something were to actually happen at a school, now you have the potential for a shootout occurring where innocent children could be hurt. Most of the times the perpetrators come into those schools armed to the teeth as if they are going into battle, and then there are other times when it's a misguided fourteen yr. old kid trying to prove a point and winds up taking their own life in the process. I remember a story recently from the Atlanta area, where an armed gunman came into a school ready to kill. But God had an angel, a woman of God there in the front office who talked him out of it without a shot being fired. This is why we have to pray with and for our children daily before they go to school.

Jesus said, "We are the salt of the earth", and it's reasons like this that make it evident. It's time for us to start being salt, come out of the saltshaker and be that light of the world Jesus said we are.

1 Thessalonians 5:17 AMP   Hebrews 13:2 AMP   Matthew 5:13-16 AMP

21

Love And Faith Working Together

On the prayer call one morning, Bishop Murphy talked about how prayer changes things, people, and cultures. This got me to thinking about a conversation I had with someone one day. It involved their work environment as I was familiar with the situation and knew the folks involved. Afterwards the Holy Spirit reminded me of something He told me a long time ago. Anybody I am willing to talk about, I should spend just as much time praying for them. I repented and prayed for them. I've been around this mountain enough times to know it's little things like this that if they're allowed to go unchecked, can hinder my faith walk. I have to walk in love even if the situation is unpleasant and causing me some discomfort. To the best of my ability I walk in love toward everybody no matter what, because love is directly tied to my faith. At first it might not be easy, but it is doable and gets easier each time. Picture a stream flowing freely. The stream is your faith. There's a beaver that has come along and he's building a dam to stop the flow. Love keeps the flow going. When we're not walking in love, the beavers show up and our faith stops flowing. Jesus told us everything hangs on these two commandments: "To love God with everything we have and our neighbor as ourselves." As you go through your day today, your love is going to be tested. It never fails that when we talk about love, in reality God is giving us the answers before the test. For me it all boils down to not reacting but responding. What will be my response? I've learned that sometimes walking in love is just keeping my mouth shut. If I react, I usually have to repent and go apologize, but if I respond, then I walk away feeling victorious because I passed the test and I represented Him well!

Galatians 5:6 NLT   Matthew 22:36-40 AMP

22

You Can Be Just Like Jesus

When we look at the life of Jesus and see what He accomplished, He was only able to do it because He had a prayer life whereby, He said and did only what the Father told him to. The same type of results are available to us (i.e. the sick can be healed, blind eyes can now see, deaf ears are opened, the dead are raised and thousands can be fed with just a lunch). I realize that some of the things I just said might seem "out there" to you but they shouldn't. If Jesus did it, He said we could also do it and greater since there will be more people like Him down here to carry on His work because He goes to the Father.

Staying in constant communication with the Father just like Jesus did will enable the Holy Spirit to guide you to where there is work to be done. We can pray continuously throughout our day by simply acknowledging and practicing the presence of God. Talk to Him as if He is sitting right there with you, because He is. Listen to what He has to say. He won't lead you astray. By now we have come to know the voice of God and recognize it when He speaks. When He does speak and He tells you what to do, know that you can do it by faith because it's His will and not yours.

John 14:12 AMP   Mark 7:32-35 AMP   John 14:26

23

The Spirit Of Detroit

As some of you might know, prior to my moving to Dallas, I lived my entire life in Detroit. I still read the *Detroit Free Press* every day and have a lot of close friends and relatives still there. A couple of years ago some of them were seriously impacted by the Judge's decision to allow, as part of the bankruptcy, that their pensions potentially be cut. To say that they were livid is an understatement. One friend of mine posted on Facebook the decision and how upset she was about it. I sent her some words of encouragement and hopefully they were received. All of this got me to thinking about "The Spirit of Detroit" sculpture that is displayed outside of City Hall. There is a Scripture verse inscribed behind it. The verse is 2 Corinthians 3:17 and it reads *"Now the Lord is that Spirit: and where the Spirit of the Lord is, there is liberty."* That is a powerful Word. No matter what the enemy can devise to come against them, if they keep a prayerful attitude and focused on God's Word it's going to be all right and suddenly God can turn this thing around.

I told my friend "You have every right to be angry and once you get over the initial shock, give God praise! You might not feel like it but do it. God has given you tools to work through all of this. The main thing any of us can do when faced with the possibilities like this is to trust God. I know the Serenity Prayer and saying to trust God might sound cliché but it's the truth. Now is the time when faith has to be put into action because the rubber has hit the road. We talk the talk, but can we really walk the talk? This situation didn't catch God by surprise. He knew from the foundation of the world that today was coming. He didn't cause it to happen, but for some reason known only to Him, He has allowed it and has made provisions for it. Watch what you have coming out of your mouth because the Bible tells us that we can have what we say, and that works on both the faith and fear side of the house. Don't let fear and doubt get in and pollute your faith. Remember we live in a twenty-four-hour cycle. Everything is okay today. Tomorrow will take care of itself. Ask God to show you what it is He wants you to do because He has a plan. We don't know all of the twist and turns it will take but the end result is it's going to be good!" I am reminded that this is all spiritual warfare and the battle has intensified. We all are going through something but if we turn to the Word of God and make it our final authority we win! I don't care how bleak the situation seems, we walk by faith and not by sight.

Mark 11:23-24   Matthew 6:34   Jeremiah 29:11-13   Romans 8:28 AMP

24

Being A Team Member

A few years ago, as I was going through the airport, I received a compliment on the hat I was wearing. It read "Jesus One Way" with a One-Way sign. The gentleman and I started talking about the goodness of God, which started me thinking how wearing the uniform, a Jesus hat and T-shirt doesn't necessarily make you a member of the team because it's all an inside job.

Today's uniforms are great witnessing tools, compromised of several diverse items (i.e. clothing apparel like a hat and t-shirt). It might be a Jesus bumper sticker, the fish or cross emblem on your car. Whatever it is that outwardly tells the world you believe God and His Son Jesus, advances that individual further into the battle and now you're on Front Street. You can talk the talk. The question is how good are you at walking the talk? Rest assured life will throw situations at you and with the right set of circumstances just like when pressure is applied to olives it produces oil, what's inside of you will come out. What we take in through our eyes and ear gate good or bad, goes into our hearts and minds, eventually coming out either in the way we act or talk. If it comes out of our mouth it goes right back into our ears reinforcing our belief system. If you're spending more time watching television or listening to secular music than you do in God's Word, when you start getting assaults from the enemy, for instance a bad report from the doctor, what will be the first thing to come out of your mouth? Will it be the Word of faith or words of fear? There are way too many distractions that can affect your focus. God's Word is the best foundation one can have, because it's hard to build a house in the middle of a storm, when the winds begin to howl, hit the frame of the house and you become worried about losing something. Water from the rain is coming in causing damage; frustrations mounts and you're saying, "If it ain't one thing it's another."

Don't let things like this happen to you. Fill up on the Word. Read, pray and listen to the still small voice of the Holy Spirit. The next time you put on your uniform proudly displaying that you're a member of the team as someone who is walking the talk, then you'll be a living epistle for the entire world to see. No matter what a storm might bring you'll be standing in faith on the Promises of God.

Romans 13:13-14 AMP   Matthew 7:24-27 MSG   2 Corinthians 3:1-3 MSG

25

Spiritual Complacency

When things seem to be going all right in our personal lives, we have a tendency to want to relax and catch our breath spiritually speaking. Does this sound familiar, "I've got some money in the bank, my health is good, family is ok, and the job is… well it's the job but I'm all right with it. This morning I think I'm going to lie in bed a little longer before I get up to pray. I've got plenty of time." Before you know it one day has kind of rolled into another and another. The quality and quantity of the time you spend with the Lord has diminished. If this is or has been you in the past, one of the things I've learned from being there myself is that we can't afford to get caught slipping.

We are constantly being warned that our adversary is on the prowl looking for someone that he can catch napping. Don't let it be you. We have to remain sober and vigilant which means not letting up on our spiritual maintenance and keeping the Word before our eyes, in our heart and mouth, because they are our life source.

It's easy to get lulled into a sense of complacency. When we find ourselves there, we pick ourselves up, knock the dust off and get back to business. There's no shame in being there, but it is if we stay.

1 Peter 5:8-11 MSG   Proverbs 4:20-22

26

He's Still Here

God is with you all the time, He hasn't left or moved. The day you got-born again God took up residence on the inside of you and now the Greater One lives big in you. This is why He'll be with you until the end of the world.

No matter what you might be facing, everything's all right as long as you stay inside of today. Future events can seem fearful if tolerated. That's why you have to speak against those thoughts as soon as they come. You can't allow them to hang around and fester. Your enemy is on a mission to get you to abort the process God has started in you by your words. The same tactic he tries to get us with we use to oppose him when we speak against whatever challenges we might encounter. It's all spiritual not emotional. We have to be on guard at all times because it's easy to allow our feelings to kick in and drive us if we're not careful. His attacks are invasive and always hit us in the sensory realm where he can get us to think or feel. We who are the blood-bought body of Christ rely on the Word of God and nothing else.

We have God's Word to remind us that this is a walk by faith. It doesn't matter what it may look like at the moment, our stance is always, what does the Word say? Don't be afraid, just stay in faith. Everything's going to be all right. God is right here with you every step of the way.

1 John 4:4 AMP   Matthew 28:20   2 Corinthians 5:7 AMP

27

It's In The Book

All of today's current events (i.e. wars, pestilences, etc.) can be found in the Bible and are nothing more than the prophecy spoken by Jesus being fulfilled. Since we know that all of this is going to occur, we're not afraid nor caught off guard, and because He told us up front this was coming, what did He tells us to do; ***don't be afraid this is not the end.***

Armed with the knowledge that certain things have to come pass takes the proverbial wind out of the enemy's sails and is nothing more than just another one of his tricks to instill fear and terror in us which we know don't come from God. The Bible says that God has not given us "the spirit of fear, but one of power, love and a sound mind." A sound mind means that you are able to think clearly, by that I mean we arm ourselves with the nothing but the Word of God coming out of our mouths when things start happening like the Ebola virus making its way to the USA. What does the Word say about it? The Psalmist wrote that *we are not afraid* of pestilence and that no plague will come near our dwelling or where we live. This is what I believe and confess whenever I get thoughts about all of this nonsense.

The things we can do to protect ourselves in times like this are: 1) Put the Word of God to work. Know what it says, take the Word, confess it, and then stand on it. 2) Wash your hands with soap, warm water or one of those hand sanitizers. Nothing beats keeping germs down like clean hands and then keeping them out of your face.

God has provided everything you need to live a victorious life. It is found in His Word. Just read the book. All the answers to life's questions can be found there.

2 Timothy 1:7   Luke 21:9-11 AMP   Philippians 1:27-28 AMP   Psalms 91

28

Praying For People Who've Done You Wrong

If you've never prayed for someone who's done you wrong, then you are missing an opportunity to receive a blessing from God that is tailored-made just for you. They could be someone close to you. One day the Holy Spirit told me that if I was willing to talk about them and what they did then I ought to be willing to pray for them also. I began praying for the things I wanted to see manifest in my life to be manifested in theirs. I prayed their children would be blessed with good health, their marriage blessed, and there would be nothing but peace between them and their spouse. I prayed everything they put their hand to would prosper supernaturally. Every time I had a thought about them those words came out of my mouth, spoken by faith because I really wanted God to keep them and do for them what He has already done for me and more. The outcome was that I had peace no matter what because I did what the Word says, and I had the subsequent results it promised.

3 John 2 AMP   Psalms 90:16-17 AMP   Philippians 4:6-7

29

Growing In God

Doesn't it seem that after you go through or maybe while you're in the middle of the challenge's life presents that you've experience a growth spurt? As painful as it may be, we are always given these God arranged, God allowed circumstances for our good. I know that for me I have to ask God what is this I'm feeling. I want to put the right label on them and not mask the truth. I've come to learn the difference between anger and disappointment. It might take a moment but whenever I seek Him, He always comes through. God shows me the best way to deal with whatever situation I'm in when I get into His Word. There is both comfort and chastisement in the Word. Our shortcomings are exposed. The course to making minor adjustments to our character can be found in the Word of God. There are times when we just have to go through something while we learn the difference between an enemy attack and self-inflicted wounds. In spite of what Flip Wilson used to say, the devil didn't make you do it! Both ways hurt, but we grow. All of this is nothing but the pruning of the Lord. Pruning is part of our growth process as we gain and lose along the way. The only reason we get the grand opportunity to "enjoy" these experiences is because we are valuable to the Kingdom due to the call God has placed on our life. As you go through this journey remember God only prunes those branches that are bearing fruit so that they may bear more fruit. It won't kill you. It just makes you better for the master's use.

Hebrews 4:12 AMP   Hebrews 12:11 AMP   John 15:2 AMP

30

Sowing Into The Kingdom

I was talking to someone once and we ended up talking about financially giving into the Kingdom. We talked about emotional giving vs. being led by the Spirit. More specifically when a special offering is being taken up and a certain dollar amount is mentioned to give. As we were talking, they said they had a problem with it. I shared with them how I once heard it said that if you don't have the money, don't get into condemnation about it because this doesn't pertain to you. There are specific people in the congregation that God speaks to through the person taking the offering. Usually the amount is a faith amount. By that I mean it's an amount that you better have heard from God because it will stretch your faith. When that type of offering is being taken up and it's a faith amount, you have to hear the voice of God and not get "caught up in the moment." For me, the Spirit will usually prompt me about it before it occurs, so when it does, I'm ready to give. Your faith has to be developed to the point that if you do give in this type of setting you can do it doubt free. You cannot be in faith and in the back of your mind you've got an "if" hanging around (i.e. If this doesn't work out I can go borrow from…) No my friend that is not faith. God doesn't want you to live like that. If your faith is not at that specific level, then give on the level you're at. If you have to go borrow to cover money you gave when you overextended yourself in a special offering, that is not being blessed. His blessings add no sorrow with it. It's moments like this the enemy will use to deceive and turn us against our spiritual leaders, eventually causing a resentment against God thinking He failed to hold up His end of the deal, when in reality you didn't have the faith to begin with for it to work in your life. God takes pleasure in your prosperity and He wants you to be blessed. To be blessed means that you are empowered to have success. We all at some point have been there, and through the course of time and experience have learned the principles of faith by removing all doubt and experience a harvest on the seeds we have sown.

Don't stop giving, just start on your level. As you do, your faith will grow and eventually you'll be giving on a different level. Remember, we don't give to be seen, but we don't mind being seen giving. It's all a trust and heart issue.

2 Corinthians 9:6-8 AMP   Proverbs 10:22 AMP   Psalms 35:27

Deuteronomy 28:8,12

31

The Rhythm Of God

Do you want to experience a sense of calmness and peace in the midst of all that is going on in this world? If so, all you have to do is get in alignment with the rhythm of God. By that I mean trust that God has a plan and purpose for your life, and He is unfolding it little by little because "Father knows best."

God's way of thinking and doing surpasses ours, and it's always in our best interest to defer to Him. I know there are times when I have the urge to take hold of the reins and want to "drive" only to wind up having or almost causing a wreck by jumping out in front of Him and moving before it's time. When you glance back over your life or as my grandfather used to say, "Hindsight is 20/20 vision" and you can see how you got to where you are. You don't have to try and swim upstream like a spawning salmon, stop resisting and get into His rhythm. There is always a rhythm to what God is doing.

The best way to get in rhythm with God is by spending time with Him in prayer and His Word. Some might say that it doesn't take all of that, and to that I ask: aren't you tired of feeling discombobulated or like the old saying "a day late and a dollar short?" You're only like that because you choose to and if you get into the rhythm of what God is doing and how He does it, all of that will fall by the wayside.

Being out of sync makes you look like a soldier out of step with the rest of the troops during the parade. Start today right where you are. Yesterday is gone and tomorrow hasn't arrived. Get in rhythm with God today, because it really is the best way.

Ephesians 1:11 AMP   Jeremiah 29:11   Isaiah 55:8-9

November

1

The Favor Of God

In the story of Joseph, God prospered him as a result of what his brothers had done to him. God's Favor brought him to be second in command in all of Egypt and an ultimate blessing to his father and brothers.

When God is working in your life people can see it. God's work brings favor and attacks. Opportunities arise and doors will open. When they do, walk in it. You'll get attacked. In your attack you'll receive favor from people because God is getting things through you. It's all part of the plan. What you have to do is remain confident that the work, which God began in you, will be completed. Just like Joseph, in the end you will openly bless those who were against you. It'll be right there in their face.

God has a purpose and the enemy is attempting to derail your purpose. The enemy will always use something or someone close to you. It's the same old tricks just repackaged to look different. He only has five plays in his book to use. They are: 1) persecution, 2) affliction for the Word's sake, 3) the cares of this world, 4) the deceitfulness of riches, and 5) the lust of other things which will come to choke the Word and cause it be unfruitful.

Let's push past negative feelings and anything that doesn't line up with God's Word. It's going to all work out, even if we can't see it right now, because our trust is in Him and His Word.

Genesis 39:1-4 AMP   Philippians 1:6 AMP   Genesis 45:1-7 AMP

Mark 4:16-19 AMP

2

Unanswered Prayer - Walking In Love

Are your prayers going unanswered? Have you've met all the "conditions" yet no manifestation? Are you beginning to wonder why? My question to you is how's your love walk? Paul tells us "faith works by love." We can't expect to receive anything from God if we are walking around hateful and embroiled in strife with people. Do you really treat others the way you want to be treated or do you set people straight at any cost under the guise of "speaking the truth in love?" Jesus tells us that we are commanded to love. This means all of the characteristics of love described in 1 Corinthians 13 were given to us so that we could govern ourselves accordingly.

I will be the first to tell you that it's not easy. After trying and failing, I have begun to get it right most of the time. One of the main things I've learned is to keep my mouth shut when every part of me wants to scream the opposite of how love is required to act. When I hold my peace, I don't have to go back and apologize for something that I shouldn't have said in the first place. Words hurt. They can't be taken back just like you can't put spilled milk back into the bottle.

Do a self-check and see if your love walk is intact. The Holy Spirit will reveal what needs to be corrected. Follow His lead.

Your love is going to be challenged. It inevitably happens every time we start talking about love. This is one of those receiving answers before the test days. I know you'll pass!

Galatians 5:6 AMP   Matthew 22:37-40   1 Corinthians 13:4-8 AMP

3

The Pages Of Life Keep Turning

While driving home one day I was quietly reflecting on my life. Looking at how God has blessed me in spite of my flaws and my basic humanness. I rest comfortably in the knowledge that He loves me. Only His love for me kept me when certain pages of my life turned, and I didn't know any better. We all have those times when we can look back and see the hand of God during various time in our lives, especially when we wanted to go one way and were prevented from going there. I know from personal experience, there were a couple of times when I found out down the road had I gone through with it, death was waiting. All I can say is God kept me from dangers I didn't see and for that I'm grateful. As we go day by day, the pages of life keep on turning. It's going to happen. There is nothing that we can do to prevent it. It's by design and for a purpose. When the pages turn sometimes, we know ahead of time from the Holy Spirit something's coming. Then there are times where the pages turn will catch us seemingly by surprise. When they do, we can either embrace or mourn it. The choice is ours. Choose the thing or the way that best represents the life Christ gave Himself for.

Today choose life and rest in God's love!

Deuteronomy 30:19-20 AMP   Proverbs 3:3-6   John 16:13 AMP

4

The Capacity To Receive

God has already given us everything that we'll ever need to be successful in this life. All we have to do is receive it. If I placed a one-hundred-dollar bill on the table and told you that it was yours come and get it. If you received what I said and believed it to be true, you would then act on it by going over and picking it up. The prior sentence was nothing more than a demonstration of faith. Faith is acting on what you believe and if you believe something then you'll act accordingly to receive it. When it comes to the Word of God, it's just as simple as believing what's written is true and then acting on it to receive.

It takes the same amount of faith that you used when you accepted Christ as your Savior, to get healed from sickness, delivered from oppression, and to realize prosperity in every area of your life. All you have to do is receive it. The Bible tells us to receive the engrafted Word of God with meekness. Webster's1828 defines meekness as resignation, submission to the divine will, without murmuring or peevishness. If we can accept and submit to the Word of God, we then place ourselves in position to receive all it says we can. In order to know what the Bible says we can have, we have to spend time in it. It's going to require developing an intimate relationship with our Bible to get the full benefits from what God has written.

Pastor Sheryl Brady once said, and I have found it to be true in my life that "The Word is a stabilizing force that causes me not to be shaken and it keeps me anchored."

2 Peter 1:3 AMP   Mark 11:24 AMP   James 1:21

5

Letting God Settle The Score

What do we do when people purposefully treat us wrong? Our immediate reaction is to retaliate in some way, but it just doesn't feel right on the inside. As should be our custom let's go to the Word of God for some clarity and direction.

When we look in the Book of Romans, the Apostle Paul admonishes us not to go "tit for tat" with those who do us wrong, but rather take the high road, looking for the good that is in them while we try to be at peace with everybody. Let me be the first to say that's a tall order. Paul goes on further to tell us that when it comes to paying back those who have wronged us God said, "vengeance is mine I will repay." We don't have to concern ourselves with trying to "get back" at people who either mistreat or take advantage of us. Paul could always be found taking the "love route" no matter what the situation or circumstance. He urges us to do the same. When you think of how much God loves you and that He forgave you for the things you have yet to do wrong, how can we with a clear conscious, continue striving to get even or settle the score with someone who has wronged us? Getting to the point where you can do this does take work. If you're diligent about it you'll get there.

There's no greater feeling than when you achieve this milestone in your walk with Christ and you let God settle the score.

Romans 12:17-19 MSG   Deuteronomy: 32:35 NLT   Hebrews 10:15-17 AMP

6

Prayer

I remember a time when I ran across a couple of instances where people were talking about prayer and confessions. The conversation touched on how we, as believers, don't hang in there very long when it comes to interceding for others. We start out good but then lose our fervency somewhere along the way. If we want our prayers to "avail much" then we have to develop "some stick-to-itness" and stay engaged until the Holy Spirit says Stop. It might be that He leads you to spend a certain amount of time one day in prayer or whenever a person comes across your mind you stop and pray for them. We have to keep praying until we get the release.

When it comes to making our confessions, they should be a daily practice. Don't stop just because you feel better or have received a breakthrough. Placing them in your Bible is a good practice because they'll be there when you read your Bible daily.

Keeping the lines of communication open between God and us requires that we pray without ceasing and make our confessions daily.

Hang in there. Don't stop praying until you get the desired results.

James 5:16   Ephesians 6:18 AMP   1Thessalonians 5:16-18 AMP

7

Sticking To The Plan

We talk a lot about how God has a plan for all of us. If we're to execute His plan successfully then we have to stay close to Him. By that I mean we have to live a holy, by the Word of God kind of life. That's a life lived by what we've learned from the Word of God. It's not based on how we feel or what is the most politically correct stance for the day. Living holy brings favor under adverse circumstances, as long as you don't compromise your core values (i.e. who you are in Christ).

Joseph didn't violate his core and sin against God by sleeping with his master's wife. His refusal landed him to become unjustly imprisoned. While there he was promoted once again to a position of authority. One thing we can glean from Joseph is when the anointing is on your life, you not only find favor with those in authority, but you become an attraction to your enemy. He takes notice, with attempts to thwart your destiny.

God's way of doing things is found in His Word. We should continually seek it. There is a process to what He does and nothing that we go through is a wasted experience. There are always lessons to be learned. We might not fully understand or use what we've learned immediately after the lesson but through the course of time it will be revealed. One day you'll be dealing with something and then a "light" comes on inside of you, that will connect the dots from that past experience to todays.

Joseph found favor in the middle of every challenge and test he had. He not only found favor he prospered. Most of us probably would've been so despondent, that we couldn't foresee any good coming out of it. This was all part of the process God allowed to bring him into the king's presence, find favor with the king, become second in command throughout the land, reunited with his family and in the time of famine in the land was able to provide for his family.

God is faithful. He won't allow us to go through anything that we can't handle together with Him. There is a purpose to the process He has you in right now. Stay in His Word, watch what you say, and continue to walk in love towards everyone. Just watch and see how it's all going to work out in the end.

Genesis 39:19-23   Proverbs 3:3-4 AMP   Genesis 41:39-43 AMP

Romans 8:28

8

Choices

Where you are in life right now is a direct result of the choices you've made. When you really think about it, we all make choices throughout the day, basically on autopilot. The majority of them we don't even give a second thought because we're on automatic. You can train or re-train your spirit to help you make better choices.

When you put the Word of God into your life on a consistent basis, you are more apt to make choices and decisions that are in line with the Word or as the church world says you'll be "walking in the spirit and not the flesh." Walking in the spirit or the flesh is nothing more than a mindset that is either in line with the Word of God or it isn't. When you're in the spirit there is a certain amount of freedom that comes along with it.

If you don't like what you're getting out of life today, then start by putting something better in. There is no better place to start than with the Word of God. When you prayerfully read the Word of God and speak it out loud it goes in and feeds your spirit man. As your spirit is continually being fed, you'll begin to notice subtle changes, which will lead to better choices and subsequently better results that are based on the Word of God.

Today take the Word in and watch the Word come alive in every area of your life!

Romans 8:1-8 MSG   Hebrews 4:12 AMP

9

It's A Fixed Fight

Sometimes when I make a mistake by doing or saying something I shouldn't have, I have feelings of guilt and shame. I might not have hurt anyone, but within myself I know I could've made a better choice. When I've had enough of feeling bad, I go to the Word and confess another one of my favorite-committed to memory Scriptures: *"There is therefore now no condemnation to them which are in Christ Jesus, who walk not after the flesh but after the spirit."* Eventually whatever I was feeling subsides and I am back on solid ground emotionally.

The enemy will attempt to use negative emotions against us if we allow it. Because we are now on the winning side, we don't have to tolerate that nonsense anymore. From time to time we all are subject to these attacks. When they come, they don't last long because we've been spending quality time with the Father. God's Word is the perfect antidote for dealing with negative feelings. It might take us a minute to get our bearings but once we do look out Mr. Devil because we're coming back fighting "with the Sword of the Spirit, which is the Word of God." When we put the Word in our mouth and speak it by faith, the fight is on, and the thing that is so remarkable about this fight is that it's a fixed fight. I read the back of the book where it says that the devil is defeated, and Christ has already secured our victory.

Stop feeling bad about past mistakes. Take out your sword and start wielding it like the weapon that it is. Fight back. Remember, it's a fixed fight. You've already won!

Romans 8:1-4   Ephesians 6:17 AMP   Revelation 20:7-10 AMP

10

Living By Faith

At certain times during this faith walk with God we will be so far out there, we can't see what we desire coming to pass nor can we successfully do anything without Him. Yet we're out there, believing God like never before, and when you eventually look back you see that you made it this far so you keep on going. At different times in my life, like now, this is how I feel. When I reach a new level of faith in God the growing doesn't stop. I have to keep using my faith to make it through this place where He now has me.

One of the things that I have to be on guard of is allowing fearful thoughts to come creeping in. When they show up, I immediately open my mouth and speak against them. I don't have time to let the enemy play mental gymnastics and get me all twisted up. Fear is nothing but faith in believing the lies of your enemy. If you want to exercise your faith correctly then put it in God and His Word where it has a much better payoff. This means you have to constantly renew your mind in and with the Word of God. By faith speak God's Word into your life. Faith and belief are two sides of the same coin. Faith is acting on what you believe.

What it really all boils down to is we speak what we believe and act accordingly. If you're not pleased with the results that you have right now, then change your speech. The Bible tells us that we can have what we say if we don't doubt. Good or bad where you are right now is a reflection of your beliefs. Does your life mirror the Word of God or the words of your enemy?

Mark 11:23   Romans 12:2 AMP   2 Corinthians 5:7 AMP

Hebrews 11:1 AMP

11

Law vs. Grace

I have come to a deeper understanding and revelation of what grace is. The things I'm about to share with you today are going to challenge your "religious thinking." Let me start this off by saying I am a tither and will tithe until the day I die. When I first started going to church, I was taught if I didn't tithe then I would be cursed, so I gave to prevent from being cursed. Who wouldn't? No one in his or her right mind wants to be cursed, so I did it. It was said that it's better to have a "blessed 90 than a cursed 100." The Book of Malachi clearly states that people who don't tithe and give offerings are cursed. That's what the law says. Our teachers were going off of the revelation they had at the time. When I read that Christ has redeemed me from the curse of the law, and how the law of the spirit of life in Christ Jesus has made me free from the law of sin and death, then being cursed because I don't follow an Old Testament law is void. No more yearly sacrifices are necessary to cover our sins. Christ's shed blood remitted them once and for all. Remitted means to pardon, forgive, relinquishment of payment.

I am a tither and will continue to tithe and teach my children to do the same because it proves to us that we trust God. If I trust God in the area of finances, then I can trust Him in every other area of my life. I don't tithe out of fear of something bad happening to me. The Bible says that God loves a cheerful giver. I can't give cheerfully if the threat of something bad happening if I don't is hanging in the balance. The two don't mix.

Christ has redeemed us from the curse of the law. Grace took its place. Once we accepted Christ as our Savior we can now walk in the righteousness of the law because grace has made it available. We are now the righteousness of God in Christ Jesus. We are no longer under the threat of the law.

Galatians 3:13-14 AMP   Romans 8:1-4 AMP   Malachi 3:8-9 AMP

2 Corinthians9:7-8 AMP

12

There Is A Shift About To Take Place

Have you been feeling a little unsettled in your spirit lately? If so, then it's nothing but your advance notification system alerting you of a shift that's about to take place. It's going to happen in the spirit realm before it manifests in the natural. That's why you feel like this, so get ready. Everything is going to be okay. This is just your warning system in action.

The Holy Spirit is our guide and He always communicates with us Spirit to spirit. What we have to do is pray, continue to seek God, go to His Word, watch what we say and how we treat people. At first, we don't understand why we feel like we do so we pray in our heavenly language and keep confessing the Word. This will keep us in faith and not fear, regardless of what's happening emotionally with you.

Are you experiencing feelings of loss for no reason at all? It could be a pruning is about to take place in your life. Think of pruning as the process of shaving off useless material. Pruning always removes lack, provides abundance and helps more than it harms. There are times when a bad situation is nothing more than pruning and you might not see it until you get further down the road.

No matter what your feelings might be at this moment, you have to trust God through the process. He's giving you a "heads up" so stay in His Word, because His Word won't change, but your feelings will change just as quickly as the weather in Texas.

John 16:13 AMP   Romans 8:26-28 AMP   John 15:1-5 AMP

13

I Will Not Be Defeated

Have you noticed how it seems like you are always in a transition of some sort? My wife and I were talking about this and how the only permanent thing in life is change. We have all the tools necessary to win, and they are found in God's Word. His promises are the only sure thing that we have in this ever-changing world and God's Word will never change.

With a lot on our plates these days, we can easily get wrapped up being discouraged or disappointed. If we're not careful those feelings will defeat us. We can't afford to allow them that much control in our life. We were born to win. God has fixed this day for you to win. Everything He promised you is waiting for you to receive it. They can only be accessed by faith. If you want to win consistently here are the keys you'll need: renew your mind in the Word of God and watch what you say. You have to constantly spend time in the Word of God. When it comes to this you can't hit or miss. You have to be consistent because your enemy won't miss with his weapons. The Bible tells us that we can have what we say and when the heat is on you have to watch what you say. If you don't want something to show up in your life, then don't say it. My brother always says, "If God didn't write it, I'm not saying it." Our words have creative power just like God's because you were created in His image. He created the world by the words He spoke. You create your world by the words you speak.

You're a world over-comer because of what Christ did on the cross. Everything you'll ever need He has already provided and put it in the budget for your life. If you want it then say so.

Ephesians 4:23 AMP   Mark 11:22-24   2 Peter 1:3-4 AMP

14

Road Blocks

One day as I was reading a devotional, part of it talked about roadblocks in our paths and how if we focus on the obstacles or if we look for a way to go around it, we will probably go off course. At the same time if we just focus on God, the obstacle will be behind us and we won't even know how we passed through it.

That really hit home with me. As I began to meditate on this, I thought about how we sometimes complain about this or that (the roadblocks), and in doing so they do not go away. If nothing else the roadblocks appear bigger than they are. If we're not careful, our grumbling and complaining intensifies while the obstacle is still there. One thing I learned about complaining is that it shows that I don't like where God has me at this point or juncture of my life.

God wasn't pleased when the children of Israel murmured in the wilderness. Since He never changes it stands to reason that He won't be pleased when we murmur or complain. I have to remember that God does not cause or make misfortune or calamity. It's called life! If it's here, He allowed it. Whatever it is, God has already given us the grace to get through it, and ten times out of ten it's not about us but to help someone else.

Whatever the obstacles are that you might be facing, remember complaining is not going to make it any better; more often than not things seem to get worse. If you want things to get better, speak words of faith over your obstacles. When you do, God is magnified, and problems get smaller or go away. Keep your focus on Him. You'll get through it and then be able to share the experience with someone else. That's when you'll know that it was all worth it.

Psalms 34:19   Number 14:26-27   2 Corinthians 1:3-4 AMP

15

How To Be Free From Resentments

Webster's 1828 defines resentment as the excitement of passion which proceeds from a sense of wrong offered to ourselves, or to those connected with us; anger. In laymen terms, resentment is hanging on to a suffered wrong that someone has done to you.

There is an old saying that fits this, "You can't let people live rent free inside of your head." While you're hanging on to whatever it is that might have transpired, trust me when I say that person has gone on living their life not giving you or whatever happened one iota of thought.

Any time you have resentment against someone simply try this for a couple of weeks, it's the best way I've found to be free from resentment. Pray for them, and when you do, ask God to manifest in their life those things you want to see Him do in yours. Pray for their family, finances, health, etc. It's not going to be easy at first but the more you do it the easier it gets. Give it a try I promise you it works.

Healing and restoration are two things that we receive from God on a consistent basis. What we send into the lives of others will surely return back into ours. That's why we have to be ever mindful of how we treat people and pray for those who do us wrong. There are people praying for us who we don't know about just as we are praying for others. It's the law of sowing and reaping. It's still in operation.

James 5:16 AMP   Luke 6:27-28 AMP   Galatians 6:7-9 NLT

16

God, I Trust You

Do you really trust God? I pose this question because I find myself increasingly leaning on God in different areas of my life more and more each day. As I grow, it seems like more things, people, and situations around me go awry, causing me to pause and say, "God, I trust you." I have increased rehearsing past victories, telling myself, "If He did it before, He'll do it again."

We can't afford to let the things of this world negatively impact us emotionally or physically, without giving the enemy some push back. We do that by going to the Word to see what it says and then speak it. When it comes to trusting God, the Psalmist tells us to basically "try the Lord" because the man that trusts in Him is blessed (happy, fortunate, to be envied). If we trust in the Lord and do good, then everything is going to be all right. That's why we have to trust God with everything and stop trying to figure things out on our own.

Learning how to trust God takes time and practice, but you can achieve it if you'll be diligent. For me, it came in stages after trying and failing a few times. I eventually put the Word to full use and got the desired results. You can too. Go for it and let God work out the details.

Psalm 34:8 AMP   Psalm 37:3   Proverbs 3:5-6

17

Chewing The Cud

One morning in my prayer time I started thinking about cows and how they chew the cud. As they graze in the fields they instinctively know when to swallow and when to spit out the sticks. I was telling a young guy at work about this and how it relates to life. He didn't believe cows did that. Being here in Texas one of my coworkers had recently recovered from a bull stepping on his foot, so we went over to him and I asked him what does "chewing the cud" mean. He explained it and what he said next was priceless. He said, "It's almost like life; you have to know when to swallow and when to spit out the sticks," I turned to him and said, "see."

In this season of life, make no mistake about it, things can get challenging. When they do, our relationship with the Holy Spirit is paramount to our survival. We have to pay attention to that still small voice. The voice that tells you to take a different way to work and you ignore it because it's a little out of the way. You get stuck in traffic and have to sit there telling yourself, "I should have listened to my first mind." Well that was God trying to help you out.

So, as you graze in the fields of life keep this in mind: *Just as a cow chews the cud, the Holy Spirit will instinctively tell you when to swallow and when to spit out the sticks as you travel along your journey.*

John 14:26 AMP   1 Kings 19:9-12 AMP   Proverbs 4:5-7 AMP

18

What Matters Most

Our Senior Pastor closed out our Harvest Week Revival one year and the title of his message was "What Matters Most." With this being the beginning of the Christmas shopping season, I began to look at what value people place on things that to me personally aren't that important.

Black Friday has been moved up a day and been renamed brown Thursday and retail stores are having pre black Friday sales. I can't see myself pitching a tent outside in the cold on Monday, to be the first one in the store Thursday night to catch a sale. What could be that important? The time spent waiting four days outside in the Texas cold to save some money on an object or thing that will be outdated in a few months could be better spent doing something more productive. All of this raises a couple of questions I asked myself: How important is God to you? Am I willing to put forth the same type of energy in my relationship with the Father that I talked about above?

You can tell what's important to people by how much energy and effort they put into something. What do you give your time and money to? When the heat of the battle intensifies have you given ample time to the Word so that you can recall it without having your Bible handy? Jesus told us to seek God's Kingdom first and everything else will be given to us. If you make that your priority, the things that used to bother you will dissipate. When given first place, God's Word will keep your mind renewed. As your faith grows so does your confidence. When you pray you get results.

Remember, it's not a waste of time to spend time in the Word of God. It sure beats sleeping outside in the cold for four days trying to catch a sale!

Matthew 6:33 AMP   Ephesians 4:23 AMP   1 John 5:14-15

19

Keep Moving

Sometimes life can deal a blow so devastating that if we're not careful it will keep us stuck right there in the past. There's an old saying that "a rolling stone gathers no moss."

We have to be the same way when certain life events occur. It could be a divorce, a close friend or family member betrayed you or maybe a downright injustice. Whatever it might be, it's time to let it go and keep moving.

How long will you allow yourself to lament over something in the past while there is so much living to be done today? God has prepared the good life for you. It's right up ahead.

All you have to do is get over this hurdle and step into all He has waiting for you. You can't drive your car down the road while looking in the rear-view mirror. The only time we should ever look back is to rehearse past victories or to see just how far we've come.

If we're to ever get over what happened to us in the past, it's going to require some forgiveness. Forgiving someone is not a feeling but a decision. You have to decide whether or not you want to be free from the past and forgive them. When it comes to forgiveness, sometimes the hardest people we have to forgive is ourselves, but it's achievable. You just have to work at it. Jesus said that our forgiveness from the Father is directly tied to the forgiveness we extend to others. When we're praying, if there are past issues and conflicts with our brother or sister then we need to resolve them and move on.

The antidote is love. Our faith can only work by love. Given the shape that the rest of the world is in these days, all it takes is for us to begin looking at everyone through the eyes of love and learn how to forgive. That's when the love God has for others can truly be expressed through us.

Philippians 3:13-14   Ephesians 2:10 AMP   Mark 11:25-26 AMP   Galatians 5:6

PS. There will be a love test today

20

Half Full Or Half Empty?

How much is in your glass? It's the same amount either half full or empty; it's all about your perspective. How do you see the glass or more importantly how do you see yourself? You're not the same person that you used to be. The old man is dead, and you have put on the new man, which is created in God's image and nature of righteousness and true holiness. We are constantly being transformed or changed on the inside where our spirit man lives. That's why things that the old you used to enjoy you don't desire anymore.

To maintain the proper perspective, we have to see things in life through the lens of God's Word, where there's always hope. God's Word allows us to see the good in everyone and everything no matter what the situation or outcome might be. It's the fuel that keeps you going, changes your demeanor, determines how you carry yourself, and how those around you perceive you.

When you spend time in the Word of God it changes you from the inside out. Our whole Christian walk is an inside job.

As you go through your day today look for the good around you and ask yourself is my glass half full or half empty? If your perception needs to be adjusted, then go to the Word of God. Let it change how you see the glass.

Ephesians 4:22-24 AMP   Colossians 3:9-11 AMP   Hebrews 4:12 AMP

21

Valiant Fighter

Nicola is now with Jesus @1:06. That was the message I received from my cousin Derrick early one Sunday morning about his sister Nicola. She, the only granddaughter left out of the thirteen grand kids, slipped away. She wasn't the first one of us to die. One died from Sudden Infant Death Syndrome, another committed suicide, one from AIDS, another died from injuries suffered in a motor vehicle accident and now cancer. Nicola fought a valiant fight and was tired.

Death is defined as the point where the spirit separates from the body. Nicola went to sleep on this side and woke up totally healed on the other side. That's the truth, not a fact. I can boldly say that because she accepted Jesus as her Savior. When I heard on Friday morning that she went back in and that this might be the end, I wondered about her salvation. The Lord told me Saturday morning that she was safe, and it's going to be all right. I talked with my cousin Derrick that Saturday afternoon and he told me he led her to Christ awhile back. This was confirmation.

So why does this feel so goofy and numb? I'm not sad because her battle is over but missing her juxtaposed against the joyful feeling of knowing where she is and who she's with, all while trying not to be a hater because to be absent from the body is to be in the presence of the Lord feels weird. You know how you have that inner feeling of invincibility as if you'll live forever? Well guess what, you will! Your spirit man goes on living when you give up the earth suit. The only thing I caution you about is make sure you've got the correct new address: Heaven. Don't know for sure? Pray this simple prayer: "Dear Lord Jesus come into my heart and my life, forgive me for the wrong I've done and save me now. I confess with my mouth and believe in my heart that God raised you from the dead and I am saved." The Bible says whoever calls on the name of the Lord shall be saved. Now you're saved. Go tell somebody. That's the best decision you'll ever make. The angels are rejoicing while the demons lament over losing another one!

Perhaps you're already saved, and the Lord has placed someone across your path that you can share this good news with and lead him or her to Christ. Go for it and don't be afraid of being rejected. I learned that they wouldn't be rejecting you; they'll be rejecting Him! Contrary to popular belief, there won't be a party going on in hades. It's a lie! It's all going down at the Lord's house up in Heaven.

We all have the same appointment as Nicola, she not as much today as yesterday, but every now and then a remnant will resurface and I have to remember all that God has forgiven me of and if I want it then I have to give it, because the exact way I give it out will be the way it comes back to me.

James 2:26   2 Corinthians 5:6-8 AMP   Romans 10:9-13 NKJV

22

Angels Are Our Servants

There is a ministry that angels have. It's to serve or minister to those of us who are heirs of salvation. Some people think that angels are better than us, but according to Scripture they are sent as I mentioned above, to minister to us.

There are various ways angels serve us. One is being God's special messenger. Both Mary and Daniel had the angel Gabriel bring them messages. To Mary he was sent to announce the birth of Christ. For Daniel he appeared answering his prayer to God, bringing understanding to Daniel and revelation of a vision. Daniel also had Michael who was his guardian angel for protection that fought spiritual battles in the heavenlies. Angels are known to take on the appearances of man and are still in operation today. We're told to be careful how we treat people because they could be angels. Have you ever been blessed by someone you didn't know and haven't seen since? Could they have been an angel sent to serve your needs for that specific purpose?

You've got help and when you speak the Word of God, angels are waiting on the sidelines to hear it so they can go to work. Have you given your angels their assignment today? Are they sitting there waiting to dust off their Nikes and go to work? God has given us everything that we'll need to be successful in this life. When you factor in the Word of God, the Blood of Jesus, guidance of the Holy Spirit and the ministry of angels, there is no way you can lose.

Hebrews 1:13-14 AMP   Luke 1:26-31 AMP   Psalms 103:20

Hebrews 13:1-2 AMP

23

How To Fight Back

When the enemy kicks up his heels and starts a ruckus in your life, there's only one way to deal with him. It's not fighting as we understand it to be. The Bible tells us to submit to God. In doing so we'll resist the devil and he'll flee. A good definition of resist is: to stand firm against, refuse to give in; this is my favorite one: say "no."

If we're submitted to God, then it will be evident with the words coming from our mouth. We were created in the image of God which means that we are just like Him, another speaking spirit. We have the same creative power coming out of our mouth with our words just like God when He spoke this world and everything in it into existence. When the attacks come, we immediately take authority over the situation by speaking Gods Word in faith and not in fear. It's possible for us to speak words of faith out of fear thinking, "What might happen." If we spend time daily in the Word, then we know that the Word will work when we speak it.

Speaking the Word (making confessions) when things are going well is a sure-fire way to build yourself up. When the attack comes, you don't even give it a second thought because God's Word just comes rolling off your tongue into the atmosphere creating your desired results. I caution you not to get discouraged if the results don't manifest themselves immediately. Stand your ground. Keep speaking the Word it will come to pass. Our whole attitude should be as if it's already here. "Due season" or our time of manifestation is not if but when. You might experience some turbulence but if you keep your confessions right, and walk in love towards all those around you, the manifestation of your desires from God's Word are right around the corner.

James 4:7 AMP   Romans 10:17   Galatians 6:9 AMP

24

You're In A Faith Fight

In case you hadn't noticed, just because you got saved, life's problems didn't go away. On the contrary, things might have intensified! It's all prophecy being fulfilled. Jesus told us that these things would happen, but there is peace to be found in Him. He tells us be of good cheer because He overcame all of it for us.

The enemy doesn't want you to have anything good to say about God. He will attempt to fill you with fear, doubt and anxiety about your situation. I'm here to tell you: stay in faith. When the enemy brings his little bag of tricks into your life there are three things to always keep in mind. The first is watching what you say. When it looks like things are heading in the wrong direction, don't let your mouth confirm it. We speak the Word instead of how things appear. The second is to use the name of Jesus intentionally and not flippantly, casually or in vain. I've learned how to properly use the name of Jesus and when I do, I want it to do something for me. Jesus said to ask for anything in His name and He would do it, that the Father may be glorified in the Son. Last and most importantly, walk in love. This is the curtain rod that everything hangs on and is the fuel that keeps your faith working.

When you're standing in faith there are times when it gets tight. If you hang in there, use the tools I just gave you and meditate on them, you'll do like Paul told Timothy "Go and fight the good fight of faith." Remember a good fight is one that you win. The greater the battle, the closer you are to your breakthrough.

John 16:33 AMP   John 14:12-14 AMP   Galatians 5:6   1 Timothy 6:12 AMP

25

Running Your Own Race

We all have an individual plan or race for our life that has been designed and pre-arranged by God. It's our responsibility to discover what the will of God is for our life and carry it out.

The writer of Hebrews tells us that it will involve some challenges along the way but to run it with patience. As we journey through our course, one of the main things we have to keep in mind is living a life that's pleasing to God; even when we're in the middle of conflicting circumstances. We have to keep looking forward and walk in love. It's a commandment.

Faith working in our life is contingent on love. It's not easy but it's doable. All we have to do is look to Jesus as He was on His way to the cross. There is no greater example of love in action than at that point in His life. If we adopt His mind-set, which was one of pleasing the Father, no matter what life throws at us, God will give us the grace to walk through it a day at a time.

As you go through your day today know that your course has been ordained of God and you're going to make it. You can finish and finish strong. At the end of the day, you'll have a testimony like Paul told Timothy, "I have fought a good fight, finished my course and kept the faith."

Hebrews 12:1-2 AMP   Matthew 22:37-40   Philippians 2:5-8 AMP

2 Timothy 4:6-7 AMP

26

New Levels In God

Hitting new levels in God means that you had to lose some of the "old" you. It could almost be compared to how a snake sheds its skin. It's called molting. Snakes usually start at the head and begin rubbing against a hard surface like a rock until their entire old skin is removed. While God is in the process of conforming us into the image of his Son, one could readily identify with the molting process. We take off the old man and put on the new one.

Once you hit that new level, all of your prior experiences both good and bad make it worthwhile. Getting a new revelation from familiar Scriptures is an awe-inspiring moment that stays with you like a good meal from your favorite restaurant. When the Holy Spirit starts challenging you to step out in boldness and you do, it fills you with joy.

This is the next level. We have only begun to scratch the surface of what God wants to show and do through us.

Romans 8:29   Ephesians 4:22-24 AMP   1 John 1:3-4

27

Stepping Out In Faith

As you continue to grow in the things of God, your level of faith gets challenged. Sometimes God will place a tremendous opportunity across your path. One that seems virtually impossible given where you're at right now and you don't see how you can do it by yourself, but there is something on the inside of you pushing you. That gentle push is God telling you that if you could do it alone you wouldn't need faith. This is what the answer to your prayers and all of your confessions look like. It feels real uncomfortable. When this occurs, the only thing I know to do is stay in the Word of God. Make sure that what's coming out of my mouth is in direct alignment with His Word. Don't let anything make you say something contrary to what you believe or want to see manifest in your life. All kinds of confusion will come up but you have to keep the Word of God before your eyes and coming out of your mouth. That's why reading the Word of God and making daily confessions is so important. It keeps your mind renewed amidst the attempts to distract and discourage.

Today, acknowledge that gentle push you're feeling is from the Holy Spirit. He's only doing what Jesus said He would in guiding and showing us things to come. You might not be able to see it right now, but this is all working for your good. It's in His plan. Just roll with it!

Ephesians 4:23 AMP   John 16:13   Romans 8:28 AMP   Jeremiah 29:11-13 AMP

28

Taking Giant Steps

One day as I was reading my devotional, it talked about the difference between baby steps and giant steps. Baby steps might be simple for us, but giant steps demand a different level of trust and faith. This started me to thinking about how we're supposed to be continually growing in the things of God.

When we first began this journey, we were like babes who had to crawl before we could walk. Now that we have learned to walk and are running this race, we're experiencing new levels of spirituality. By that I mean we are receiving new revelations and manifestations in and from the Word of God. Just because we have achieved a new level doesn't mean that we stop doing the things that got us here. Rather, we are now required to do more. Spending more time in the Word and prayer is a sacrifice, but there's a payoff. I've heard it said that sacrifice puts a demand on the supernatural. It's as if God is provoked by our sacrifices causing Him to release His super on our natural.

When we forgo the natural things that we like for the things of God, it will bring increase into our lives. An increase in the revelation received from God's Word is something you'll gain. Scriptures that you're familiar with all of a sudden will take on new meanings. Your sensitivity to the Holy Spirit will be enhanced as you faithfully pay greater attention to that still small voice guiding you safely through the uncharted waters you now find yourself in.

Now that the steps you're taking are giant ones, keep moving forward, and don't stop growing. You've been given much, and it requires much. God knew from the foundation of the world that you could handle it and that's why you're here today!

Ephesians 4:14-15 AMP   Romans 12:1-2 AMP   1Kings 19:12   Luke 12:48

29

Shifting Your Focus

What's taking up most of your time these days? Maybe it's time to now cut some things or people out of your life to make room for other things; namely the Word of God.

With the proliferation of smart phones and the subsequent attention given to the various social media outlets, which I call time stealers, you wonder where your time has gone. It's time to put the phone down, proclaim a fast from social media and other things that easily distract us away from what God has called us to do.

Change is required for this next level if we're to go forward and continue growing in every area of our life. One thing I learned along the way about change is that it doesn't hurt to let things go. It only hurts when we hold on to whatever or whoever it is that we should let go. We can't drag that old stuff into where we're going. It might have been useful at one point but it has outlived its usefulness and it's time to let it go. God is doing a new thing in us. We have to let the Word of God apprehend and seize everything in us that's not in alignment with His purposes for our life.

You get more out of something when you put more into it. If your desire is to have a greater manifestation of the Word in your life, then give yourself over to it. Search the Word. Meditate on it day and night. Be diligent about making whatever adjustments have to be made and let the Word consume you. Shift your focus back to where it needs to be, on God's Word and reaching the lost. At the end of the day it's really all about leading others to Christ and nothing else.

Hebrews 12:1 AMP   Isaiah 43:18-19   Philippians 3:12-14 AMP   Psalms 1:1-3

30

Spiritual Maintenance

Maintaining our relationship with Christ is predicated on us taking the time daily to be in His presence. That means we have to consistently set aside time daily for prayer, reading the Bible and then giving voice to His Word. All of these steps are the foundation to our walk with Him.

When we pray, we begin a dialogue not a monologue with God. It's a two-way street, where both parties act as a transmitter and receiver. God in the person of the Holy Spirit is always speaking to us. He speaks through the Word. As you read, a thought gets quickened to you, answers or wisdom is given that pertains to a specific situation. God speaks in that still small voice. The one that tells you not to go that way and you go anyway. Confessing His Word or giving voice to it, not only allows angels and the Holy Spirit to go and begin to bring into manifestation that Word which you have spoken by faith, but it also increases your faith. When your spirit man hears the Word of God spoken out of your mouth, a deposit is made. When the time is right the Holy Spirit will remind you of that Word. You can then withdraw it and have it to use at the right time. All of this is a direct result of your investment in maintaining your relationship with Christ.

When you do you your part God will do His. You first have to give Him something to work with and which comes from the effort you put forth in the daily upkeep of your spiritual life.

1 Kings 19:12   Psalms 103:20 AMP   Mark 11:23-24

December

1

Distractions

The Bible tells us not to be ignorant of Satan's devices so that he won't get an advantage over us. While in this stage of our development it seems to me that the Word of God is telling us not to get distracted and tune in a little quicker to the Spirit of God when distractions come along.

One of the things we can do is ask the Holy Spirit in our Morning Prayer time to help identify when the opportunity to be distracted is coming and what's the best way to handle it. They won't always be glaring like a "major" catastrophe. Most of the time they're more subtle irritants that if not handled prompt and correctly will take us temporarily off course. One thing that I've done is developed a mental checklist that I can run through instantly. There are only two questions on it: How does this fit into what I'm doing? Or Where I'm going? Ten times out of ten it doesn't.

There are times where we have to turn down the volume of noise happening in our life. There can be so many things competing for our attention that we can easily lose sight of the big picture if we're not careful. One of the biggest distracting culprits we have today is the smart phone. It is the main reason you feel like time is flying. It was just the summer and now it's almost Christmas. At the same time we're planning next summer's vacation. Because you can do so much on your phone when you pick it up you go from one thing to another. Every few minutes you're checking it while answering a text or email. It has become such a major part of my life that I forgot my phone at home one day and didn't realize it until I had reached my destination, which was too far for me to "run back home." I felt like something was missing all day.

As you go through your day, pray and ask the Holy Spirit to help you identify the things distracting you, so you can turn down the noise volume in your life.

2 Corinthians 2:10-11 AMP   John 14:26 AMP

2

Facing Your Giants

According to the Word of God, we know that faith removes mountains. Mountains can be sickness or some type of indebtedness, but giants are something entirely different. A giant might be facing issues that you have been avoiding in a relationship or within yourself. How about needing to correct a past mistake and you're fearful of making the approach? Those are the type of giants I've had to face. One thing I've learned is just because I don't or won't deal with it doesn't make it disappear. If anything, it grows bigger in my mind, eventually becoming a Goliath. That's not the way God designed this thing to be. We have to confront our giants just like David, armed with the knowledge that God will not let this giant slay us. We can overcome it, because we trust in Him.

Confronting a giant not only challenges but it also takes us out of our comfort zone. Yet it causes us to grow in God and in different areas of our lives. You soon begin to notice how things that used to bother you don't anymore. You now view things differently and you develop some well-earned wisdom from it.

Someone once helped me face a giant. When I did, they told me, "See how that fire breathing dragon you were afraid of, was nothing more than a wagging tail, with a puff of smoke coming out of it. It wasn't really all that bad now was it"? And you know what it really wasn't. Today, face the giants in your life because you can overcome them.

Mark 11:23   1 Samuel 17:45-51 NLT   1 John 4:4 AMP

3

We Need To Pray

The holidays are a difficult time of the year for those who have lost loved ones. It's even harder if they transitioned earlier this year or passed away recently. People all around us are dealing with some sort of loss. My heart and prayers go out to not only those I know but to the ones who I might not know personally who are in need of some comfort.

When I pray in the spirit, my spirit prays the perfect prayer. There are times as I am praying that God will bring certain people to my consciousness. I understand that they need someone to stand in the gap for them. So I do it. Every one of us is here because someone somewhere prayed for us. It could've been grandma, our mothers, or maybe someone we don't even know whom the Holy Spirit got them up in the middle of the night and they walked the floor praying in the spirit. They didn't know who it's for but have acquiesced to His gentle leadings because they know in their spirit what's at stake.

If you know of someone the Holy Spirit brings to mind or perhaps you see their face, say a prayer for them. You don't have to know all of the particulars in their life, just that you have been assigned to pray and it's a divine set up. Ask God to meet them at the point of their need whatever that might be. He knows what it is, all He needs is someone to ask and it will be done.

Romans 8:26-27 AMP   Ezekiel 22:30   Isaiah 61:1-3

4

Growing Pains

Growing up in the things of God is not easy. We're supposed to be on our best behavior no matter what we might be going through because Jesus commanded us to walk in love at all times just as He did. He is our example, God in the flesh. All the way to the cross He was showing us what love is. Showing how love behaves when you have "a God given right" to stand up for yourself yet say nothing and keep moving toward your goal. That's what He did.

Some of the things you're experiencing right now are working for your good. You are being molded into the image of God Himself. You're growing and that means being stretched and pulled in every which way but loose. When we grow, our feelings can be all over the place. That's why you sometimes feel all out of sorts on the inside. You're growing and that means an encounter with grief. Grieving over parts of the old you that have been a constant companion for quite some time. For me, God has been working on the things that I say and when I say them. Things I used to think were funny, clever and quick wit are now unacceptable. If I say them now, I get a sickening feeling in my gut that wasn't there before which means that's a no-no. As I enter this new phase of my spiritual development, I look at the attitude of Christ and how He had joy knowing full well what was laid before Him and that it was God's plan to redeem (His man) humanity.

Remember, God has a plan. He is working all of this it out for your good. You'll be okay. They're just growing pains.

Matthew 22:37-40   Hebrews 12:2 AMP   Romans 8:28 AMP

5

Knowing The Will Of God

When it comes to knowing what the will of God is for your life, there is one thing that has to be in place-knowing His voice.

In order for you to know the voice of God, you have to spend time with God building a relationship with Him just like a parent does with their child. If you're a parent, your child can be in a crowd. You can't see them, but you know when your child cries or calls your name because you've spent time with them and you know their voice. It's the same way with God. If you spend time with Him in prayer and His Word, you'll know when He talks to you.

As you read the Word, depending on your situation at the time, God will reveal insight and wisdom to help you. After you spend time praying in the spirit, answers to things that are before you will intuitively come. There are times when God is trying to give you advance warning, notice, or confirmation. He'll place a recurring thought about something like He does me concerning these messages we share.

Whether it's through reading the Bible, hearing sermons preached or an inner witness, God's always talking to us about His will for our life. Spirit to spirit is His only form of communication. Do you know His voice when you hear it? If so, do you act on what you've been told?

2 Timothy 3:16-17AMP Romans 8:26-27 AMP   John 16:13 AMP

6

Fighting Back

One morning before I could begin praying, the Holy Spirit began talking to me about fighting back and how the Apostle Paul tells us about the type of weapons we have at our disposal to fight with.

This is all spiritual warfare. We have to recognize and address it as such. You might get a bad report, experience symptoms in your body, get cut off by another driver while driving your car or some other slight irritant. It's all designed to throw you off your game and get you to start speaking against what you know to be true from the Word of God. To fight a spiritual battle in the flesh will get your brains knocked out every time. You fight it in the spirit realm because it's *spiritual warfare*. We have been given the Word of God, the blood-bought authority to use the name of Jesus and to pray in the spirit. Those are our weapons and faith in those is all we need. The battle is not ours it's the Lord's. There is no way we can lose. We do our part, then stand back and see the salvation of the Lord come through just as He promised.

Speak the Word of God over whatever the enemy is using against you and the angels assigned to you will immediately go to work, causing that Word you've spoken to come to pass. No matter where the attack is coming from find a Word, call your prayer partner, and get in agreement. When you use the Blood of Jesus along with the name of Jesus, your victory is assured.

If you take a hit get up, dust yourself off, and get back in there with your victorious self!

2 Corinthians 10:4 AMP   Romans 8:26-27 AMP   John 14:13-14 AMP

Psalms103:20

7

The Process Of Receiving From God

I've learned that there is a process God allows us to go through in order to receive the things He has already laid up for us.

When things seem to be going sideways, do you try to get in there and help God out by trying to get Him to follow your plan for the manifestation rather than trusting His? What I'm learning is to trust His timing in the process and stay in faith. When things seem to be going against what I'm expecting to manifest in my life, I keep confessing what the Word says and stand my ground.

It's a process just like making coffee is a process. You have coffee grounds and put cold water into the pot where the percolation takes place. Once completed, it's poured into a cup where sugar and cream can be added to achieve a desired taste and the process is complete. Receiving from God is the same way. He has to get us prepared for what He has for us. If we were to receive something prematurely it could be a curse instead of a blessing. A good father wouldn't give keys to his car for a six yr. old to drive. That would be irresponsible and detrimental to the child's safety. Once they've reached a certain age and have received the proper training, you can give them the keys. They are mature enough to handle the responsibility.

As you go through your day keep in mind that God is preparing you for something good. You're in the process. He's working everything for your good!

Mark 11:23-24 AMP   Proverbs 3:1-6 NLT   Romans 8:28 AMP

8

A Circumcised Heart

As I was in prayer one morning, I ran across a Scripture that talks about being circumcised which is something that most men know about. I then began thinking about how it's our heart that needs to be circumcised. To be circumcised means that there is a cutting away of the flesh. When we talk about our hearts being circumcised, we have to let the Word of God perform it.

When you take the Word in prayerfully every day, it will fill you with hope and joy. Things happening in your life will suddenly become clearer as if you cleaned a dirty pair of glasses. God said that He would "remove the stony heart out of our flesh and give us a heart of flesh." Scripture says that a man's heart, which is the seat of his will, affections, passions and understanding, should all be in subjection to God through His Word.

When your heart is right no matter what people do or say that could quite possibly harm you, you don't have to mount a defense against them because you trust God to judge it fairly. You only get this mind-set by taking in the Word daily, over and over again building yourself up.

Today let the Word of God perform a little outpatient surgery on you and circumcise your heart. The worst thing that can happen to you is that you'll become a better person.

Romans 4:9-12 AMP   Hebrews 4:12 AMP   Ezekiel 36:26   1 Peter 2:21-23

9

Getting Good Orderly Direction

Good Orderly Direction (G.O.D.) is an acronym I picked up years ago and remembered one morning. We are always in need of direction. If we're to be successful, it has to come from above. Personally, there are things that I desire to do, but I must ask God how do I get there? There's only one answer. God has to lead.

One way that He chooses to lead is the still small voice. When you hear it, pay attention and know that it is God in the person of the Holy Spirit, guiding you along the way. The Holy Spirit is a gentleman and won't force Himself upon you. He is always there showing what steps to take. Another way God leads is through His Word. The Bible is full of wisdom and direction for just about every area of life. You can find out how to raise your children, keep your marriage together, how to handle your money and deal with just about any problem that could come up. You have to spend time in the Word to know that help is available.

As God leads, remain flexible to His course corrections. Let Him work out the details of your journey. God has a plan. If you allow Him, He'll see you through it to the end.

1 Kings 19:12   John 16:13 AMP   Psalms 37:23   Psalms 119:133

10

Show Your Appreciation

With the busyness that seems to have consumed everyone these days, many people don't show or aren't shown any appreciation for things that have been done or that they do.

When we show people that we appreciate them and the things they do, we are in essence acknowledging the great things God has done for us through them. How can we not do more than say "Thank you" to them?

God has given me prime examples on how to conduct myself in this area. When I had job interviews for promotions, my brother encouraged me to send thank you notes to my interviewers. A few years ago, my parents went to China. The Lord placed a couple from Texas on the trip with them. The wife assisted my father with my mother immensely, as she was progressing in the early stages of Alzheimer's. Upon their return, my dad sent them a gift for their house to express his gratitude. When my parents came to visit me, circumstances permitting, they would go down to the Austin area and see them.

It's a classy thing to articulate your appreciation in a tangible way. When we give cards, a gift or money, it makes people really feel appreciated that they have done something good. When we bless others, we make room in our lives to be blessed. When you activate this level of spiritual growth in your life it becomes a perpetual constant state of exchanges.

We don't bless others just to get blessed. By blessing others, we in turn get blessed. Your being blessed is directly tied to your giving.

This is the next level so adjust yourselves accordingly!

Psalms 103:1-5 AMP   Galatians 6:7 AMP   Luke 6:38 NLT

11

Hang In There

Our relationship with God is not based on how we feel or what's happening in or around us. It should be based on one thing; His Word. Our feelings and circumstance will change but His Word won't. I don't know about you, but His Word is the only constant thing in my life.

God is faithful and He cannot lie. You might be waiting on the manifestation of something from His Word. Hang in there. God is an on-time God because with Him it's always now. As humans, we live in time, but our God lives in eternity and speaks through time. There is no time as we know it when it comes to God. His Word says that a day is as a thousand years and a thousand years as a day. So as you stand on the promises of God, due season is not if but when. His Word will come to pass. The question is what are you going to be doing in the interim? While waiting will you serve the Lord or just hang out until? The one thing we should always be doing is helping others to get what we've got in Christ.

Christ is our example of being a servant, especially if you're someone who is in leadership. He was the quintessential Servant Leader. It's on us to follow His lead. We can follow His lead through His Word as it orders our steps or by the Holy Spirit as He guides us into all truth. Either way, we can't go wrong. We'll reach our expected end.

Don't stop confessing and speaking God's Word into your life when things don't look like you think they should. Hang in there and continue to speak those things.

1 Corinthians 1:9 AMP   Numbers 23:19   2 Peter 3:9   Romans 4:17 AMP

12

Let's Pray

We should continually pray for those in authority. With the events that are taking place today; I see why God wants us to pray for our leaders. Bishop Jakes said it best when he said; "When we send people to Washington, we want our voice to be heard and not be punished by the people we send." No matter which side of the political spectrum you're on they all are in need of our prayers.

God's Word admonishes us to get engaged in prayers of supplication, intercession and the giving of thanks for all men, for kings and all those in authority. We have to intercede and supplicate for all of whom the Lord has placed on your heart. We have family members and loved ones who need Jesus, so we pray that a laborer would come across their path. Someone they would listen to and accept Christ as their Savior. There are people you know who have stepped away from Christ, have been deceived about certain issues, or have had their understanding darkened. They are in need of our prayers also.

I challenge you to set aside time daily to pray for specific people you know or who the Holy Spirit brings to your remembrance. We are all in this together. Your prayers have an impact.

1 Timothy 2:1-5 AMP   Ephesians 4:17-18 AMP   James 5:16 AMP

13

Prayer Of Agreement

One way that we get others to assist us with our prayers is by asking them to come into agreement with us. When you ask someone to join their faith with yours, you are combining faith forces as you enlist some help and not so much relying on theirs alone as some people often do when they ask others to pray for them.

There is strength in numbers. The more people that we can get to join corporately in prayer puts the enemy on the run. Keep in mind that this is warfare we're engaged in. The Bible says that one can chase a thousand and two can put ten thousand to flight. Do the math and see for yourself and see how it's better to have more people standing in faith with us. Being on one accord in prayer has tremendous effect in the spiritual realm. The disciples had great manifestations in the early church when they came together in one accord for prayer.

One of the primary purposes God placed us here is for one another. Having a prayer partner is another great tool to have in your arsenal. This is someone that you can share things with and know that it won't go any further than the two of you and the two of you get into agreement with each other in prayer whenever warranted.

Ladies and gentlemen, we're at war. You don't have to be out there all alone. When it comes to prayer partners, knowing they have your back when things get tough is a real confidence booster. If you don't have someone to get in agreement with you, ask the Holy Spirit to guide you to the person God has set aside just for you. We all need somebody to be in our corner. From time to time we're going to need help so don't be afraid to ask.

Deuteronomy 32:30   Matthew 18:19-20   Acts 2:1-4 AMP   Romans 8:26-27 AMP

14

Your Prayer Has Been Answered

The moment you prayed in faith; your prayer was answered. Where some of us lose it is somewhere between "I believe" and "I receive." This is the place and time that your speech cannot be contrary to what you've prayed for just because you don't see it manifested yet.

When a farmer plants seeds, he doesn't dig up his seed immediately after they were planted because he doesn't see anything coming up. No, he waits patiently and waters it while he awaits his harvest. It's a process. We can dig up ours if we start speaking words of doubt and stop walking in love. We have to water our seeds with the words we speak while we wait, and we do that by thanking God in advance for the manifestation. Number one rule in prayer is to only ask once and thank God for it until you receive it. This is the proper way to live when you're in between "I believe" and "I receive."

Some answered prayers get manifested immediately, some don't. If your prayer is in the latter group, more than likely there are certain things that have to be in alignment. Then your now will happen. Stay the course. Don't get weary in well doing because due season is not if but when.

Mark 11:22-24   Mark 4:26-29 AMP   Galatians 6:9 AMP

15

It's In Him

One morning as I was basking in the presence of the Lord, I began meditating on how Jesus told us that we are to live by the Word of God. John, in his writing told us that Jesus is the Word. I was then led to a Scripture where Paul is preaching. In his discourse he tells them that it is in Him (Christ) that we live and move and have our being.

God, through Jesus, has given us everything that we will ever need. It's in Him. One of the things Kenneth Hagin taught in his book *"In Him"* is when you read your Bible especially the Pauline epistles underline wherever you see "In Him, In Whom and In Christ." I underline it and when I go back and read through a verse and see it, I receive a new revelation because it's in Him.

Today as you go through your day just meditate on the truth that it's in Him. Everything we'll ever need is in Him. All of our provisions are in Him and we have no lack. Your healing is In Him. Whatever you need is in Him!

It's in Him!

Matthew 4:1-4   John 1:14 AMP   Acts 17:28

16

He's Taking You Somewhere

God has prepared a path for all of us to take. When we spend time with Him daily in prayer and the Word, we discover not only the correct way to go but also how fast or slow we should move. Once we find it, we have to work in order to stay on it. It's very easy to veer off course and become distracted with the day-to-day affairs of life, but God has made arrangements so that if you do, there are valuable lessons to be learned that only the experience could teach.

There are times when the roads He has us traveling doesn't make sense. How many times have you been believing for the manifestation of something from God, and be led to do something totally out of the ordinary that to you, it doesn't make sense? You discover later that you needed that step to get where He's taking you. It happens to all of us from time to time.

I'm reminded of the man in the Bible that was blind from birth. Jesus spits on the ground to make a mud pie and put it on the man's eyes. Jesus tells him to go wash in the pool of Siloam and the man comes back seeing. It's times like this when we have to trust the guidance of the Holy Spirit because the answer to our prayer might not look like we thought it would or come the way we expected it to come. God has a plan. He's working out every detail to bring you to an expected end. He has to do it His way and that makes sense! This road leads to the good life. That means everything we do should be about the Kingdom and living in Him.

Ephesians 2:10 AMP John 9:5-7 Matthew 6:33 Acts 17:28

17

Are You Eating Fast Food Or Five Star?

When our church had its "Harvest Week Revival" one year, Dr. Bill Winston was our guest speaker. Something he said had a real impact on me. He talked about how God only moves when we are ready to receive and that we have to redo our minds because we are what we eat, and we need to start eating on another level. That got me to thinking about when we eat the Word of God or spend time in the Word, do we treat it like going through the drive thru at McDonalds? Do we place the order, pay for it, drive to the next window, pick it up and off we go? Or do you go in, sit down, wait to be served and enjoy a full course meal as if you're at a five-start restaurant, that lasts longer than a drive thru restaurant experience?

You only get out what you put in or like the Bible says, "you reap what you sow." Do you want to get more Word results in your life? If so it's going to take putting more Word in. Spending time daily in God's Word has a payoff that you can only receive when you do it. As the Word of God transforms your thinking, you might feel a little uncomfortable because it's going to mean you have to give up old paradigms for new ones. You will grieve the old ones who have become dear friends that can't go on to the next level. When you go to a five-star restaurant, your dress and table manners reflect that you know how to carry yourself and that you belong in this environment, or else people will be talking about you on their way home from dinner. I'm pretty sure you know what I'm talking about. From time to time we've seen or experienced it ourselves. When it comes to the Word of God, change your mind set and start thinking on a five-star level. In order to do differently you have to think differently and that takes a constant renewing of the mind.

Let the water of God's Word wash your mind, as you get prepared to enjoy five-star manifestations from the Word you've sown!

Galatians 6:7   Romans 12:2 AMP   Ephesians 5:26

18

Going All In

In the game of poker when a player makes a decision to bet his entire stake on the hand that he is holding, that's called "all in." He's confident that the hand he's holding, the cards he's been dealt, will win. We as people of faith should exemplify the same all or nothing stance when it comes to our walk with Christ and His Word. It should be our final authority.

The enemy is going to strike fear and terror into the hearts of people with all of the viruses that have found their way to the forefront of our lives. With Cova-19, Ebola or the Enterovirus D-68 that is affecting children, the media is giving it a full steam ahead approach in their reporting. You have to be careful not to take a steady diet of that stuff. Zig Ziglar used to say that he read his Bible and the newspaper every morning so that he could see what both sides are up to. Be aware of your surroundings and what's going on in the world. When you hear about these things you can be concerned; just don't get fearful. Let all of it be nothing more than a guide to where you focus your prayers.

When you hear these various reports, don't let the words of your mouth snare you. Speak the spirit-filled Word of God. You have the same creative power with the words you speak just like God did when He spoke this world into existence. Watch what you say because you're creating your world. My brother says, if God didn't write it he isn't going to say it. That's the correct attitude to have. The only way to know what's written is to spend time reading your Bible.

Are you all in or not? Don't be like those who have no hope. Either God meant what He said or He didn't. You have the Word of God so exercise your faith. Go all in. You'll experience for yourself how every Word that comes out of His mouth is true and God's promises do come to pass.

Proverbs 6:2   John 6:63 AMP   Mark 11:23

19

Praying The Word

When we go the Bible and find a Word to pray that is relevant to whatever situation or person we're praying for, what we actually are doing is giving voice to God's Word. When we do, we are releasing that Word into the atmosphere. There's a song by Myron Butler & Levi "Speak Into The Atmosphere" that solidifies my point. You have the creative power in your mouth to create your world. What does the Word have to say and are you speaking it? What you have and where you are right now in life, is a direct result of what you've been speaking, whether it's the Word of God or the world, you've got it! Giving voice to God's Word activates the angels assigned to you and puts them to work on your behalf.

I'm a staunch believer in reading my Bible daily, because I want to keep the lines of communication open, so that whenever God wants to speak into my life, I'm ready, willing and able to receive. Sometimes I can look up a Scripture and inadvertently get led to a Word that is relevant to another situation I might have.

Spending time in the Word of God is never a waste of time because there is life in the Word!

Hebrews 11:3 AMP   Psalm 103:20   John 6:63

20

It'll All Work Out In The End

God is working this thing, whatever is going on in your life, out. Every step is designed, and every misstep has been taken into account for the plans and purposes He has for your life. It wasn't a waste of time. You are fulfilling your God-ordained destiny. Keep walking, putting one foot in front of the other. Don't look back. At this stage of development, don't give up. When things aren't going the way you want, wait. The Bible tells us that after we have done what God has given us to do according to His Word, to be patient, because our reward is coming.

Regardless of how things might sometimes look, hang in there and continue to stand on His Word. You've probably heard it said before how delayed doesn't mean denied. It's true. This is the time where one day we'll look back and see how God was putting everything into its proper alignment for us to receive it. It's all part of His plan for our life. His plan is for us to have and to enjoy the good life. Our part is to stand on His Word. Don't give up. Just wait. No matter what it looks like or come what may, know that it will all work out in the end for your good.

Hebrews 10:36   Ephesians 2:10 AMP   Romans 8:28

21

It's Not A Dream

After you've been through some things and have quite possibly suffered a loss and maybe some setbacks, when God turns that thing around it might seem like a dream.

God will never leave you hanging. When life happens, as it most assuredly will, you have to take the hits and trust God. No matter what comes your way, keep moving. Always keep your confessions right. Don't talk about what it is but rather say what you want it to be. You're not lying about your situation, what you're doing is calling what you want it to be into existence. We have to "call those things that be not as though they were." You have to give your angels something to work with. They are ministering spirits waiting to go to work on your behalf. All you have to do is speak God's Word in faith and they go to work. God will not let you suffer a loss of any type and not have your restoration already planned. What we have to do is follow the gentle leadings of the Holy Spirit as He guides our steps along the path to the good life that has been pre-arranged for us.

God wants to do some wonderful things in your life today. Once He gets started, they will be so amazing it might seem like a dream.

Psalms 126 AMP   Romans 4:17 AMP   Ephesians 2:10 AMP

22

Blessed And Grateful

We adopted three foster children a couple of years ago. They have been a real blessing. I remember one time when we began fostering a new family it made me reflect on how far God has brought me and the things that He not only has given me, but the lives I am entrusted with. We've grown so large now that we had to purchase a van so that we can all ride together. I never imagined doing the things I am doing let alone reaping the rewards for doing them.

I grew up and used to deliver mail in the "hood" back in Detroit. I had relationships with people who were doing the best they could, but I never knew any family who lost their children because of abuse or neglect. I'm pretty sure there were some, but today's standards have raised the bar and it seems like there is an influx of children. Now that could be due to my ignorance prior to getting involved but now that I am, I thank God for the opportunity to have been chosen. I am blessed and grateful.

There are so many children, literally hundreds of thousands who are out there looking for their "forever family." It makes me cry when I think about it. I'm talking about children who might be as young as five years old who have been in several foster homes. It's no fault of their own. They didn't ask to be born and like all of us we don't get the chance to pick our birth parents. Think about how many places you have lived as a child or since becoming an adult. It's not hard to see how God has blessed you and be grateful.

I don't know who this message is for, but I feel led to share it with all of you. Being a Foster Parent is a good place to start. There is such a blessing that comes when you open your heart and home to a child. Words can't accurately describe it.

Luke 6:38 AMP   Ephesians 1:3-6 AMP

23

DO IT NOW!

At the end of every year, you hear people voicing when the New Year comes there are certain things they plan to change. It could be related to their health, like going to the gym, beginning a new diet or to stop smoking. It could be a desire to spend more time reading their Bible and get closer to God. Why wait for a calendar date to make the necessary changes you feel led to do? The only thing standing between your success and failure is you haven't made the decision to do it. When the New Year rolls around, you'll most likely be in the same spot with the same unfulfilled desire. Go ahead make the choice and decide to do it now!

Every year the majority of "New Year Resolutions" fail because they lack the determination required for success by not making a decision. Once the decision is made, bring your mind into alignment with your desire. Then move on to establish parameters that reinforce your decision, making any behavioral changes required for success.

I attempted to quit smoking cigarettes several times and successfully failed, until I made the decision on December 4, 1995 to quit. I gave it to God and haven't had one since. I owe it all to God. If He did it for me, He'll do it for you.

Identify with the area of your life you desire to make some changes. Make a decision not a resolution. Do it now.

Deuteronomy 30:19 NLT   Ephesians 4:22-24 AMP   Acts 10:34 AMP

24

True Love Gives

When I think of Christmas, I think of it as the beginning of God expressing His love toward us, in that He sent His only begotten Son into the world. There was a twofold purpose for Christ coming into the world. 1) He was going to destroy the works of the devil. 2) Through Him we would have eternal life.

Jesus Himself told us that He came to give us the abundant life, a life that is overflowing with goodness. That's what true love is. When you give it a serious, meditative moment of thought, you can't help but say "Thank You" to a God who loves you so much. He gave everything for you upfront. An expression they used to say back in the day, He "fronted you" all that you would ever need for this life before you even made it here.

Throughout the day, look at everything around you through the eyes of love. God made it all just for you. Why? Because He loves you and thought you might enjoy it. A simple "Thank You God" repeated throughout the day will change your whole perspective!

1 John 3:8   John 3:16 AMP   John 10:10 AMP   2 Peter 1:3 AMP

25

The Gift

As we celebrate the birth of Jesus, lets take a moment to reflect on how He is the gift that really does keep on giving.

His birth is the ultimate gift that God could've ever given us. He unselfishly stripped Himself of His deity and took on the fleshly attributes of man. All so that He could show us how to conduct ourselves while we sojourn here on earth. He completed His assignment by willingly offering Himself up to be the perfect sacrifice for our sins. This is where He became all we were so that we could become all that He was. This is the great exchange. Everything we'll ever need was consummated on the Cross. When He ascended, we were given the Holy Spirit who now dwells within us. He (the Holy Spirit) came to guide and show us the way to go. If we follow His gentle promptings we can navigate through this life with remarkable ease. All we have to do is follow His lead.

Today, as you spend time giving and receiving gift, don't lose sight of the Ultimate Gift that God has given to all who will receive the gift of His son. Keep in mind that it was in His death that we really received our gift!

I want to wish you a Merry Christmas from my family to yours!

2 Corinthians 5:21 AMP   John 16:7-13 AMP   John 14:16,26 AMP

26

Unanswered Prayer: Wrong Motive

There are hindrances to our receiving manifestations when we pray. One is our love walk, another one is our motives. This is usually the culprit when people are believing for things like money, cars etc. Why do you want it? When you receive it what will you do with it?

The Bible warns us that maybe the reason we don't have the things we desired is because we ask for the wrong reasons. Why do you want more money? God is not against us having money because He gives us the ability to get wealth for Kingdom purposes and not to keep up with the Jones' but to be a distribution center, further advancing God's agenda on the earth. That's why He takes pleasure in our prosperity so that we can "spread the wealth." The promotion on your job, the new house, car, all those things that you desire, He wants you to have but can He trust that the things won't have you? When it comes to your money do you regularly and consistently tithe and give offerings? Will you open the doors of your new home for others? Will you be willing to go the extra mile, offer to pick someone up and take them to church in your new car?

These are some of things we have to check our heart's motives when it comes to receiving from God. As would any father, He wants only the best for us and will provide access to it when we're ready.

James 4:3 AMP   Deuteronomy 8:18   Psalms 35:27

27

Sharing Your Faith

When you're in the middle of one those "God allowed" character-building moments, it can get real tight. There may be times when you don't think you're going to make it. You can't see past the current dilemma that has suddenly sprung up. People of faith around you keep the encouragement coming and someone says that "everything you're dealing with is for somebody else." Even though you can't see it at the moment, eventually God will inexplicably have you cross paths with someone who is going through the same thing you did. Suddenly it will have been worth it. I had one of those moments happen to me.

A friend of mine from Detroit called and began sharing with me some challenges he was experiencing. I listened because I've learned that the best way to work through things and begin to heal is to talk about it. As he was talking, everything he was telling me reminded me exactly of something I went through back in the 90's. So much of his situation were almost identical to mine. I knew where he was both emotionally and spiritually. I shared with him what happened to me, how I got through it, and where I was now. I was able to give him some insight into his situation and a couple of suggestions of things that I did to help me along the way. By the time we hung up he said that it had been on his mind to call me all day and was glad he finally did, as he now felt better. I prayed with him. I was so grateful that God used me to share with him the things I went through and to offer some hope in the middle of his storm.

God allows us to experience all sorts of things as we go through life. More often than not you'll get a chance to share it with someone. Be grateful that you survived. Tell someone else that they will also.

Proverbs 27:17   Romans 8:28-30 AMP   1 Pet 5:10 AMP

28

God Is Still Working In You

One thing is for certain, God is constantly at work in you and in your life because He's always talking, leading or guiding. Do you know His voice? Are you listening? Are you paying attention and taking heed to what He says?

If we want to hear God clearly, sometimes we have to turn down the volume on the noise in our life. God will use people who cross your path to bring you something. More importantly, you might have a Word for them, so you have to remove any pre-conceived notions of folks and remain open minded. It's not always all about you and what you can get. The old saying "it's better to give than to receive" is still true to this day. Our whole focus should be on trying to be a distribution center for Kingdom purposes. We tend to take a lot of things for granted but every now and then, it'll do you good to look around and see how blessed you really are. Be willing to bless someone else. We have a lot to be grateful for and giving to others is the best expression of just how much gratitude you have for the things God has given you and the position He's placed you in.

If God can get it to you, He's probably trying to get it through you, to meet the needs of others.

1 Kings 19:11-12   Proverbs 10:22 AMP   Luke 6:38 AMP

29

Are You Really Grateful?

Have you ever awakened in the morning and felt somewhat off balance? There's nothing major going on or wrong. You just can't quite put your finger on it. That happened to me recently and I didn't want to let it hang around, so I got busy and delved into the Word.

As my youngest son and I were sitting outside enjoying the cool morning breeze that day, I began to meditate on the things that I am grateful for. To be able to enjoy this moment outside, watching the branches sway from the breeze is a blessing. The things we unknowingly take for granted in our daily routine should be counted as blessings. If you were able to get out of bed and no one had to take you to the bathroom, dress and feed you is a great starting point. I have a roof over my head, money in the bank, I'm in good health and my family is doing well *according to the plan God has for their lives*. The lyrics to a song that says, "it is well with my soul." It really is because everything's in divine order as I choose to trust God.

We have a lot to be grateful for. Every now and then it would behoove us to take stock of the things we have. Recognize that there are people in the world, maybe right next door who don't have half as much as we do. Even if what you have isn't a lot, there are some who don't have that much. What about those, especially children, who don't know where their next meal is coming from? Think about that the next time you throw away some good food.

The position God has placed you in is unique for you. Today let the mind-set of Paul be in you. He learned to be content no matter what.

1 Timothy 6:6-8   Psalms 139:1-4 AMP   Philippians 4:11-12 AMP

30

This Is A Test

The teacher presents the lesson plan to you in its entirety. You've been given all the information that you'll need to pass the test. Holy Spirit has borne witness to your spirit as you read the Word. He's even sent His Word through various speakers for quite some time now to adequately prepare you for this. Never lose sight that testing doesn't come from God. It only comes because of who you are and what you've been taught. That's why He allows it.

Distractions will come to throw you off and attempt to discourage you. Every new test seems like it's the greatest one you've ever had. When you see it for what it actually is, it's the same thing as before just dressed up differently. Your enemy only has a few plays in his book. They are all designed to influence you with the things of this world, attacks on your thoughts, feelings or for the Word's sake. The only power your enemy has is the power of suggestion. If he can get you to act or speak his suggestions, then he thinks he won. But he hasn't. We all make mistakes and slip up every now and then. When we do, repent, go to the Word of God, speak it and pray in the spirit.

As for the test, it is an open book test, which gives you the upper hand. Review your notes and all the information you've been given. Testing has begun. You will pass.

James 1:13-14 AMP   Mark 4:14-19   Jude 20 AMP

31

Leave It All Back There

As we approach yet another new year, I want to encourage you to not carry any unnecessary baggage from this year into the new one. When I say baggage, I'm referring to unforgiveness. The Apostle Paul admonishes us to forget those things which are behind and reach for that which lies ahead. God has so much in store for us that to get hung up, stay mentally and emotionally engaged in something that happened a long time ago is not worth the energy it takes to keep it alive. I promise you that whatever, whoever did to you, they have definitely moved on. Don't you think you should too? There's an old saying: "Stop letting people live rent free inside your head" and it is so true. What you need to do is serve them an eviction notice for non-payment of rent. Don't give them thirty days or until the end of the month to leave, put them out now.

Forgiveness is not a feeling it's a decision. At some point in our lives we all stand in need of it. You have to decide that you want to be free. I'll be the first one to tell you it takes work. There was a time I realized something someone had done and said about me years ago began to bother me. The only reason it came up is because I found out there existed a strong possibility that I might have an opportunity to run into them, which brought up feelings that didn't originally exist when it occurred. Nevertheless, I had to go to work forgiving them, which for me means praying God's best for them. Everything I want God to do in my life, I want to happen in theirs. I want their marriage to be blessed and for them to walk in divine health. I pray that they prosper in their finances and all of their relationships with family, friends, and coworkers. Whatever they put their hand to do, I ask God to put his super on their naturals.

If your desire is to be free from past hurts, experience the goodness of God in your life and not carry unnecessary baggage into the new year, then go for it and know that it takes work. Trust me when I tell you the rewards of leaving it behind are great. All you have to do is just let it go!

May you have a blessed and prosperous New Year!

Philippians 3:13   Luke 11:4 AMP   Romans 2:4 AMP

Thank You

First and foremost, I would like to thank my Lord and Saviour Jesus Christ, for laying down His life for me and giving me the wonderful gift of eternal life and being able to share it with others so they can enjoy it also. To my wife Doris and my children, my parents-RIP Mom and Dad, my sister Edd-Lania and Bro In Love Jerran, my brother and sister Carl and Marsha January, my bro Patrick "Fat Pat" Van Buren, Ginger, Bill (RIP), my "Resting In His Word" teammates: Cheryl, Dan and Randy; thank you all for your love and support over the years. I love all of you more than words can ever say. Ken and Kristine Bresser for leading me to Christ that Sunday afternoon. To Bishop Keith and Pastor Debra Butler, Bishop T D and First Lady Serita Jakes, Bishop Joby and Pastor Sheryl Brady, for pouring the Word of God into my life not only by preaching but walking the Word out in your life so others like me can see. To Carolyn Gilleylen, you're work and input was invaluable. Thank you! To Odessa Costner, Venus Gamboa and the staff at West Bow Press for your guidance in helping me put it all together.

My PHSOM classmates and TPHND Blue Team members: It's harvest time

To all of the twelve steppers out there; "Keep coming back, it works if you work it." There are so many more I want to thank that I can't mention you all. Just know that when I think of you, I thank God for you being in my life and I'm grateful! For more information visit www.botvm.com

Printed in the United States
by Baker & Taylor Publisher Services